William E. Dearie Sr.
150 Truman Pl.
Centerport, NY 11721

William E. Dearie Sr.
150 Truman Pl.
Centerport, NY 11721

William E. Dearie Sr.
150 Truman Pl.
Centerport, NY 11721

THE PICTORIAL HISTORY OF
BOXING

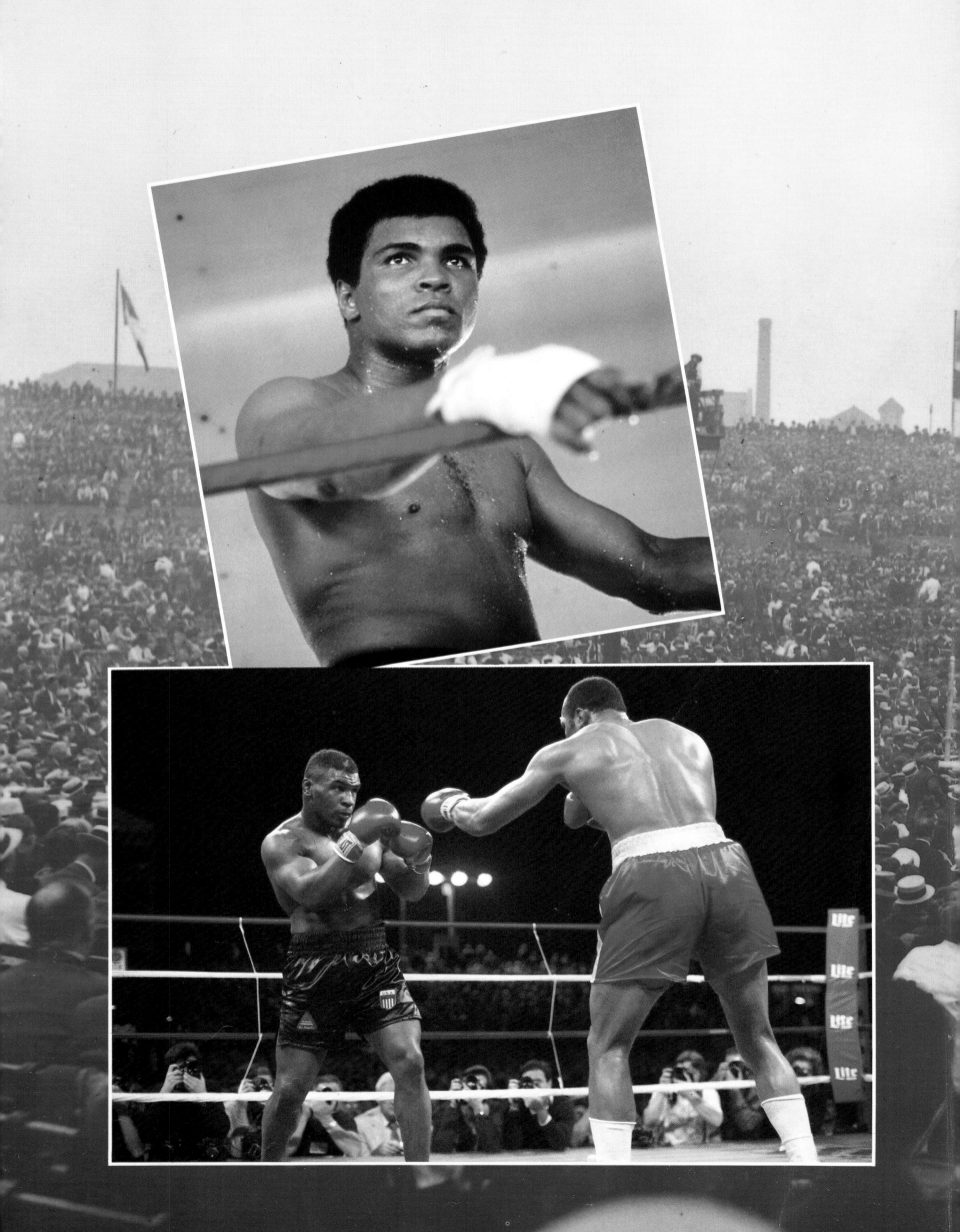

THE PICTORIAL HISTORY OF
BOXING

PETER ARNOLD

FOREWORD BY
BERT RANDOLPH SUGAR
Publisher-Editor of Boxing Illustrated

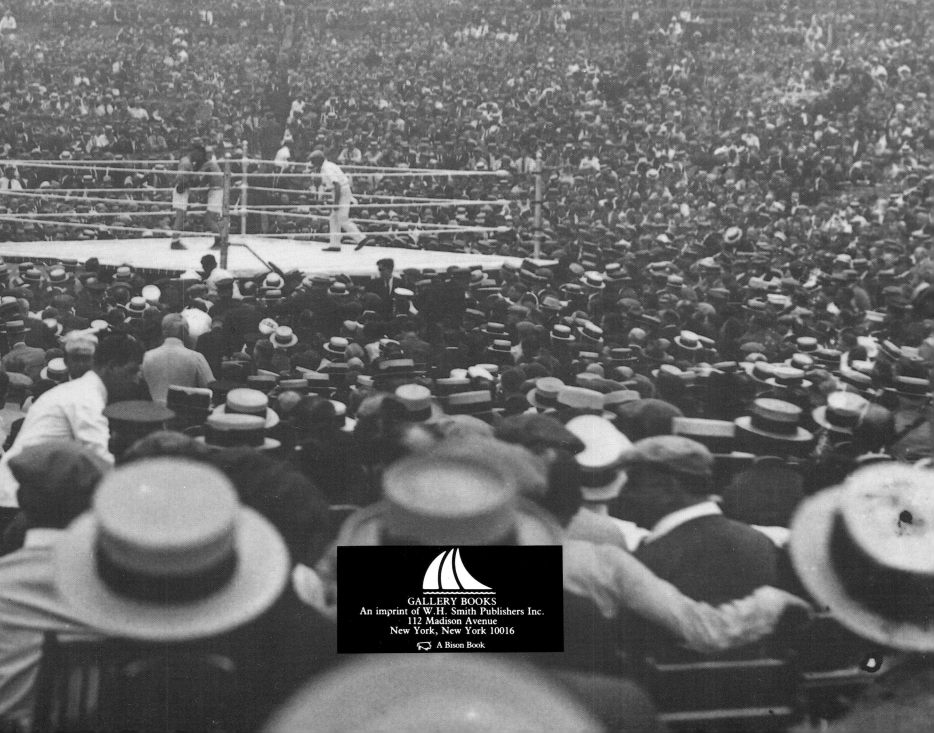

GALLERY BOOKS
An imprint of W.H. Smith Publishers Inc.
112 Madison Avenue
New York, New York 10016

A Bison Book

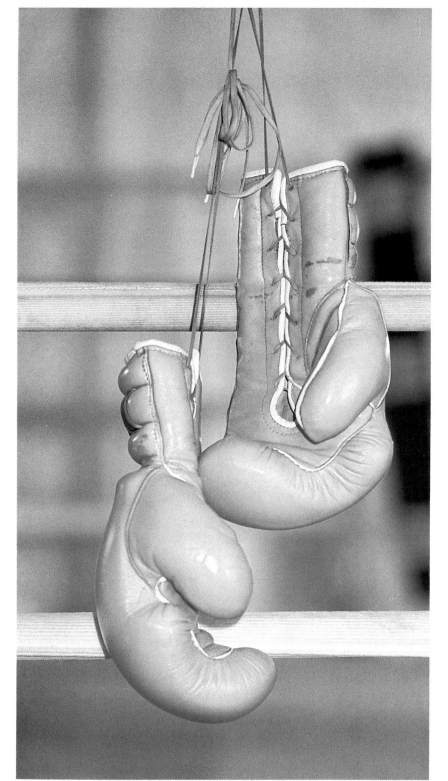

PART I
Modern Boxing Replaces the Prize Ring

Published by Gallery Books
A Division of W H Smith Publishers Inc.
112 Madison Avenue
New York, New York 10016

Produced by
Bison Books Corp.
15 Sherwood Place
Greenwich, CT 06830

ISBN 0-8317-6899-1

Printed in Spain

1 2 3 4 5 6 7 8 9 10

PAGE 1: *Bob Fitzsimmons.*
PAGES 2-3 MAIN PHOTOGRAPH:
*Dempsey versus Carpentier at Boyle's
Thirty Acres, Jersey City, in 1921, the
first fight to take over $1 million at the
gate.*

PAGE 2 INSET ABOVE: *Charismatic
champion Muhammad Ali.*
PAGE 2 INSET BELOW: *Mike Tyson in
his fight with James 'Bonecrusher'
Smith on 7 March 1987 at Las Vegas.*
THIS PAGE: *Modern boxing gloves.*

PART II
The Golden Boom Days

PART III
From The Greatest to Iron Mike

Foreword

Those of us who have not yet fallen over under the collected weight of our memories can still recall a little bird named Sharpie who, every Friday night, jumped up and down like Rumpelstiltskin on our 23-inch black-and-white television sets singing out, 'Look Sharp, Feel Sharp, Be Sharp,' to the accompaniment of three chimes in F#, A#, and C#. To the faithful it meant but one thing: 'The Gillette Cavalcade of Sports was on the Air.' And for the next hour – or less, if the union scale for rounds wasn't met – those who mainlined boxing would be treated to watching the superstars and lesser novas of boxing do battle; the winner to go to bigger and better things, the loser condemned to backsliding down boxing's social scale.

By the early 1950s boxing had not only become a staple on television, it had made prime time a veritable gymnasium. To cop Red Skeleton's famous line – 'Our Monday meeting, originally scheduled for Tuesday this Wednesday, has been postponed till Thursday this Friday and rescheduled for Saturday 'cause Sunday's a holiday' – boxing appeared on TV every night except Sunday, a holiday. Monday night the DuMont network carried the fights 'live' from St Nicholas and Eastern Parkway Arenas; Tuesday the fights emanated from New York's Sunnyside Gardens; Wednesdays found Bill 'The Bartender' Nimo filling glasses with Pabst Blue Ribbon Beer between rounds on CBS; Thursday the Newark fights were carried live over a mini-network extending from Schenectady to Washington; Friday was Gillette's – and Sharpie's – night out on NBC; and, to cap off a long week, ABC carried Ray Arcel's fights on Saturday. With, of course, Sunday a holiday.

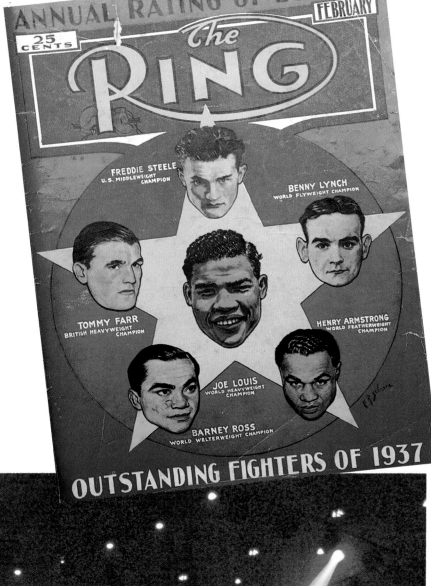

LEFT AND RIGHT: *Covers of*
The Ring *from the Joe Louis era,
just before the Second World War.*

LEFT BELOW: *The scene at the world
welterweight title fight between
defending champion Lloyd Honeyghan of
Britain and challenger Maurice Blocker
of the USA in London in 1987.*

Television not only opened up boxing like a flowering rose to those millions of fans who wouldn't have known the difference between a left hook and a sky-hook, but it also introduced us to some of the most flavorful nicknames this side of a Dick Tracy rogue's gallery: 'The Bronx Bull,' 'Sugar Ray,' 'Bobo,' 'The Rock,' 'The Onondaga Onion Farmer,' and 'The Cuban Hawk,' to name but a few, were all transported into our living rooms every week. In fact, it seemed we were served Ralph 'Tiger' Jones on Fridays more times than fish.

In the homeopathic discipline of medicine minute quantities of a substance are administered which, if dosed in massive amounts, would have produced effects similar to the disease being treated. Boxing's equivalent in the 1950s was Chuck Davey. For if boxing suffered from a severe case of overexposure, its excesses were never more apparent than in the case of Davey, a college-educated white southpaw out of Detroit who became TV boxing's 'Glamour Boy.' In 1952 alone he appeared seven times on the Wednesday night fights, becoming almost as familiar as Bill 'The Bartender.'

Boxing seemingly existed for one purpose alone – to make sponsors happy. Gillette was happy although hardly ecstatic, having paid $250,000 for the second Marciano-Walcott fight in 1953, a fight in which Jersey Joe looked for – and found – a comfortable resting place after just 145 seconds of the first round, forcing Gillette to run their commercials like a string of pearls for the remainder of the scheduled time period. Pabst was delighted, even if Chuck Davey was the permanent condiment for their brew. In fact, the only unhappy sponsor seemed to be Buick, which sponsored the 1957 heavyweight championship bout between Floyd Patterson and Tommy 'Hurricane' Jackson over NBC. When the network cut late to a commercial between the ninth and tenth rounds, thus depriving the viewers of the 'action' in the ring – the stopping of the fight – Buick staged

its own 'Hurricane' and blew its advertising agency out of the water. Forthwith.

John Crosby, writing in the *New York Herald Tribune*, may well have discovered why the sponsors were so pleased with boxing on television. One CBS executive, according to Crosby, decided to try a little experiment of his own one night. Watching the Pabst Wednesday Night Fights over his own network, the executive determined to follow the advice of the between-rounds barkeep who sternly advocated visiting the refrigerator between rounds and to repay the kindness of the beer company for bringing him the fights for free. Gulping furiously he managed to stay up with the announcer's 'rounds,' retrieving a new bottle from his refrigerator every time he was told to. The result – the losing fighter was knocked out in the tenth; the executive was flat on his back by the end of the ninth.

But boxing soon became a casualty of television's version of Gresham's Law – that good programming will ultimately drive out bad programming. By the end of the 1950s there were too many boxers posing as life's losing stuntmen, with good fighters as rare as that proverbial day in June – or July, or any month for that matter.

And so, TV boxing sort of faded into the sunset. But even today, three decades later, it leaves a wonderful memory that grows strong and intoxicating every time one remembers those Friday Night heroes of yesteryear. It is, therefore, a pleasure to be asked to write a foreword for a book that pays full faith and credit to boxing's traditions. And to those, like this correspondent, who remember. Only too well.

Bert Randolph Sugar
Chappaqua, New York
7 June 1988

ABOVE: *John L Sullivan in 1883, the 'champion pugilist of the world.' He was the last great bare-knuckle champion.*

PART I

Modern Boxing Replaces The Prize Ring

The Prize Ring Days

Nobody can say when boxing started but certainly Egyptian hieroglyphics from about 4000 BC suggest soldiers fought with hands and forearms bound, and ancient Greek vases and murals show men fighting with fingers and wrists bandaged in anticipation of the modern boxing glove. Homer and Virgil mention fighting with the fists, while boxing was part of the ancient Olympic Games hundreds of years before the birth of Christ and was part of Roman gladiatorial displays. Indeed the Romans used a vicious form of boxing glove called a *caestus* which was covered with iron or brass studs and frequently led to the death of one of the fighters.

Modern boxing, however, did not arise from these gloved contests, but from the prizefighting which became increasingly popular in Britain in the seventeenth century. Boxers fought with bare knuckles, and matches were popular in the traveling fairs, which might sport a boxing booth, in which professionals would put on exhibitions or accept challenges from the locals. Samuel Pepys reported seeing such a 'prizefight' in 1662.

Naturally men proficient in boxing gained local reputations and the concept of 'champions' developed. Men would be supported by their friends who might put up a 'purse' of money for a challenge to another champion. There would be plenty of betting upon the outcome. Sometimes a member of the aristocracy would become the patron of a champion and take him on to his staff, supporting him in contests against all comers. The first known report of such a match in England is from the *Protestant Mercury* of January 1681 and concerns a battle between the Duke of Albemarle's footman and a butcher.

Men proficient at boxing would roam the land, issuing challenges to the locals on village greens. They would attract a crowd and get them to form a circle by holding a rope. This was the original 'ring.' To accept the challenge a local would 'throw his hat into the ring.' If there were no challengers, two of the party would box each other. After the fight the crowd would be

invited to throw money into the ring to show their appreciation, a habit which still survives to the present day in some of the more intimate professional arenas of today when the money is called 'nobbins.'

The rules in these fights were not formalized, but many came to be accepted by custom. The boxers were stripped to the waist, below which they could not hit or grab each other. Neither could they kick bite or poke fingers in the eyes. Most

TOP: *Ancient Greeks boxing with fingers and wrists bandaged. In the ancient Olympic Games competitors performed nude and women were not allowed to watch.*

ABOVE: *Jack Broughton, who published the first rules of the prize ring after his opponent died.*

LEFT: *Tom Johnson and the giant Isaac Perrins fighting at Banbury, Oxfordshire on 22 October 1789. Johnson won in one hour 15 minutes.*

ABOVE: *Jack Randall (left) and Turner sparring at the Fives Court, a boxing venue near Leicester Square, London that was popular in the early nineteenth century. Randall was the original 'Nonpareil,' so-called some 90 years before Jack Dempsey was given this sobriquet.*

RIGHT: *Richard Humphries (left) and Daniel Mendoza during their third fight, on 29 September 1790 at Doncaster, which Mendoza won. Mendoza had a gate built and charged spectators passing through it, the first example of a paying 'gate' in boxing.*

other things were allowed, like grabbing by the hair. Wrestling formed a big part of the fight, the object being to throw or knock the opponent to the floor. The assailant was then allowed to throw himself upon him as heavily as possible but was not allowed to strike or otherwise hurt a man while he was down. The round ended when a man was down and there was a 30-second break before the next round.

As fights grew in popularity, it was necessary to have a less flexible ring, so stakes were fixed into the ground to take the rope and the 'ring' became square. It became the habit to attach the boxers' purses to these stakes, where they could be kept in sight. The money itself came to be known as 'the stakes,' a term still in widespread use in gambling. Soon there was an inner and an outer ring, the space between being for the patrons and officials, like the timekeeper and the boxers' own umpires who were there to protect the interests of their fighter. As the sport developed each boxer was allowed to have in his corner two helpers, who were usually other boxers who could perform the role of substitutes, or box a secondary bout. They were called 'seconds,' a name which still survives today.

Fights lasted until one man could not continue. At the end of the 30-second break between rounds, the timekeeper blew a whistle or hit a gong, and each man had a further eight seconds to come up to a line scratched across the center of the ring. If he could not 'toe the line' or 'come up to scratch,' he lost. He was 'counted out of time,' the 'count-out' having now become popularly known as the 'knockout.'

The art of pugilism came to be taught by the masters of fencing. James Figg, from Thame in Oxfordshire, was one of these. In 1719 he opened an academy in London where he instructed gentlemen in the use of the small backsword and the quarterstaff. His business card, designed by the famous painter and engraver, William Hogarth, described him as a 'master of ye noble science of defence.'

Figg also taught boxing and was proclaimed champion of England by one of his clients, Captain Godfrey, a sportswriter. Figg became accepted as the first of the prize-ring boxing champions by beating off several challengers.

Boxing enjoyed a strange reputation. It rapidly attracted unsavory characters and became illegal. Fights were set up near county borders, so that if the sheriff arrived it was easy to flee his jurisdiction. Elaborate decoy fights were arranged to throw the law off the scent of the big matches. At the same time George I had authorized the building of a ring in Hyde Park for casual battles, popular with the men who carried the sedan chairs around London, and this was in use for nearly 100 years. The aristocracy, particularly royalty, were very keen on prizefighting, and the growing numbers of avid followers of the sport became known as 'The Fancy.'

The next great name in prizefighting was Jack Broughton, who as champion beat George Stevenson so severely that Stevenson died. As a result Broughton, who also had his academy of gentlemen, drew up and published in 1743 his rules, the first to be written down and gain some acceptance. They were intended to lessen the risk of permanent injury. Broughton also invented padded boxing gloves, called mufflers, but these were for the protection of his clients in practice, not for fighting in the ring.

Broughton's patron was the Duke of Cumberland, brother of the Prince of Wales, but the friendship did not survive the loss of Broughton's championship. The Duke had thousands of pounds wagered on Broughton but Broughton's opponent, Jack Slack, closed both his eyes with one tremendous blow. As Broughton groped around the Duke berated him and

ABOVE RIGHT: 'Gentleman' John Jackson, a champion boxer who ran an Academy where fighting skills were taught to members of the aristocracy. Jackson provided a bodyguard of 18 pugilists at the Coronation of George IV.

RIGHT: 'The Boxer's Arms,' published in 1819, was a code of arms for both amateurs and professionals. The code mentions the 'mill proper between two champions rampant' – a pun, as the word 'mill' is slang for a fight.

THE BOXER'S ARMS.
Dedicated to the Pugilistic Club, to Amateurs & the Fancy in general

ABOVE: *Jem Mace, the 'Father of Boxing' and champion of the world from about 1866 to 1882. He taught the 'noble art' in South Africa, Australia, New Zealand and America, discovered triple world champion Bob Fitzsimmons and influenced Jim Corbett, who followed Mace in applying his knowledge of science to boxing.*

ABOVE RIGHT: *Tom Sayers, one of the most remarkable of bare-knuckle boxers. He weighed around 150 pounds, yet became the English champion in 1857, beating men much bigger than himself. He was beaten only once. His last fight was the great 'world' championship with John C Heenan of America, which ended in a draw.*

Broughton said: 'I can't see my man, Your Highness. I am blind but not beat – only let me be placed before my antagonist and he shall not gain the day yet.'

After Broughton there was a period of corruption, when the title was bought and sold, but toward the end of the eighteenth century the championship regained respectability with men like Tom Johnson, Big Ben Brain, Richard Humphries and Daniel Mendoza. When Humphries beat Mendoza in their first fight in 1788 he sent a message to his backer: 'Sir, I have done the Jew and am in good health.' Mendoza released a black pigeon to take the bad news back to his friends living in the East End of London.

'Gentleman' John Jackson, a dandy, took the title from Mendoza by holding his hair with one hand and battering his face with the other. Jackson ran an upper class academy whose patrons included the poet Lord Byron, who wrote about him in verse. He formed the Pugilistic Club, an early attempt to impose order and authority on boxing.

Jem Belcher, Hen Pearce (the 'Game Chicken'), John Gully and Tom Cribb were succeeding great champions. Cribb, on his way up, had beaten a black American slave, brought over to challenge the British pugilists, and as champion he had two fights with another black man, Tom Molineaux. They were the first white versus black contests for the championship. Cribb won them but needed the help of a little gamesmanship and a lot of cold rain, which dispirited the Virginian, in order to win the first contest.

There were some notable deaths in the still illegal prize ring in the 1830s, including Simon Byrne, after a savage 99-round challenge for the title of James Burke, 'The Deaf 'Un.' Burke was charged with manslaughter, but acquitted. These deaths led to a softening of Broughton's rules, which had lasted nearly 100 years. They were replaced with the London Prize Ring Rules of 1838. The main change was that at the start of each round a boxer had to reach the center of the ring unaided and could not be carried or supported there by his seconds as Byrne (and Burke) had been several times.

'Bold Bendigo' from Nottingham was another in the line of famous champions. His real name was William Thompson and he came from a family of 21, being the third of triplets known as Shadrach, Meshach and Abednego (corrupted to 'Bendigo'). He beat men much bigger than he was, as did Tom Sayers who was less than a middleweight, and was forced to concede about six inches and more than 40 pounds when facing the American champion John Camel Heenan, a New Yorker, in the first great international bout in 1860.

Reporters came from all over the world to see this fight which nevertheless had to take place in secrecy. Fans who bought rail tickets for the fight and caught the special trains at London Bridge Station did not know the destination, which

LEFT: *Tom Cribb (right) was challenged by Tom Molineaux, a former slave from Georgetown, South Carolina, in 1810. Molineaux was following the example of Bill Richmond, another former slave who had been a victim of Cribb. Molineaux put up a tremendous show but lost in 39 rounds. In this return 'The Black' was beaten in 11 rounds.*

LEFT BELOW: *An unidentified prizefight of the era, showing the two seconds of each boxer.*

ABOVE: *'The great contest between Sayers [right] and Heenan' which took place on 17 April 1860. The engraving is by J R Mackrell and J B Rowbotham from a painting by J B Rowbotham and A J Brown. Over 12,000 watched the fight which attracted more attention than any previous contest held in Britain. The ring was broken into after 37 rounds and again after 42, when Heenan was threatening to strangle Sayers. After 2 hours 20 minutes the referee declared a draw.*

turned out to be Farnborough, 25 miles away. The writers Dickens and Thackeray were there with the aristocracy and the politicians. The fight was undecided. Police intervened after 42 rounds with both Sayers and Heenan having taken great punishment, and a draw was announced as the boxers fled and the spectators brawled. The opponents became great friends, but within 14 years of the fight, both had died.

The last of the great British bare-knuckle champions was Jem Mace, another small man but with a strong physique which he had developed at his work as a blacksmith. With prizefighting becoming more difficult to stage in Britain, he traveled the world, fighting in America, South Africa, Australia and New Zealand, and everywhere encouraging the sport by teaching the best methods of boxing to novices, and by promoting competitions. He is known as 'The Father of Boxing,' and he was a great advocate of boxing with gloves. Mace's last competitive fight was in 1890, when he was 59; he wore gloves and with him virtually died the bare-knuckle era in Britain.

Some of the great practitioners of the art – Broughton, Jackson, Cribb, Tom Spring, 'Bold Bendigo,' Tom Sayers, to name but a few – have huge and impressive memorials erected to their memory in various parts of Britain.

The Science Comes to America

It is generally accepted that the first prizefight in the United States to be conducted under the English rules and watched by an audience, took place in New York in 1816. It was, in fact, only a grudge fight between Jacob Hyer and Tom Beasley. Hyer won (his only fight) and laughingly claimed the championship of America. Most observers, however, gave this honor to his son, Tom Hyer, who won the title by beating George McChester, known as 'Country McCluskey,' at Caldwell's Landing, New York, on 9 September 1841 over 101 rounds. In that year James Ambrose, an Irish boxer, arrived in the States, and he was to become Hyer's bitterest opponent.

Many of the early fights in America were between sailors and immigrants from England and Ireland, who would scrap on any waste ground near the bars in the ports at which they arrived. In the 1830s Sam O'Rourke, the Irish champion, came to the United States, claiming to be the champion of the world because James Burke, the English champion, had refused to meet him. He opened a boxing school in New Orleans and in 1836 Burke followed him there and fought him. But O'Rourke was a gangster and after three rounds his mob tried to kill Burke, who was lucky to escape with his life.

An Irish-American called Tom McCoy was not so lucky in 1842 when he fought an Englishman, Chris Lilly, over 120 rounds and subsequently died. This caused prizefighting to be made illegal in the United States, and led to the imprisonment of one of Lilly's seconds, the newly arrived James Ambrose,

mentioned earlier. Ambrose had taken the ring name 'Yankee Sullivan.' He became a politician and mobster, and on his release from prison went out of his way to abuse Hyer and his supporters, until on 7 February 1849, the two met for the American championship and a stake of $5000 a side. Hyer knocked out Sullivan in the sixteenth round.

Hyer tried to tempt the English champion, William Perry, 'The Tipton Slasher,' to America but without success and, failing to induce Sullivan's backers to put up $10,000 for a return, he retired.

Most of the good fighters in America at the time were of Irish descent. The next to become champion was John Morrissey, born in County Tipperary but living in Troy, New York. He, like Sullivan, was a gangster who later entered politics. He made money by using his mob to ensure the victory of a friend on whom he bet heavily and then he proclaimed himself champion and accepted a challenge from Yankee Sullivan to fight for the title at Boston Corners, New York, on 12 October 1853. Once again Morrissey's mob had an effect on the result. Sullivan was in front when the mobsters moved to his corner before the thirty-seventh round and with their taunts enticed him to leave the ring and fight them, at which point the referee gave the verdict to Morrissey.

Morrissey defended against John C Heenan, who came from the town in which Morrissey's own parents had settled, Troy, New York. Heenan had gone to California to work for the

BELOW: *Tom Hyer in 1849, when he beat Yankee Sullivan for $5000 and the American title.*

BELOW: *Yankee Sullivan who challenged Hyer but was knocked out in the sixteenth round.*

LEFT: *The scene at the prizefight between champion Tom Hyer (right) and challenger Yankee Sullivan on 7 February 1849. Referee Steve van Ostrand is on the ropes, left. The seconds, or bottle men as they were then known, kneel in the corners.*

BELOW LEFT: *A similar scene 14 years later when Joe Coburn and Mike McCoole, both Irish-born, fought in Maryland for the American title. Coburn won in 63 rounds.*

RIGHT: *Joe Goss, from Northampton, England, weighed only 150 pounds but had a distinguished prize ring record. He went to America, beat Tom Allen and claimed to be American champion.*

BELOW: *Goss was beaten after 1 hour 24 minutes by Paddy Ryan (right) from Troy, New York, in 1880. As Jem Mace, the English champion, had more or less retired, some acknowledged Ryan as champion of the world.*

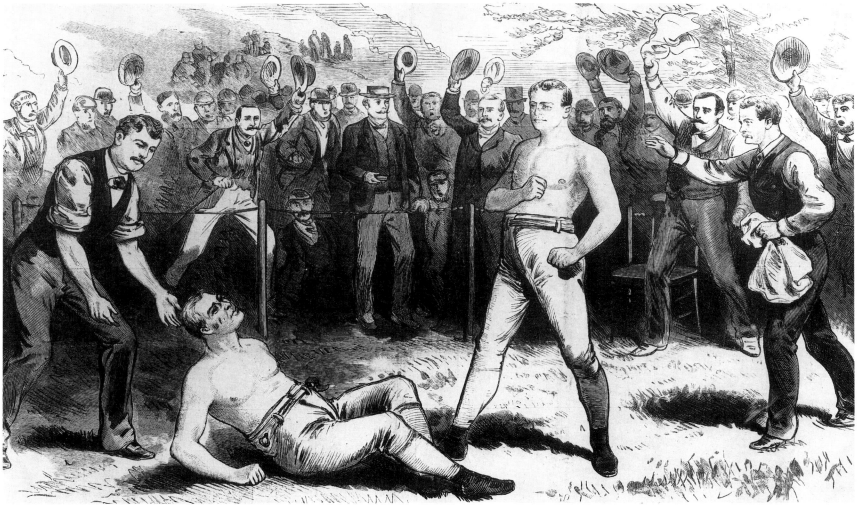

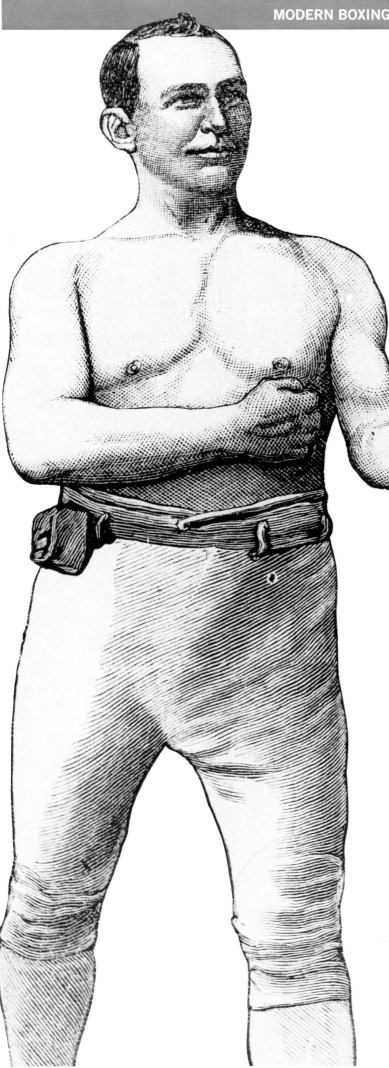

England to fight a draw, as already noted.

When Sayers retired, Heenan claimed the world title and sought to prove his claim by settling matters with the new English champion, Tom King. Heenan was not quite so good as he had been against Sayers, however, and lost in 35 minutes, after which both men retired.

Meanwhile, with Heenan out of the country, two Americans claimed their native championship – Joe Coburn and Mike McCoole. They fought to decide matters on 5 May 1863, at Charleston, Maryland, and Coburn, another Irishman by birth, from County Armagh, won by a knockout in 63 rounds.

When the English champion King retired six months later, Jem Mace, who had lost the title to him, was recognized as English champion again, and Coburn set sail to try to become world champion. He and Mace agreed to meet for £500 a side in Dublin in 1864, but on the day Coburn refused to fight unless his friend, James Bowler, was the referee. This was unacceptable to Mace, and in the end the two fought a 75-minute exhibition, without a referee or title at stake.

With public opinion now against prizefighting in England, Mace went to Australia, while many of the other British fighters decided to come to America, which became the center of the fistic activity. Mace eventually followed them to America too.

Meanwhile on the 'local' front in America Coburn had decided to retire, so McCoole claimed to be champion. This was disputed by Tom Allen from Birmingham, England, who had settled in the States and beaten many Americans. The two fought at Foster Island near St Louis in 1869, when McCoole was given the title on a questionable foul in the ninth round, having been outclassed for eight. He thereupon declined to meet Allen again, so when Mace arrived in America it was Allen who was given the shot at the world title against him. They met at Kennerville, Louisiana, in 1870, and Mace won the fight in ten rounds.

Coburn now appeared out of retirement to challenge Mace. The two fought twice in 1871. The first fight was in Canada and after more than an hour of little action the Canadian authorities stepped in and stopped the proceedings, reading the riot act. The rematch was at Bay St Louis, Mississippi, and again the police stopped it, this time after 12 rounds lasting 3 hours 48 minutes. Again it was declared a draw, although Mace appeared to be winning comfortably.

Mace was by now 40 years old and although he did not retire altogether, he devoted most of his time to teaching the sport. Allen and McCoole fought again, at St Louis in 1873. Allen forced McCoole to retire in the seventh round and called himself 'world champion.' Joe Goss, another Englishman, from Northampton, did not regard Allen as even the best Englishman, however. He himself had twice lost to Mace but had drawn once and although he had lost to Allen in England, he had beaten him in America. He now challenged Allen and beat him on a disqualification at Covington, Kentucky, where Allen, having taken a beating, deliberately fouled in the twenty-seventh round.

Goss's first defense of his crown came four years later when he was 42 years old. His challenger was Paddy Ryan, a handsome man who had been born in County Tipperary but had settled in Troy, New York, apparently an almost obligatory itinerary for American champions of the era. Ryan was a man of imposing strength, who weighed 200 pounds and was known as 'The Trojan Giant.' It was his first professional fight when he fought Goss at Colliers Station, West Virginia, in 1880. With all his advantages he still needed 84 minutes to dispose of Goss, who did not come out again after his seconds claimed a foul (which was disallowed) in the eighty-sixth round. Ryan thus became the first American who could claim to be champion of the world. However, lurking in the wings was one of the greatest Irish-American fighters of all, John L Sullivan.

Pacific Mail Steamship Company at Benicia, and fought as 'The Benicia Boy.' His fight with Morrissey at Long Point, Canada in 1858, was a painful one, for he broke his right hand on a post in the first round and was forced to retire in the eleventh. He immediately challenged Morrissey to a return, but Morrissey retired, leaving Heenan the undisputed champion. With the backing of the editor of *Spirit of the Times*, Heenan challenged the English champion, Sayers, and went to

17

The Boston Strong Boy

John L Sullivan was born on 15 October 1858 in Roxbury, Massachusetts, in the highlands of Boston. Both his parents came from Ireland and his father and paternal grandfather were both useful with their fists. John L grew to be a well-muscled man of 5 feet 10½ inches, weighing around 196 pounds, and immensely strong. According to legend he lifted a street car back on to its tracks. His fans called him 'The Boston Strong Boy.'

Sullivan was good at many sports but excelled at boxing. From about the age of 20 he began fighting and beating local boxers. A victory over Dan Dwyer established him as the best in Massachusetts. He boxed an exhibition with Joe Goss, who claimed the world championship, and had the better of it, and was then invited to show his prowess farther afield by beating Professor John Donaldson twice in Cincinnati.

Sullivan's fame spread to New York in 1881 when, on a barge

anchored in the Hudson River, he fought John Flood, known as 'The Bull's Head Terror.' The men fought in very thin tight gloves and Sullivan repeatedly knocked Flood down, winning rather easily in only 16 minutes.

With his manager, Billy Madden, Sullivan went to Philadelphia to record some quick wins and then, on 7 February 1882 at Mississippi City, he challenged Paddy Ryan for the championship of the world. The match was made with a sidestake of $2500 a side and caused widespread attention in America, many of the leading writers of the day being asked to record their impressions for the press. Sullivan proved much too strong for Ryan, handing out punishment with both punches and throws and knocking him out in the ninth round after only 10½ minutes of action.

Sullivan, helped by this wide reporting of his victory and by a boastful, outgoing and fun-loving nature, began to acquire a charisma of legendary proportions. Fans who had met him, or who claimed to have met him, would even go so far as to invite acquaintances 'to shake the hand of a man who had shaken the hand of John L Sullivan.'

A man of equal cockiness was the Birmingham-born Englishman Charley Mitchell who, while Sullivan was making himself top of the world, was winning middleweight and heavyweight competitions in London. He came to New York in 1883, beat Mike Cleary and issued a public challenge to John L. They met at Madison Square Garden over three rounds, wearing gloves. Mitchell weighed only 165 pounds but he was a quick and clever boxer and actually put Sullivan on the floor with a shot to the chin in the first round. An enraged Sullivan knocked Mitchell out of the ring in the second and had his man down again in the third, when the police stopped the fight. But Sullivan had been made to look clumsy by the taunting contemptuous Mitchell and built up a hatred for him that was to last through future encounters.

Sullivan registered more quick wins and then hit upon the device that was to increase his fame still more. At a suggestion that some of his victims were 'easy,' he went on a tour of the United States, offering $100, which he gradually increased to $1000, to anybody who could stand up to him for four rounds.

Many of Sullivan's contests were fought with gloves, and one, a six-round match on 29 August 1885 at Cincinnati with Dominic McCaffrey, was billed on the program as being under Marquis of Queensberry Rules and was described as 'six rounds to decide the Marquis of Queensberry glove contest for the championship of the world.' Some 50 years later, some experts suggested that this fight should be recognized as the first world heavyweight title fight, and this view is still held by some. It loses a little credibility by the fact that the referee, Billy Tait, left the ring, and indeed the town, without giving a verdict and gave Sullivan as the winner only when asked who had won by a fan in Toledo two days later.

LEFT: *John L Sullivan, 'The Boston Strong Boy,' ensured his fame after becoming champion by touring the United States and challenging all-comers to stand up to him for four rounds. He began by offering $100, a figure he gradually increased as nobody won it. This woodcut shows Sullivan standing over a Cornish miner in 1887.*

RIGHT: *Another woodcut shows Sullivan in magnanimous mood. Having won the title from Paddy Ryan in a bare-knuckle contest in 1882, he fought him again on 13 November 1886 at the Pavilion, San Francisco, and succeeded in knocking out his opponent in the third round. He is seen here helping Ryan back to his corner.*

In 1887 Sullivan broke a bone in his arm in a six-round draw with Patsy Cardiff, and then sailed for England and Ireland. Welcomed by the Prince of Wales, for whom he boxed an exhibition, he announced that one of his objects in coming was to wring the neck of 'that scoundrel Charley Mitchell.' 'Sullivan is bluffing,' said Mitchell, and so belittled the champion that Sullivan, anxious to get at Mitchell again in the ring, agreed to fight him for £500 a side.

Because of the illegality of prizefighting in England, they decided to meet on the training ground of Baron Rothschild's stables at Chantilly in France. The two parties arrived for the battle on 10 March 1888, with the officials and a handful of spectators who were mostly British. One was an American, Sullivan's clandestine girl friend, Ann Livingstone, who used her prowess at playing a boy on stage by dressing as one for the journey and maintaining her disguise for the fight.

The crafty Mitchell, at a huge weight disadvantage, had engineered other things in his favor: an English referee, a large 24-foot square ring to give himself plenty of dodging room, and even a slight slope rising from Sullivan's corner to his. As if the gods were on his side a cold rain, which had made the ground so wet it was soon a mudheap, returned as the fight began and was blown by a strong wind into Sullivan's face as he sat in his corner.

John L's anxiety to batter Mitchell, even after he injured his arm on Mitchell's elbow, played into the Englishman's hands. Mitchell darted around the ring while Sullivan lumbered after him in the mud, trying to land his killer punch. So keen was Sullivan to inflict pain that he refused to allow his seconds to claim a foul when Mitchell hit low. Mitchell gained the initiative by going down whenever Sullivan had him cornered, thus avoiding any severe blows, while at the same time delivering

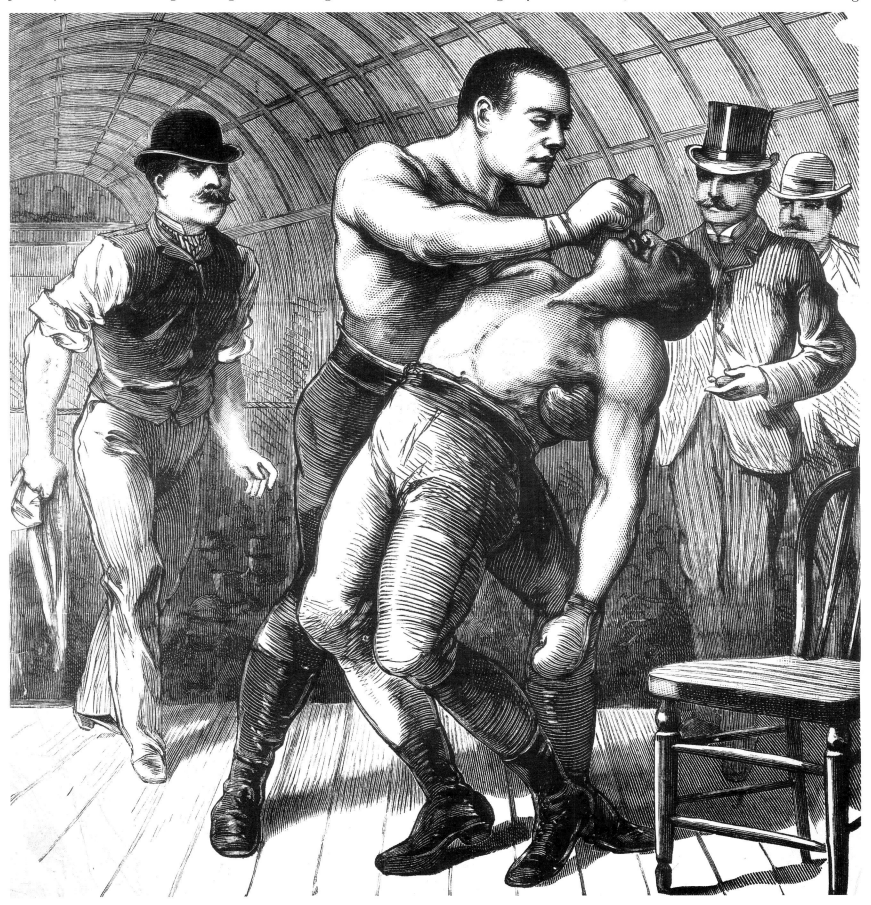

19

LEFT: *One of Sullivan's great rivals was Jake Kilrain, of Quincy, Massachusetts. When Sullivan declined a challenge to fight Kilrain, Richard K Fox, editor of the* Police Gazette, *proclaimed Jake as American champion.*

ABOVE: *Charley Mitchell was the opponent who enraged Sullivan most. Hardly more than a middleweight, Mitchell gave Sullivan a hard fight that ended in a draw on 10 March 1888.*

quick punches of his own, one of which closed Sullivan's eye.

In the thirty-ninth round, after 3 hours and 10 minutes, somebody leaped into the ring and announced the fight a draw. The referee left the ring and, despite Mitchell's protests, that was that. Both men were shortly arrested by the police. Each was sure he would have won.

A man who detested Sullivan even more than Mitchell did was Richard K Fox, the influential owner of the *Police Gazette*, the leading American boxing paper. He harbored a grudge over a snub Sullivan had inflicted on him in a restaurant, and

BELOW: *The* Police Gazette *belt that Sullivan called a dog collar.*

ABOVE: *An artist's close-up impression of the finishing moments of the last great bare-knuckle championship bout, held at Richburg, Mississippi in July 1889. Sullivan (left) is about to send Kilrain crashing to the ground.*

BELOW: *A rare photograph of the same fight. It is the seventh round and the boxers are in a clinch. It was reported to be a very hot day. Sullivan eventually won the long grueling fight in the seventy-fifth and last round.*

this grudge grew deeper when Sullivan beat his protégé, Paddy Ryan. After the Mitchell draw Fox published reports of a 'secret fight' which, according to the English sporting peer Lord Lonsdale, the originator of the famous boxing belts, had taken place between him and Sullivan in New York. Lonsdale claimed to have knocked Sullivan out in the last round.

Sensing the 30-year-old Sullivan was now fading, Fox issued a challenge to him on behalf of Jake Kilrain. Kilrain had just drawn in France with the British champion, Jem Smith, when darkness had stopped the action after 106 rounds. Sullivan declined the challenge whereupon Fox, in a public presentation, gave Kilrain a magnificent belt and proclaimed him champion of America by default.

Sullivan's incensed Boston fans immediately collected $10,000 and gave Sullivan an even more splendid belt, 48 inches long and 12 inches wide, with nine gold panels and 397 diamonds, some of which picked out Sullivan's name. It bore the legend 'Champion of Champions.' At the presentation Sullivan boomed that the *Police Gazette* belt was a dog collar.

The publicity stirred by the two belts meant that the showdown between the two men had to follow and the fight was fixed for 4 July 1889. Sullivan was deprived of champagne for six months and William Muldoon, an ex-wrestler and physical fitness expert, was engaged to get him into peak condition.

Charley Mitchell was in Kilrain's corner at Richburg, Mississippi. The fight was under prize ring rules, with Kilrain managing to throw Sullivan several times, but Sullivan's blows gradually knocking the resistance from the challenger. Several times near the end Kilrain had to be carried back to his corner. Eventually a doctor warned that should he toe the line again he could be going to his death. The corner threw in the sponge and Sullivan retained his title after 75 grueling rounds.

This was the last heavyweight championship fight under the London Prize Ring Rules. For a long time John L Sullivan had preferred to fight with gloves and his next defense of his title was to take place under Queensberry Rules.

The Queensberry Rules

There is no doubt that without the Queensberry Rules, or something like them, boxing would not have survived until today. Under the London Prize Ring Rules which preceded them, boxing was already illegal in most countries where it was practiced. The adoption of the Queensberry Rules allowed the authorities to take a more lenient view and while boxing was not to be without its future legal difficulties it gradually regained respectability.

John Sholto Douglas, the Eighth Marquis of Queensberry, was an all-round sportsman, particularly at home with horses, and he rode many winners of steeplechases and hurdles races. At Cambridge University he boxed to a high standard and became an amateur champion.

Although his family estates were in Scotland, he preferred to live a full life in London where he belonged to the Pelican Club, a leading sporting club of the day whose members promoted fights. In fact they arranged for a rather notorious bare-knuckle encounter in 1889 between Jem Smith and Frank Slavin in which Slavin was abused and robbed of the verdict to suit the gamblers. This was 22 years after Queensberry had drawn up his rules.

Queensberry was helped by a friend and fellow student at Cambridge University, John Graham Chambers. The two came to America to compare the boxing here with the local product. Chambers, however, was not the Arthur Chambers who came to America to claim the world lightweight title in 1872, although because the two men shared the same name they have been confused in reference books.

The main innovation was the introduction of gloves. Another, which saved the boxer unnecessary hurt, was the concept of a three-minute round, with the need for a boxer knocked down to 'come to the scratch' unassisted in 10 seconds. This meant that many a bout ended quite soon, whereas under the old rules a badly hurt boxer would have been dragged to his corner by his seconds, partly revived, and sent back for more suffering.

With necessary amendments, the Rules have not altered much in the succeeding 120 years. The main change is that bouts themselves, as well as rounds, have time limits. The original Queensberry Rules still assumed that a contest would

The Queensberry Rules, published in 1867, were as follows:

1 To be a fair stand-up boxing match in a 24-foot ring, or as near that size as practicable.

2 No wrestling or hugging allowed.

3 The rounds to be of three minutes duration and one minute time between rounds.

4 If either man fall through weakness or otherwise, he must get up unassisted, 10 seconds to be allowed him to do so, the other man meanwhile to return to his corner; and when the fallen man is on his legs the round to be resumed and continued till the three minutes have expired. If one man fails to come to the scratch in the 10 seconds allowed it shall be in the power of the referee to give his award in favor of the other man.

5 A man hanging on the ropes in a helpless state, with his toes off the ground, shall be considered down.

6 No seconds or any other person to be allowed in the ring during the rounds.

7 Should the contest be stopped by any unavoidable interference, the referee to name the time and place as soon as possible for finishing the contest, so that the match must be won and lost, unless the backers of the men agree to draw the stakes.

8 The gloves to be fair-sized boxing gloves of the best quality and new.

9 Should a glove burst, or come off, it must be replaced to the referee's satisfaction.

10 A man on one knee is considered down, and if struck is entitled to the stakes.

11 No shoes or boots with springs allowed.

12 The contest in all other respects to be governed by the revised rules of the London Prize Ring.

RIGHT: *The Eighth Marquis of Queensberry, whose name lives on with the 12 rules that form the basis of the rules used today. It is probable that his friend Chambers did most of the work in drawing up the rules.*

ABOVE LEFT: *Jake Kilrain, five years before his epic bare-knuckle battle with John L Sullivan, boxing Mike Cleary, with gloves. The contest was held at Madison Square Garden, New York, on 26 June 1884.*

ABOVE: *A woodcut of an 1885 meeting between Alfred Greenfield and George Fryer in Industrial Hall, Philadelphia. The two put on a display wearing gloves which was described as exciting and artistic.*

RIGHT: *Dominic McCaffrey knocks out 'Sparrow' Golden with a classic straight left at the Palisades in 1886. McCaffrey fought Sullivan on 29 August 1885 in Cincinnati in a fight billed as 'the Marquis of Queensberry gloves contest for the championship of the world,' where 'the fight will be under Marquis of Queensberry Rules.' Some authorities, including* The Ring *magazine, consider this to be the first world heavyweight title fight and Sullivan, therefore, the first champion.*

ABOVE: *Peter Jackson (right) fighting James J Corbett at the California Athletic Club on 21 May 1891. The result was a draw that established Corbett's claim to a title fight.*

BELOW: *Charley Mitchell, the Englishman who fought often in America, gets a right home on his opponent Sherriff, in an early glove contest at Long Island in 1883.*

end only when one man was unable to continue. The promoters themselves soon began to impose a limit to a fight – at first 45 rounds. Nowadays no bout is longer than 15 rounds. A limit on a bout meant the need for a scoring system. The idea of assessing the boxers' performances round by round and awarding 'points' to determine a winner began in Britain.

John L Sullivan, the last bare-knuckle heavyweight champion, preferred boxing with gloves. Of the London Prize Ring Rules he said: 'They allow too much leeway for the rowdy element to indulge in their practices. Such mean tricks as spiking, biting, gouging, strangling, butting with the head, falling down without being struck, scratching with the nails, kicking, falling on an antagonist with the knees, are impossible under the Queensberry Rules. Fighting under the new rules before gentlemen is a pleasure.'

The first champions with good claims to world honors to win their titles wearing gloves are as follows:

Heavyweight:	James J Corbett (1882)
Light-heavyweight:	Jack Root (1903)
Middleweight:	Jack Dempsey (1884)
Welterweight:	'Mysterious' Billy Smith (1892)
Lightweight:	George Lavigne (1896)
Featherweight:	George Dixon (1890)
Bantamweight:	Billy Plimmer (1892)
Flyweight:	Jimmy Wilde (1916)

The Marquis of Queensberry performed a great service to boxing, revolutionizing it into the popular sport that it is today. Before he died in 1900 he achieved less fortunate fame in the literary world, when he was sued by Oscar Wilde, an action which brought about Wilde's downfall.

The First Heavyweight Title Fight

The champion of the world, John L Sullivan, went on the stage after his whipping of Jake Kilrain. He toured America as the hero of a melodrama called *Honest Hearts and Willing Hands*. He

BELOW: *James J Corbett, acknowledged generally as the first heavyweight champion.*

boxed only exhibitions, he returned to his champagne and generally he did not live like a champion should.

During this period he was to meet his next opponent, James Corbett. He embarrassed Corbett by taking him into a saloon and making his famous boast: 'I can lick any sonofabitch in the house.' They met again at the Grand Opera House at San Francisco, where John L had agreed to box an exhibition with his young challenger. On the night, to the audience's disappointment, Sullivan insisted on sparring with gloves in evening dress. In the end the men took their jackets off and went through the motions but Corbett claimed he had learned enough. He told his manager, William A Brady, that Sullivan was a sucker for a feint.

Sullivan, pressed by challengers for his title, issued a challenge himself. Addressed to the 'bluffers who have been trying to make capital at my expense,' he named his preferred opponents, first Frank Slavin of Australia, second Charley Mitchell of England, 'who I would sooner whip than any man in the world,' and third James Corbett of California, 'who has done his share of bombast.' The condition for fighting was a $10,000 side bet. Only Corbett could raise this cash and in March 1892 the two men signed for the fight – which would be fought with five-ounce gloves at the Olympic Club, New Orleans – for a $25,000 purse and the $20,000 stakes.

Corbett, eight years younger than Sullivan, was born on 1 September 1866 in San Francisco, one of 12 children of Irish parents. He became a clerk, then a teller in a bank, then went on to enjoy a successful amateur boxing career before turning professional at 19, when he was coached at the Olympic Club by Professor Watson. He progressed, twice beat Joe Choynski, an excellent local rival, and attracted national attention by beating Jake Kilrain. He underlined his claims for a shot at Sullivan by taking on the outstanding West Indian, Peter Jackson, in 1891. For some time Jackson had been a natural challenger for Sullivan, but Sullivan had drawn the color line. Corbett conceded Jackson 30 pounds, and the two boxed a grueling and exhausting draw over 61 rounds.

William A Brady, a theatrical impresario, took over Corbett's managership and billed him as 'the next heavyweight champion of the world.'

Corbett was very different from Sullivan. He was well educated (his mother wanted him to be a priest) but enjoyed the bustle of the streets and the fighting. He took his training seriously and studied fighting techniques, bringing science to the heavyweight ranks. At 6 feet 1 inch tall and weighing 178 pounds, Corbett was handsome and a neat dresser and became known as 'Gentleman Jim.'

Both men trained hard for the fight, but it was easier for Corbett. Sullivan did not have William Muldoon to help him this time. He stopped drinking of course, but the effects of the recent years of soft living could not be shrugged off easily.

The match was to be the climax of a three-day Carnival of Champions, on each day of which a world championship was to be decided. On the first day George Dixon was to defend his featherweight title against Jack Skelly, on the second Billy McAuliffe was to defend his lightweight title against Billy Myer, and finally the great John L Sullivan himself was to defend against Gentleman Jim.

New Orleans was full of fight fans and the hangers-on of the fight game, not all of them the most savory of characters – there was money around and consequently gamblers and conmen, not to mention ladies of the night. Corbett arrived from his training camp in New Jersey quietly and confidently. He even continued his training on the journey, a gymnasium having been fitted up in the baggage car attached to his train. Sullivan traveled from Good Island like a king. There were many to shake his hand at every stop, to drink his health, to participate in the progress of a legend. Sullivan was 4-to-1-on in the betting. Nobody around him could contemplate defeat.

The open-air arena was covered by tarpaulin which was rolled back to allow the crowd of 7000 or so to breathe some air. They soon saw tactics which were unfamiliar to them and which they did not like. Sullivan, who was as fit as any 34-year-old who had drunk as much alcohol in his life as he had, came in swinging his powerful blows at Corbett's face. Any one of them, had it landed correctly, could have ended the fight. But Corbett swayed and dodged, easily avoiding his opponent's fists, while contenting himself with straight lefts to Sullivan's body. Even when Corbett was trapped on the ropes, a position usually painful when he was facing Sullivan, a twist of the shoulders would extricate him, and Sullivan would find himself attacking the air.

The crowd booed. This was not the blood-and-guts sparring they were used to and expected. It seemed to them the smart young challenger was making a fool of their hero with his ducking and dodging.

Soon, however, it was clear that the great Sullivan was becoming tired through his own efforts. It was noticeable that Corbett was now getting in stinging blows to Sullivan's face, and John L began bleeding from the nose. The crowd's jeering was now in the past. After an hour Sullivan staked all on a desperate attack but his challenger evaded his lumbering punches as easily as before.

In the twenty-first round a weary John L was dropped to his knees by a right to the chin. Hauling himself up he was put on the floor three more times, the third time leaving him unable to rise. An unmarked Corbett had become the first heavyweight champion of the world.

Sullivan had lost his invincibility, but he was magnificent in defeat. When he recovered he stood in the center of the ring and demanded silence. 'I was beaten fairly by a fellow American and I am glad the championship stays in this country,' he said. Then he left weeping and his fans wept with him.

Sullivan had one great victory left. He beat the bottle. Not only did he stop drinking, he turned evangelist and earned a living touring America preaching against the evils of alcohol.

RIGHT: *James J Corbett in 1909, six years after his retirement from the ring, but still with a fine figure and with the air of a man living up to his nickname of 'Gentleman Jim.'*

BELOW: *The mustachioed John L Sullivan in his prime. He became a legend, his aura of invincibility and his swagger in private life helping to popularize the fight game. His final defeat was dignified, and his later conversion to preaching against alcohol extended the legend.*

The First
Fight Film Attempt

Corbett is recognized by historians as a man who altered the face of heavyweight boxing. Until Corbett the great battles had been, on the whole, trials of strength and endurance. Champions like Mace had clearly possessed skill and expertise, but to the American public a champion should be in the mold of Ryan or Sullivan, the sort of man to be on the right side of in a bar-room brawl – a 'fighting man.'

To American fight fans Gentleman Jim Corbett was all wrong. He had worked in a bank, he dressed well but conservatively, he took trouble over his appearance and he fought not as one who enjoyed a scrap but as somebody who seemed to plan a fight like a game of chess, working out moves and strategies. Defensive maneuvers were as important, even more important than mixing it in the center of the ring.

On winning the championship Corbett did try to do the right thing by offering a title shot to Peter Jackson, whom Sullivan had refused to meet and with whom Corbett had fought that great 61-round draw a couple of years earlier. Since then the 32-year-old Jackson had engaged in a hard 10-round battle for the British Empire title in London, knocking out the Austra-lian Frank Slavin. However he became ill and as a result the match fell through.

There were no other obvious challengers around so Corbett went off on tour with a play specially written for him, *Gentleman Jack*. John L had trod the boards, but Corbett appeared to be more interested in acting than fighting. What's more, he was good at it. The fans, already resentful that Corbett had toppled their idol, were not keen on his 'image.' He was never to receive the rewards or the popularity that his place in boxing justified.

One who mocked Corbett's acting abilities in the sporting papers was none other than Charley Mitchell, now 33 years old. He repeated the vilification campaign that had so annoyed Sullivan and, persuading a sporting club to put up a $20,000 purse, provoked Corbett into accepting a challenge.

The two met on 25 January 1894 and Mitchell used his usual tactics of jeering at his opponent to unsettle him. It didn't work with Corbett. Both Mitchell and Corbett had fought Sullivan in the same manner – by avoiding a toe-to-toe battle and countering shrewdly. But Mitchell could not keep away the younger, taller, heavier, stronger and just as clever Corbett, and he took a beating before his third-round knockout.

Corbett took part in a fight involving the first use of a motion picture camera to record a fight. The fight, on 8 September 1894, was reported as legitimate, but it is now accepted as one which was arranged. It took place at the Edison Laboratory in Orange, New Jersey in a studio called a kinetographic theater, but more popularly known as the 'Black Maria.' This was built on a circular track, so that it could be swiveled round to follow the sun. It was only 15 feet wide, the padded walls representing two sides of the 'ring,' while ropes were stretched across to form the other two sides. Corbett's opponent was a local man, Peter Courtney. The camera began filming at the start of a round, but as the film lasted only 90 seconds, so did the rounds, time being called when the film ran out. The intervals between rounds, when the camera was reloaded and sometimes the studio re-aligned, lasted longer than the rounds themselves. Corbett 'knocked out' Courtney in the sixth round.

With the most persistent challenger to Corbett being Bob Fitzsimmons, whom Corbett despised, Gentleman Jim decided to retire. He announced that the winner of a match be-

ABOVE: *Corbett's first defense of his title was against the Englishman, Charley Mitchell. The two met at Jacksonville, Florida, on 25 January 1894; Corbett (right) proved too strong* *for Mitchell who was knocked out in the third. The artist has caught the likeness of the boxers, but was certainly not at the fight – the clinch is most unlikely, and the boxers wore gloves.*

tween Steve O'Donnell, in whom he had an interest, and Peter Maher, would be the new champion. Alas for Corbett, Maher won with a first-round knockout, and Corbett had to congratulate him on being his successor. Neither the Irishman Maher nor the public took this abdication seriously, and Maher has not gone into the sporting records. However Maher's victory did inspire the first attempt to film a genuine fight.

Fitzsimmons had beaten Maher in a scintillating match in 1892, and public interest was enormous when the two arranged to meet 'near El Paso' on 14 February 1896. Racketeers, reporters, swindlers and genuine fight fans poured into the town. Among them were the backers of Edison's Kinetoscope, who had arranged with promoter Don Stuart to film the fight. The talk around the bars was that the new 'moving pictures' would make somebody a fortune. Fitzsimmons got to hear of this and thought that some of this extra money should be his. He set about tackling the promoter about it.

Fitzsimmons received no joy from Stuart, who pointed out that according to contract Fitz was paid to fight, not act, and that 'all privileges appertaining to the contest were at the absolute disposal of Dan A Stuart.' Fitz said that in that case there would not be any moving pictures. At which Judge Roy Bean, who administered the law in nearby Langtry and had invited Stuart to hold the fight there, fingered his gun suggestively and told Fitzsimmons to get back to his business.

The atmosphere in El Paso became overpowering. Maher got dust in his eyes and the fight was postponed for a week, leaving the edgy populace to entertain itself in as many devious ways as possible. Already squads of Texas Rangers were in town to prevent the fight taking place in Texas. Mexican soldiers were at the border to stop it there. Bat Masterton, the Western marshal, was also in town with a band of gunmen, having been engaged by the promoter to protect the boxers and the Kinetoscope.

Eventually the train for the fight left El Paso carrying the fans to the unknown venue, which they discovered to be Langtry. From there the contingent entered Mexican territory.

A wooden tower was erected for the Kinetoscope and at 5 pm on 21 February the fight began. Well before 5.02 pm it ended. Maher split Fitzsimmons's nose with the first punch. He was following up his advantage when Fitz made him miss, sunk a left to his body and knocked him clean out. The fight was over in 95 seconds, before the Kinetoscope crew had started to film.

Three weeks later the boxers re-enacted the fight for the Kinetoscope and Fitzsimmons got paid. But it was to be another year before a real fight was filmed.

BELOW: *The contest between Bob Fitzsimmons and Peter Maher in Texas in 1896 should have been the first genuine fight to be filmed, but the fight ended before the Kinetoscope was ready.*

RIGHT BELOW: *Jack Dempsey, 'The Nonpareil,' receiving a belt signifying his world middleweight championship from Edward Mallahan, a well-known sporting patron, in 1886.*

The Original Jack Dempsey

It has always been easy to recognize *the* champion of the world. He is simply the man who can beat all others. But how can a lighter man prove his worth? He can profess that he is the best man at his weight in the world. Before the weight divisions as we know them now became formalized in the twentieth century, this is what boxers did. Whatever weight a champion fancied became the weight limit. Bob Fitzsimmons, for example, won what had come to be regarded as the middleweight title, and promptly set about raising the weight limit by a few pounds.

Of course anybody could proclaim himself champion and it is impossible to say dogmatically before the twentieth century who the champions at lighter weights really were. Lists of nineteenth century champions published today vary from reference book to reference book and from expert to expert. However some men so stood out so clearly that there is general agreement on their claims.

One of the earliest was the man from whom Bob Fitzsimmons won the middleweight title. He was born John Kelly in County Kildare, Ireland, on 15 December 1862. Taken to New York as a boy, he became a cooper. In 1883 he volunteered himself as a substitute at a boxing show and, giving himself the name of Jack Dempsey, he emerged as the winner when he succeeded in knocking out Ed McDonald in 21 rounds.

He weighed no more than 150 pounds, and when George Fulljames of Toronto, who held the Canadian title, offered to fight anybody for the vacant world middleweight title, Dempsey accepted the offer. On 30 July 1884 at Great Kills, Staten Island, he knocked his opponent out in 22 rounds and was acclaimed by Americans as the 'middleweight champion of the world.' Because nobody could be found to beat him he was called 'The Nonpareil' – having no equal. Dempsey knocked out another Canadian, George LaBlanche, 'The Marine,' in 1886 and next year fought Johnny Reagan at Huntingdon, Long Island in a bout remarkable for being held in two rings. After eight rounds the rising tide meant the boxers were fighting in two inches of water, so the two boxers, the officials and 25 spectators boarded their tug and found a better spot 25 miles away. Dempsey won in 45 rounds.

Dempsey drew with Professor Mike Donovan, a former 'champion,' in six rounds and then met with his first reverse. In a return with George LaBlanche, Dempsey was on top in the thirty-second round when LaBlanche missed with a hook and then, pivoting on his heel, brought his arm back and knocked Dempsey out with his elbow. He was awarded the fight by the referee, but the boxing world objected and it was generally agreed that Dempsey remained the champion. The 'pivot punch' was rapidly outlawed.

Dempsey beat his next challenger, Billy McCarthy, but lost his title on 14 January 1891. He fought Bob Fitzsimmons in New Orleans for a record purse of $12,000 in front of an enormous crowd of 4000 spectators. Fitzsimmons was on top right from the beginning, knocking Dempsey down as many as three times in the fourth round. In the eleventh round he was down four times, including being knocked out of the ring on one occasion. In the next two rounds he was down five more times, until in the thirteenth round, when he clearly could not rise from a right to the jaw, the sponge was thrown in. It was his first defeat, except by a disqualification.

Dempsey fought a few more times, losing once more, but in 1895 he became ill and he died on 1 November in Portland, Oregon. His lawyer, coming across his grave, wrote a poem which was published four years after Dempsey's death. Sufficient funds were raised to erect a tombstone on which the poem was engraved.

The Nonpareil's Grave

Far out in the wilds of Oregon,
  On a lonely mountain side,
Where Columbia's mighty waters,
  Roll down to the ocean side;
Where the giant fir and cedar
  Are imaged in the wave
O'ergrown with fire and lichens,
  I found Jack Dempsey's grave.

I found no marble monolith
  No broken shaft, or stone,
Recording sixty victories,
  This vanquished victor won;
No rose, no shamrock could I find,
  No mortal here to tell
Where sleeps in this forsaken spot
  Immortal Nonpareil.

A winding wooden canyon road
  That mortals seldom tread,
Leads up this lonely mountain,
  To the desert of the dead,
And the Western sun was sinking
  In Pacific's golden wave
And those solemn pines kept watching
  Over poor Jack Dempsey's grave.

Forgotten by ten thousand throats,
  That thundered his acclaim,
Forgotten by his friends and foes,
  Who cheered his very name
Oblivion wraps his faded form,
  But ages hence shall save
The memory of that Irish lad
  That fills poor Dempsey's grave.

Oh, Fame, why sleeps thy favored son
  In wilds, in woods, in weeds,
And shall he ever thus sleep on,
  Interred his valiant deeds,
'Tis strange New York should thus forget
  Its 'bravest of the brave'
And in the fields of Oregon,
  Unmarked, leave Dempsey's grave.

Dempsey's last defeat was inflicted by Tommy Ryan, who was the world welterweight king. Ryan was born in Redwood, New York and was a brilliant all-round boxer with a big punch. He was later to become middleweight champion. He took his welter title by outpointing 'Mysterious' Billy Smith in a fight held in 1894.

Smith was born in Eastport, Maine, on 15 May 1871. At first he boxed under his real name, but switching his attentions to California he decided to become Billy Smith, which he thought was more of a fighting name. He ran up a string of wins and claimed to be welterweight champion of the world. A fan wrote

to the New York *Police News*, a boxing paper, asking who this Billy Smith was. The 'Mysterious' Billy Smith was identified and the name stuck. Smith regained the title in 1896 when it fell vacant and held it till 1900.

A great champion of the 1890s was George Dixon of Canada, a featherweight. Other men had claimed the title before him, notably Ike Weir of Ireland, 'Torpedo' Billy Murphy of New Zealand and the brilliant Young Griffo of Australia. It was difficult for an Antipodean to get recognition in America, however justified the claim, and it was not until George Dixon knocked out Fred Johnson of England in 1892 (Young Griffo having by then outgrown the division) that a champion was universally agreed. Dixon was only 5 feet 3½ inches tall (being hardly more than a bantamweight) and so dark-skinned that he was known as 'Little Chocolate.' He was a very busy boxer and held the title, off and on, until 1900 when he lost it finally to Terry McGovern. After this he had 57 more fights, winning

RIGHT: *Jack Dempsey, the handsome Irishman from County Kildare, who was taken to New York as a boy and became one of the great middleweight boxers. He was only 33 when he died, but his skill was such that he will always be remembered; he had one of the most striking sobriquets, 'The Nonpareil,' and is the subject of boxing's best-known poem (see facing page).*

Copyrighted By John Wood N.Y. 1886.

LEFT ABOVE: *Dempsey (right), the* Police Gazette *champion of America, was challenged by Jack Burke of London, on 22 November 1886. The fight took place at San Francisco, and Dempsey is shown attacking at the final bell. He got the decision.*

LEFT: *Jack Dempsey acknowledging the applause at the Olympic Club, New Orleans, on 14 January 1891. His opponent, Bob Fitzsimmons, does not look so happy. However, Fitzsimmons gave Dempsey his first bad defeat, and took his title. Dempsey lived for less than five years afterward.*

only 11. In the 1892 Carnival of Champions, in which Corbett won the heavyweight title, Dixon knocked out Jack Skelly.

The third world championship billed in that carnival saw Jack McAuliffe retain his lightweight crown when he knocked out Billy Myer. The Irish McAuliffe, boxing out of New York, should not truly have been regarded as champion, however. In 1887 the British champion, Jem Carney, arrived in Boston to fight McAuliffe, the American champion. After five hours the Englishman was well on top. The audience interrupted the seventieth round when McAuliffe was practically out, and when it appeared that Carney had knocked McAuliffe clean out in the seventy-fourth round, the crowd, led by a gambler named Dick Roche, again invaded the ring and forced the

referee to declare a draw. Thus McAuliffe was able to retire 'unbeaten' in 1897, one of the few champions to do so, while Carney, who was also unbeaten and the better man, is comparatively unknown. Incidents like this make it impossible to be too dogmatic about the early champions.

There is no doubt about Billy Plimmer of Birmingham, a classical boxer who won the bantamweight championship of England in 1891. He came to America the following year to outpoint Tommy Kelly for the world title and remained in the States for three years, beating all comers. He lost the title to Tom 'Pedlar' Palmer, a Cockney, in 1895. Palmer's career virtually ended in 1907 when he was jailed for manslaughter following the death of a man on a train.

The Fighting Blacksmith

Bob Fitzsimmons has already appeared twice in this history, but it was not until 1897 that he enjoyed what was to prove the greatest victory of his career.

Fitzsimmons was born in Helston, Cornwall, on 26 May 1863, the twelfth child of a policeman. When he was nine the family emigrated to Timaru, New Zealand and Bob became a blacksmith. In 1880 Jem Mace visited New Zealand and organized an amateur lightweight competition which was won by Fitzsimmons, who then decided to turn professional. In 1881 he beat five men in one night to win another Mace tournament, for middleweights. In 1883 he went to Australia and built up a string of victories, but then lost a few fights, and when he sailed for America in 1890, his record was far from impressive.

However he registered three quick wins in the year of his arrival and in January 1891 was a surprise winner of the world middleweight championship when he knocked out Jack Dempsey, 'the Nonpareil.' Finding he had run out of middleweights in 1892 he had a tremendous battle with Peter Maher, a heavyweight, to whom he conceded 13 pounds. Maher rushed in at the bell and Fitzsimmons knocked him flat. Then, as Fitz went for the knockout, he was knocked to the ground himself by a desperate left from Maher. He rose groggily and was grimly trying to avoid a knockout when the bell ended the first

round . . . early. Fitzsimmons's cornerman, Joe Choynski, had managed 'accidentally' to kick the bell, and in the confusion Fitzsimmons recovered his wits. He survived the second round, and in an exciting fight subsequently broke Maher's nose, forcing him to retire after the twelfth.

Four years later, as described, Fitz knocked out Maher in the first round at Langtry, in a fight advertised at the time as being for the 'heavyweight championship of the world.' It wasn't, of course, but it brought the day nearer when James J Corbett would accept a challenge for the real championship.

Meanwhile 'Ruby Robert,' as he was known, 'lost' his first fight in six years' campaigning in America in strange circumstances. On 2 December 1896 he fought Tom Sharkey in a notorious 'fix.' The match was in the Mechanics' Pavilion at San Francisco, with 15,000 present and more locked outside. The referee was Sharkey's friend, the notorious gunman Wyatt Earp, and thereby hangs a tale.

Fitzsimmons was giving away 20 pounds, but only the bell saved Sharkey from a first-round knockout. From then on Fitz was always on top and in the eighth round two powerful blows to the body dropped Sharkey's guard and a left hook to the chin knocked him out. With Sharkey counted out and restored to his corner, Fitz was shocked to see Earp hand him the check for the

RIGHT: *The prosperous Bob Fitzsimmons in 1899, with his monogram on his watch-chain. He was the world heavyweight champion, had been the world middleweight champion before that, and could pride himself on his achievements as an English boy who had set out for New Zealand to be a blacksmith.*

LEFT: *Gloves held high as Fitzsimmons (left) seeks an opening on his way to taking the world title from James J Corbett in 1897. Not only is the style of boxing different from today's, the style of trunks is surprisingly more revealing. Over the years this picture has frequently appeared in books with Corbett's trunks tastefully lengthened.*

$10,000 purse money. Earp announced that Fitzsimmons was disqualified for hitting low and buckled on his gun belt to show that he would tolerate no objections from the fans. It seems that Wyatt Earp was part of a conspiracy with Sharkey's cornermen. The $10,000 had been bet on Sharkey at 3 to 1 and the conspirators shared the $40,000 resulting. The whole case came to court but Fitz lost on the grounds that boxing was illegal in California.

Before the Sharkey fight contracts had been signed for Fitzsimmons to fight Corbett for the world title. This was the fourth attempt to bring the two together. One fight failed when Fitz was under arrest, charged with manslaughter, following the death of a sparring partner. He and Corbett hated each other. On one occasion Corbett had actually tweaked Fitzsimmons' nose in public, nearly causing an impromptu fight.

On appearance Fitzsimmons was the unlikeliest heavyweight champion there ever was. To start with he was no more than a top-heavy middleweight. He was pale and freckled and his thin red hair was rapidly receding, making him look bald. He was 5 feet 11¾ inches tall, but all his strength and muscle was in his blacksmith's shoulders. He looked lanky and his legs were so spindly that in his early days he padded out his tights to make them look more muscular.

The title fight was at Carson City on 17 March 1897. An open-air arena was specially built for it. Bat Masterson and his crew again controlled the crowds and looked after the offensive weapons of the 4000 spectators. The movie cameras were there, this time with the approval of the boxers, and as the fight was at noon and the sun was shining, conditions were ideal for them. Fitzsimmons's wife Rose was also there as a spectator,

and was to play an important part in the outcome.

Fitzsimmons was now almost 34, three years older than his opponent, and physically inferior in every respect except chest measurement. He was conceding 13 pounds – at 157 pounds he was still a middleweight by today's standards.

Corbett had the better of exchanges from the start. He was the better boxer and caught Fitzsimmons with several good blows to his face, which was soon covered with blood from the challenger's nose and mouth. Rose now took a hand. Moving to her husband's corner she told him to keep hitting Corbett in the 'slats.' 'He can't take it to the body,' she said.

In the sixth Corbett had Fitz groggy and desperately trying to survive. Finally, a left smashed him to his knees. Fitzsimmons rose and grimly held on for the rest of the round. Corbett's failure to knock him out in that round was a turning point. Gentleman Jim stayed on top but as the fight continued it seemed that the body blows of Fitz were gradually slowing him down, while Fitzsimmons himself seemed to have recovered from the punishment he had taken.

In the fourteenth Fitz caught Corbett with thudding blows to the mouth and head and then, after throwing a right with right foot forward he suddenly, without changing the position of his feet, drove a powerful left to Corbett's body just below the ribs. It made famous the 'solar plexus.' Corbett's face drained of color as he collapsed to the boards. He tried to beat the count but couldn't.

Fitz had won the heavyweight championship, the $15,000 purse, Corbett's $10,000 stake, and about $13,000 for the film fee. The film proved very successful – it will be remembered too as the first film ever made of a championship fight.

The Boilermaker

After winning the heavyweight title Fitzsimmons followed the example of the previous two champions by going on the stage for two years. It was a logical decision because his wife Rose, who toured with him, had already appeared on the boards as an acrobat. Their specially written play was called *The Honest Blacksmith*. Audiences loved it and Fitzsimmons was able to ignore all the challengers who clamored for a title shot, most of whom he had already beaten anyway.

One he hadn't met was a huge iron worker called James J Jeffries. Jeffries was born on 15 April 1875 in Carroll, Ohio. His family moved to California where he was apprenticed to a boilermaker; this work helped develop his physique until he stood 6 feet 2 inches tall and weighed 220 pounds, all of it muscle. He joined Corbett's training camp for the fight with Fitzsimmons. Corbett was surprised at his fitness and speed and no doubt Jeffries learned something of the boxing art from Corbett. He began a promising career, beating an ailing Peter Jackson and Tom Sharkey, and was invited to New York where he was unimpressive in beating a veteran, Bob Armstrong – in doing so he also damaged his own hands.

William A Brady, Jeffries' adviser, persuaded Fitzsimmons that easy money could be made by fighting the clumsy Jeffries, and Fitz agreed to defend at Coney Island on 9 June 1899. Meanwhile Tommy Ryan, the new middleweight champion, was engaged to coach the young giant for the fight, and he persuaded Jeffries to fight from a crouching stance which made him hard to hit.

Fitz did not take Jeffries seriously and at a party before the fight even sipped some champagne. He got a shock at the weigh-in when Jeffries gave him a hug and let him know his strength. He got a bigger shock in the fight when his best blows bounced off Jeffries without seeming to have any effect. Fitzsimmons was now 36 years old. He had come in at 167 pounds, no less than 38 pounds lighter than Jeffries. In the second round Fitzsimmons was put on his back by a straight left from the determined challenger.

Fitzsimmons fought a brave uphill battle until the eleventh, getting in more blows and making a mess of Jeffries' face, but wilting every time Jeffries caught him with one of his bombs. Finally two blows to the heart and one to the chin stopped the champion's assault, and as he stood helpless, a left and right to the chin knocked him out.

The new champion's strength led Jack London, the novelist, to call him 'The Iron Man of the Ring,' but it was an earlier nickname, 'The Boilermaker,' which lasted the longer. He was only 24 years old and did not intend to be idle. Only five months after his victory, on 3 November, he was back in the Coney Island ring defending against Tom Sharkey.

Sharkey was an Irish sailor and an experienced professional who had already gone 20 rounds with Jeffries and had since won an unsatisfactory fight with Corbett on a disqualification. With a sailing ship surmounted by a star tattooed on his chest and a huge cauliflower ear, he looked every inch a tough scrapper, and he was, but he could not match 'The Boilermaker' in size or strength.

The fight was the first indoor fight to be filmed. It required 400 arc lights of 200 candle-power each to be hung over the ring. The heat was tremendous and 'The Boilermaker,' who perhaps would have known, said afterward it was like fighting in a furnace. It did not seem to affect the boxers who put on an all-action show. Jeffries had Sharkey down in the second round with a fierce uppercut, but from then on each gave as good as he got. In the seventeenth Sharkey hit Jeffries with what 'The Boilermaker' said was the hardest punch he ever felt, but he did not go down. In the following round he returned the compliment with a blow which broke two of Sharkey's ribs. Still Sharkey would not give in and in the twenty-fifth and last round was fighting back with all he had left, but he was in a sorry state. Besides the punishment he had taken, his head (and Jeffries') was blistered by the lights. 'No braver man than Sharkey ever lived,' said Jeffries. 'I was sure one of us would be killed.' In fact Sharkey went to hospital, and Jeffries, who won the decision but lost 20 pounds in weight, was held by police for a while in case his opponent died.

Jeffries then accepted a challenge from the former champion, Gentleman Jim Corbett. Corbett had been running a saloon but had kept in condition and knew that he could outbox Jeffries as easily as he had Sullivan. He secretly went into training for a year before persuading Brady, now Jeffries' manager and formerly his own, to agree to the fight. Originally October 1899 was suggested but Brady heard of the training

RIGHT: *Jim Jeffries with his wife in 1909 appear a prosperous and happy couple. Jeffries had retired about five years earlier and had, moreover, retired unbeaten. Sadly Jeffries bowed to pressure and made a return the following year, losing his unbeaten record to Jack Johnson.*

BELOW LEFT: *One of Jeffries' hardest fights was with Tom Sharkey, who nearly died afterward. In later life Sharkey went to live with Jeffries and the two men became inseparable.*

BELOW: *Jeffries (left) shakes hands with Bob Fitzsimmons at Coney Island, New York, on 9 June 1899. The referee is Ed Graney, the fight Jeffries' challenge for Fitzsimmons's world title. Jeffries was too young and strong for the 36-year-old 'Ruby Robert.'*

Corbett had put in and put the fight back to 11 May 1900 to ensure 'The Boilermaker' was ready. The bout was again at Coney Island.

The experts thought that the 34-year-old Corbett had little chance with the strong young champion, to whom he was conceding 1½ inches and 37 pounds. But Jeffries could not forget the days when he was the former great champion's humble sparring partner, and the more confident man was undoubtedly Corbett. He danced round Jeffries for 20 rounds (it was another 25-rounder) and the fight became an exhibition. Indeed, Corbett began to show off.

Corbett admitted later that he was already planning the program for his second spell as champion. However something went wrong in the twenty-third round. Jeffries, for once in his career, feinted and caught Corbett with a terrific punch to the chin as the challenger bounced off the ropes. Corbett could not remember the punch when he was revived later.

Gus Ruhlin was dispatched in 1901 and Bob Fitzsimmons, aged 39, tried to regain the title on 25 July 1902. Fitzsimmons was a fighting phenomenon. In 12 years' campaigning in America he had lost only once – to Jeffries – discounting the foul fiasco with Sharkey. The fight was in San Francisco and this time Fitz used different tactics. He did not try to outpunch

Jeffries but instead boxed him and was so successful that he cut the champion around the eyes and broke his nose, so that Jeffries' face was a bloody mess. However one punch paid for all. In the eighth, when Fitzsimmons was a mile ahead, a huge right caught him in his midriff. He gasped and dropped his hands and a left to the chin landed him on his hands and knees, from where he could not get up.

After Gentleman Jim Corbett's great effort, the public desired that he should have another try, and on 14 August 1903 at the Mechanics' Pavilion, San Francisco, he climbed through the ropes again. This time the 37-year-old was caught earlier and dropped in the third round. He was down again in the fifth. He had time to show he could outbox Jeffries any time but when a right to the ribs sank him in the tenth, his corner threw in the sponge.

'The Boilermaker' had now run out of worthwhile opponents. There was one man, Jack Monroe, an inexperienced miner, who had dropped him on an exhibition tour a few years earlier and he was now brought forward by promoter Jack Curley as a contender. Jeffries knocked him out in the second round in August 1904, and soon afterward announced his retirement, unbeaten. However 'The Boilermaker' was to appear on the boxing scene once more.

Rushcutter's Bay, 26 December 1908

When Jeffries retired he determined to keep an interest in the title and nominated the winner of a bout between Marvin Hart, whom he favored, and Jack Root to be the new champion. Root was the former light-heavyweight champion, a title which was at the time held by the 42-year-old Bob Fitzsimmons. Fitzsimmons will go down in history as the first man to hold world titles at three different weights – certainly an impressive achievement.

Jeffries refereed the Hart versus Root bout and raised Hart's arm after a tenth-round knockout. Hart, despite the fact that he had beaten the formidable Jack Johnson, an up-and-coming black boxer, was not regarded by the sporting public as a true heavyweight champion. He is the least-known and regarded of all those on that role of honor.

He did not hold the title long for he was soon challenged by a stocky Canadian, Tommy Burns. Burns was born Noah Brusso in Ontario on 17 June 1881. He weighed about 180 pounds, as light as any heavyweight champion except Fitzsimmons and possibly Corbett, and at only 5 feet 7 inches tall was by a long way the shortest. He fought Hart at Los Angeles on 23 February 1906 and clearly outpointed his opponent to take the title.

The clever Tommy managed his own affairs and set about making as much money as he could from his success, while at the same time attempting to convince an apathetic public of his claim to the title. He was one of the busiest of all champions. He knocked out 'Fireman' Jim Flynn in the fifteenth and last round of his first defense and then fought 'Philadelphia' Jack O'Brien, the light-heavyweight champion, in Los Angeles. Jeffries, who kept in the public eye by refereeing fights in

LEFT: *Jack Johnson (right) became the first black heavyweight champion when he followed Burns (left) to Australia and took the title in a specially built arena at Rushcutter's Bay, near Sydney, on 26 December 1908.*

BELOW: *Jack Johnson early in his career. No boxer has inspired such fear, with the possible exceptions of Sonny Liston or Mike Tyson.*

Palmer in London's East End 'Wonderland' for half the gate-money, then nipped over to Dublin to knock out the Irish champion, Jem Roche, in 88 seconds. Paris was the next port of call, where another British heavyweight, Jewey Smith, lasted five rounds and his old adversary, Australian Bill Squires, lasted eight. His European spree had lasted six months and he had registered five successful defenses.

Burns's triumph was colored by two men in the background. One was Jeffries, who many thought was still the world's best, and the other was the menacing black boxer, Jack Johnson, who had been long campaigning for a title shot. It was rumored that Johnson was on the way to Europe to challenge Burns there, so Burns fled to Australia, less from fear than for the purpose of suggesting fear – in order to boost the gate when Johnson should follow and the two would inevitably meet.

In Australia Burns teamed up with a caterer, Hugh D McIntosh, and they planned the forthcoming fight. First of all Burns whipped up interest by two defenses in little more than a week, knocking out two local boxers, the obliging Bill Squires who had arrived from Europe with Burns, and then Bill Lang.

Less than four months later came the big fight. It was scheduled for a special arena built by McIntosh at Rushcutter's Bay on the outskirts of Sydney, for Boxing Day, 26 December 1908. Burns accepted a mammoth £6000 for what he realized might well be his last big pay day. Johnson was quite happy just to get the chance and accepted a quarter of this fee. There was huge publicity for the black versus white battle, much of it in racist terms. More than 16,000 fans bought tickets and many more couldn't get in. The gate totaled £26,200 and McIntosh was on the way to a fortune which financed, among other things, his Black and White chain of milk bars.

Johnson stood 6 feet 1¼ inches and weighed about 200 pounds. In retrospect it is easy to see that Burns stood no chance, but this wasn't the universal opinion before the fight. However it took only 20 seconds or so for the fans to see it this way, for this is how long it took for Burns to be down. He rose and fought with great courage but Johnson appeared to be able to do as he pleased. Even inside, where he was at his best, the champion could make no impression.

Throughout the fight Johnson smiled at, mocked and talked to Burns, and gave the impression that he could win at any time. A great rally by Burns in the seventh seemed to be enjoyed as much by Johnson as the crowd, the bigger man encouraging Burns and responding with some of his own best shots. The crowd cheered when Burns drew blood from Johnson's mouth but it was a minor success. Gradually the game champion was cut and battered into submission. In the fourteenth he sank to the floor and rose so ripe for the knockout that it seemed even Johnson could not prolong the agony further. He didn't get the opportunity. The chief of police climbed into the ring and the referee, Hugh McIntosh himself, was forced to intervene in order to stop the carnage.

A black man was world champion for the first time. It was hard for some to take. The story of Johnson's ruthlessness went round the world. At the ringside was Jack London, the famous novelist, and a man with extreme racist views. He highlighted the golden crowns in Johnson's teeth which shone when Johnson laughed his contempt of his opponent. He campaigned against the champion, urging boxers everywhere to 'wipe the golden smile off the nigger's face.' Johnson himself referred to this in his autobiography, saying that during the fight he was watching a lone, rapt, colored spectator sitting on a fence, concentrating with open mouth and bulging eyes on making all the moves, with Johnson, swaying, feinting, ducking. On one violent maneuver, according to Johnson, the man fell off the fence, at which Johnson laughed heartily, and this gave rise to London's canard.

Johnson, justifiably or not, gained the unenviable reputation of being regarded as the most hated champion of all.

California, made it a draw after 20 rounds but most thought this favored O'Brien.

Burns put the record straight with a decision over 20 rounds six months later, then knocked out previously unbeaten Bill Squires from Australia in the first round. Next Burns took off to cash in in London and did so, knocking out the British champion, Gunner Moir, in the tenth round. Burns collected £3000 as a flat fee, win or lose, but he upset the National Sporting Club, a body of gentlemen, by insisting on the fee being paid before the fight. The NSC therefore refused to pay £6000 for a bout with Sam Langford, which was a pity. Langford was a black boxer whom many boxing observers thought was the best in the world at the time.

However, in quick succession Burns knocked out Jack

'Lil Arfa' and the White Hopes

John Arthur Johnson was born in Galveston, Texas, on 31 March 1878, one of a family of two boys and three girls. His father had been a fighter but was now a school janitor. Johnson as a boy was said to be timid, but a variety of hard jobs and a liking for train-hopping soon made him an expert with his fists. He began boxing in the 1890s and took part in the sort of contest that black boxers were generally forced into in those days: the battle royal. A number were cast into the ring at the same time – the survivor taking the money.

In 1901 he fought Joe Choynski, a heavyweight contender, and was knocked out. But most of the time he won and for six years he traveled the country fighting in Los Angeles and Philadelphia and later in New York and many other eastern venues. Mostly he fought black fighters, and by beating Denver Ed Martin over 20 rounds at Los Angeles on 3 February 1903, he won what was billed as 'the colored heavyweight championship of the world.' He lost a 20-round decision to Marvin Hart, who was shortly to become world champion, in San Francisco in 1905, and in two rounds knocked out the ancient Bob Fitzsimmons, an ex-champion, in Philadelphia in 1907. He fought the leading black boxers of his day: principally Joe Jeannette and Sam McVey. Many bouts were no-decision contests but Johnson generally had the edge. He met Sam Langford, another great black boxer but a middleweight, only once, winning on points in 1906. Langford often claimed that Johnson avoided him thereafter.

Johnson was called 'The Galveston Giant' by the sporting papers, but liked to call himself, in a self-mocking but menacing way, 'Little Arthur,' Arthur being his second name. This was transcribed by the papers, in a patronizing attempt at his manner of speech as, 'Lil Arfa.'

In 1908 Lil Arfa, now aged 30, finally achieved a shot at the world championship and, as related, made up for a lot of the indignities of the battles royal and the insults which Burns and the white race heaped upon him generally, by systematically beating the champion into submission.

BELOW: *Jack Johnson (left) and Sam McVey square up before their contest in Los Angeles on 27 February 1903. Johnson won on points over 20 rounds.*

In his previous fight three weeks earlier Johnson had won what was described as the 'colored heavyweight championship of the world.'

There seemed to be one man in the world who might beat Johnson: James J Jeffries, although in retrospect we can see that this optimism was 90 percent wishful thinking. Jeffries, during his career, had appeared indestructable and was unbeaten, but he had retired five years earlier and had since been enjoying a life of ease on his alfalfa farm, resisting all pleas to come back. However, the demand of the white public, led by Jack London, for Jeffries to come back and whip Johnson, became so great that he finally agreed, and promoter Tex Rickard secured what at the time was the greatest fight in history. It cost him a combined purse of $101,000 plus $10,000 'under the counter' for each man. The boxers also received over $100,000 for the picture rights. The venue was Reno, Nevada, the date 4 July 1910 (Independence Day) and Rickard refereed the fight himself.

The atmosphere of the match was a deplorable indication, not only of the sportsmanship of the day, but the racial tensions. Johnson had received threats that he would be shot by a gunman in the crowd, the band repeatedly played a tune with the line 'All coons look alike to me,' Johnson was booed and jeered, and Jeffries, introduced as 'champion of the world,' was received with prolonged cheering. The fight started at 2.30 pm with about 10,000 or so spectators and as many clamoring outside the arena. Jeffries outweighed Johnson by 19 pounds and was less than three years older. But although he was the betting favorite he was noticeably not in the condition of the old days,

The hatred that the white people of America felt for Johnson and the admiration and support that he received from the black section of the community led to race riots in many parts of the United States. There was the wish and the search for a 'white hope' to beat him. There was even a 'white heavyweight championship of the world.'

Johnson returned to the States and boxed some exhibition and no-decision contests, including one with the film star Victor McLagen. Then in October 1909 he put his title on the line by fighting Stanley Ketchel, the middleweight champion, who could punch almost as hard as a heavyweight and was seen as an opponent who might possibly beat him. Johnson had such physical advantages that no doubt the two protagonists did not see it this way and it seems probable that there was agreement between them that they would make the bout look good, and, possibly, that Johnson would deliberately refrain from knocking out Ketchel.

However in the twelfth round Ketchel, who was nothing if not a natural fighter, saw an opening and smashed a hard right to Johnson's jaw. Johnson went down but was in control of his senses and rose with revenge in his heart for what he saw as a 'double-cross.' As Ketchel leaped in for the kill, Johnson met him with a murderous right uppercut that knocked Ketchel cold and removed several of his teeth. According to Johnson's autobiography, one of these teeth was found embedded in his glove – but the story is so good that succeeding historians have recorded all numbers of teeth from one to five.

40

FAR LEFT ABOVE: *Sam Langford, two years younger than Johnson, was regarded by many as an outstanding fighter who did not get the chance he deserved. Little more than a middleweight, he fought heavies.*

LEFT: *Joe Jeannette fought such great black boxers as McVey, Langford and Willis, but like them, he never had a title chance. In one Jeannette-McVey fight there were 38 knockdowns.*

ABOVE: *Johnson at the wheel of a sports car, with his manager George Little in the passenger seat. It was Johnson's high profile, his love of the good life and his preference for white women that so annoyed white Americans of his time. Johnson retained his love of fast cars and was killed driving one in 1946.*

while Johnson, on the other hand, was at his peak, a magnificent specimen of fitness.

It became clear that Jeffries could not trouble Johnson. Johnson toyed with him, smiled, talked to him, 'How do you feel, Mister Jeff?' and even sneered at James J Corbett in Jeffries' corner. As Jeffries bombarded his body he said to Corbett, 'Hallo, Jimmy, did you see that one?'

In the fifteenth Johnson cracked Jeffries to the floor and as the old champion wearily rose he was knocked down again. On the third knockdown it was clear he wouldn't beat the count and fans clambered into the ring to save him the indignity of a knockout. Rickard actually reached 'ten' but the result that has gone into the records is 'referee stopped contest.'

The result caused race riots throughout the United States. Rampaging blacks celebrated and vindictive whites sought revenge for the defeat of their champion. There were even lynchings. Eleven died on the first night alone. In severe riots in towns from Washington to Los Angeles thousands were killed, injured or arrested. The film of the fight was banned.

Rickard swore that another black would not hold the title and the search for a 'white hope' increased. Johnson was inactive in 1911, and in 1912 he disposed of Jim Flynn in Las Vegas. In 1913 the most promising of the 'white hopes,' Luther McCarthy, collapsed and died during a bout.

Meanwhile other means were employed to get rid of Johnson. His liking for white women, two of whom he married, was a prime cause of the hatred he inspired. The instrument used for his downfall was the Mann Act, a law which prohibited the transportation of women across state lines for immoral purposes. A white prostitute, Belle Schreiber, testified that Johnson had taken her to California for just such purposes. Johnson was convicted and sentenced to a year and a day's imprisonment but skipped bail and fled to Europe.

In Paris he defended his title by knocking out a wrestler, André Sproul, and by being given a mysterious draw against fellow-American Jim Johnson, against whom he broke his arm. This was the first all-black heavyweight title fight. Although he was out of condition he outpointed a Pittsburgh dentist, Frank Moran, but received no money because the promoter disappeared and the First World War broke out.

Johnson fled to Buenos Aires where he was sought out by an unscrupulous promoter, Jack Curley. Curley promised the homesick Johnson a deal he couldn't refuse. If he fought the latest white hope, Willard, he would not only make $35,000 but would be granted a pardon by the United States government. According to Johnson part of the deal was that he should lose the title but this has always been in dispute among boxing writers. Certainly the deal with the US government was a figment of Curley's imagination. But in any case Jack signed and the fight between Jack Johnson and Jess Willard was on.

RIGHT: *Jack Johnson's associations with white women ultimately caused his downfall. While in New York Johnson met Etta Terry Duryea, who is pictured here with him at the races in England. At the time of their meeting Etta was married, but she eloped with Johnson and married him once she had obtained a divorce. Two years later she shot herself, leaving a note criticizing Johnson. Within three months he had married another white girl, aged 19, whose mother brought a charge of abduction, and soon after he was indicted under the Mann Act.*

BELOW: *The Johnson versus Jeffries battle at Reno on 4 July 1910. Johnson (left) proved too strong and skillful for Jeffries, who had been living a relaxed life for six years. His victory sparked race riots across America.*

The National Sporting Club

Sporting clubs which promoted boxing matches were a common phenomenon in the early days of boxing. Even in prize-ring days there was John Jackson's Pugilistic Club where the Royal Dukes of York and Clarence, as well as an ancestor of the Marquis of Queensberry who devised the famous rules, were patrons. The position of this club was such that at the coronation of George IV in 1820 it provided a bodyguard of 18 boxers to Westminster Abbey where it was feared that the supporters of Queen Caroline, who was banned from the ceremony, might cause a riot.

In the 1880s the Pelican Club, first of Piccadilly then of Gerrard Street, London, among whose members was the Queensberry of the Rules, staged important fights before the city gentlemen who formed the membership. But a notorious match between Jem Smith and Frank Slavin, which took place at Bruges in Belgium under the Club's direction, led to its downfall. Squire Abingdon Baird had a large bet on Smith and hired a gang of ruffians to intimidate Slavin and, in fact, to hit him with sticks. When, despite all, Slavin appeard to be on the point of knocking out his man in the fourteenth round, this mob invaded the ring and the referee was forced to declare a draw which saved the unsporting squire his money. The Pelican Club insisted Slavin should have the stakes, but soon after it ceased operating.

This proved to be beneficial for boxing, for one of the men associated with it, John Fleming, joined up with Arthur 'Peggy' Bettinson, a former amateur champion, and they founded the National Sporting Club, with its headquarters in a former theater at 43 King Street in Covent Garden, London. Members came from the aristocracy and the business classes, and the idea was that boxing would be watched in comfort and without the rowdy element. In fact cheering and even talking weren't allowed during the rounds. Members wore evening dress and sat in silence, applauding politely only at the end of the round!

Boxers, too, were required to obey the rules rigidly. These became the National Sporting Club Rules, an updated version of the Queensberry Rules, and they became general throughout boxing. The club became the unofficial ruling body on British championships. As early as 1892 it staged a famous contest billed as being for the 'British Empire heavyweight championship,' an exciting affair in which Peter Jackson of the West Indies beat the unfortunate Frank Slavin of Australia. Thus it was to the benefit of boxers who were seeking recognition to box at the NSC.

The NSC won an auspicious legal case in 1901, when one of its favorite boxers, Jack Roberts, the British featherweight champion, knocked out Billy Smith, who died two days later. Roberts and the club officials were charged with the manslaughter of Murray Livingstone, Smith's real name. An important aspect of the case was whether Livingstone had died in a prize fight or in a properly regulated boxing match. The President of the NSC, Lord Lonsdale, gave evidence of the organization and standards of the club and its matches and the jury found the defendants 'not guilty.' This did not make boxing legal and all boxers were at risk of being charged should their opponents die. However, there was clearly an easing of the situation regarding boxing in England and the judiciary were only too happy to shift some of the responsibility for the supervision of the sport onto this representative club.

ABOVE: *Jim Sullivan was a favorite at the National Sporting Club, the second British middleweight champion to be recognized by the NSC. He took the title from Tom Thomas on points on 14 November 1910 in a contest over 20 rounds that was said to be one of the best ever seen. Sullivan lost in challenges for the European and world championships to Georges Carpentier and Billy Papke respectively. He is seen here wearing a very early Lonsdale Belt.*

In 1907 the NSC promoted the Tommy Burns versus Gunner Moir world heavyweight title fight, and Burns offended secretary 'Peggy' Bettinson, Lord Lonsdale and the rest, by demanding his purse in advance. It was pointed out to him that the NSC's integrity was world famous and his late apologies failed to mollify the club. When Jack Johnson arrived in London in his pursuit of Burns, he turned to the NSC for help and was given the fare to follow the disliked Burns to Australia. Johnson was popular with the NSC and promised, in return, that should he win he would repay the favor by defending against Sam Langford under the auspices of the club. This he failed to do and an angry Bettinson decreed that a black man would not be allowed to fight for a British title, and none did until after the Second World War.

The NSC really got a hold on British boxing in 1909 and paved the way for worldwide standardization by formalizing eight well-defined weight classes. They also persuaded Lord Lonsdale to lend his name to challenge belts – the famous Lonsdale Belts – to be presented to winners of championship

LEFT: 'Bombardier' Billy Wells was another NSC favorite, a handsome man well liked by women, who were beginning to take an increasing interest in boxing. He will go down in boxing history as the first British heavyweight champion to have won the NSC Lonsdale Belt.

ABOVE: Boxing at the NSC in December 1913. Georges Carpentier, the European heavyweight champion (white trunks) is swinging a right to the ribs of British champion Billy Wells. Carpentier knocked out Wells in the first round and with this victory he retained the European crown.

bouts. The belt was to denote official possession of the title, a tradition that has lasted. A boxer winning three championship contests won a Lonsdale Belt outright.

The eight weights, and the first holders of the British championships, were as follows:

Heavyweight (over 175 pounds): 'Bombardier' Billy Wells
Cruiserweight (175 pounds): Dick Smith
Middleweight (160 pounds): Tom Thomas
Welterweight (147 pounds): Young Joseph
Lightweight (135 pounds): Freddy Welsh
Featherweight (126 pounds): Jim Driscoll
Bantamweight (118 pounds): Digger Stanley
Flyweight (112 pounds): Sid Smith

In America there was already a 175-pound division known as light-heavyweight and after the Second World War the British adopted this term. Later a new cruiserweight class was to be inserted between light-heavy and heavyweight.

Boxing was less formal in America with promoters making their own claims of championships and surviving as best they could against the laws of various states. The first state to permit boxing was New York State where the Horton Law, in operation from 1896 to 1900, permitted fights, decisions, purses and side-stakes. The Frawley Law, however, in operation from

1901 to 1918, confined boxing to private clubs only and limited bouts to ten rounds. Referees were not allowed to give decisions, hence the number of no-decision bouts on the records of boxers of the era. To win a title a challenger had to knock out the champion. Newspaper reporters gave their verdicts, of course, but these carried no official weight.

This was a bad period for boxing in New York, but it was cleared up by an Englishman, William Gavin, who arrived there in 1919 wanting to begin a kind of National Sporting Club called the International Sporting Club. On discovering that he would be unable to render decisions even in his private club, Gavin persuaded Jimmy Walker, Speaker of the Senate, to sponsor a bill calling for the legalization of boxing throughout the state. The Walker Law came into effect in 1920, permitting referees to give decisions and placing boxing in the control of a Boxing Commission. This formula was followed in most of the other states.

In England the National Sporting Club began to lose its control of British Boxing when commercial promoters like the Australian Hugh D McIntosh and the theatrical impresario C B Cochran began to stage tournaments at venues like Olympia, which attracted the public in huge numbers, making it possible to offer purses in excess of those the NSC, with its limited seating, could afford. In 1929 the British Boxing Board of Control was formed as a controlling body, the NSC retaining its influence for a while by providing the early members.

RIGHT: *The first NSC British bantamweight champion, Digger Stanley, pictured here on his retirement. Brought up in a boxing booth (it was alleged that his father sold him for £1), he won the British title in 1910 from Joe Bowker. Both Britain and the International Boxing Union recognized Digger Stanley as world champion until 1913.*

BELOW: *Almost exactly six years after his demolition of Wells, years taken up with a world war, Carpentier returned to the NSC to take on the man who had just taken Wells's British title, Joe Beckett. The result was a one-round knockout in favor of 'Gorgeous Georges'.*

Tex Rickard Promotions

The Olympic Club of New Orleans, which put up the purse for the Bob Fitzsimmons versus Jack Dempsey title fight in 1891, were the first important promoters in the USA. Prior to that boxers mainly earned their money in the ways of the prize fighters – by finding backers to put up side-bets, winner-take-all, and by collections among spectators. The Olympic Club also promoted the first Fitzsimmons versus Maher fight and the famous Carnival of Champions in 1892, with three title fights on succeeding days. The California Athletic Club of San Francisco promoted the Corbett versus Jackson fight in 1901 and James W Coffroth became an individual promoter by staging several shows involving champions in San Francisco in the early years of the century.

The biggest of all the promoters, however, was George 'Tex' Rickard. A Texan farmer and well-known gambler, Rickard astonished the boxing world by his promotion of the fight between Joe Gans and Oscar 'Battling' Nelson in 1906.

Rickard owned the gambling saloon in the small desert town of Goldfield, Nevada. It was a prosperous mining town and the leading citizens wanted to publicize it and bring investment from the east. They formed a committee but Rickard decided to do the trick himself by staging a great fight there.

Joe Gans was the world lightweight champion, an extremely skillful black boxer born in Baltimore in 1874. In his day boxers of his color frequently had to lose to orders, but Gans was so good he eventually became champion in 1902 and even boxed a draw with Joe Walcott, the welterweight champion. Gans made famous the phrase 'bringing home the bacon,' this being the gist of telegrams he would send his mother after winning, letting her know they could eat well for a while.

Battling Nelson was a rough, hard-hitting, fair-headed Dane, born as Oscar Nielson in Copenhagen in 1882, and who had been brought to Illinois as a boy and become a scrapper with a not-too-nice regard for the rules. He knocked out Jimmy Britt in a match advertised as for the 'white' lightweight championship, and he badly wanted to get his hands on Gans.

Jeffries just having retired, boxing's heavyweight scene was boring. Rickard decided that with the right hype he could boost a Gans versus Nelson encounter into a money-spinner. Crowds had not flocked to see lightweights before and his venture was met with surprise and apathy. This changed to astonishment when Rickard announced the fighters' purses would be $30,000. This was outlandish, an unheard of sum, and at first the rest of America regarded it as a joke. Rickard had the $30,000 in gold in his window. Pictures were taken of it and sent across the country. Tex told the reporters that this was a race battle between two men who hated each other and they faithfully reported the intelligence to the punters. Tex built a huge open-air arena to hold nearly 8000 fans for the fight. And he was right. The crowds flocked to Goldfield and Rickard made a healthy profit with his first promotion.

The fight was a classic, fought under a fierce sun, with the 32-year-old Gans, the 'Old Master,' outclassing his tough but crude challenger. Then in the thirty-third round Gans broke his hand, and had to ship some fierce punishment. But he regained control one-handed and in the forty-second of the scheduled 45 rounds Nelson, in frustration, deliberately struck him in the groin. The foul was so blatant and obvious that there was no argument over the disqualification.

Gans successfully defended five more times but, already ill

with consumption, was knocked out twice by Nelson two years later, and two years after that he was dead.

The aggressive Nelson held the title for just over 18 months and then met a man who was as contemptuous of the rules as he was. Ad Wolgast came from Cadillac, Michigan, and met Nelson at Port Richmond in 1910. Wolgast was only 22, six years younger than Nelson. Gradually he wore down the Dane in a brawl that contained so many fouls that Nelson was moved to ask the referee what rules he was following. The fight was to a finish and Wolgast knocked out his man in the fortieth round.

Wolgast was a busy champion and was making his sixth defense in just over 16 months, none of which had gone to a decision, when he had his most famous fight. This was with the 21-year-old Mexican Joe Rivers, and took place at Los Angeles on Independence Day, 1912.

RIGHT: *The deal being signed for one of the biggest of all boxing matches, that between Jack Johnson and James J Jeffries. Johnson is seated second left, with his manager, George Little, on his right. Jeffries is seated extreme right. The promoter, 'Tex' Rickard, is standing behind Johnson.*

LEFT: *George 'Tex' Rickard, the greatest of all boxing promoters, who guaranteed an astonishing $30,000 for the lightweight title fight between Joe Gans and 'Battling' Nelson in 1906. Rickard offered $101,000 for the Johnson-Jeffries fight in 1910 and promoted the great Dempsey fights of the 1920s.*

BELOW: *Oscar 'Battling' Nelson, who helped initiate Rickard's boxing career with a fierce fight at Goldfield, Nevada, in 1906. Rickard's receipts were a remarkable $69,715, and he never looked back after this fight.*

In those days champions frequently traveled with favorite referees and Wolgast had a third man, Jack Welch, who was to prove very useful in this particular encounter. Wolgast underestimated the inexperienced Rivers, who was another tough customer and a particular favorite with the local crowd. He split the champion's nose with the first punch of the fight and within three rounds both men were covered in blood. It was

one of the goriest of fights and in true Wolgast tradition everything went. In the eleventh round both missed with swings and grabbed each other, overbalancing and nearly rolling out of the ring. By the end of the twelfth Rivers was on top, but the thirteenth proved to be an extraordinary round.

After Wolgast had taken a shattering blow to the head and Rivers a left to the body that doubled him up, Wolgast advanced in a crouch. Rivers measured him with a left and shot over a perfect right to the chin. At the same time Wolgast released a swinging left that started at knee height and thudded into Rivers' body, according to most spectators, below the belt. The punches landed simultaneously. Wolgast was knocked down and lay motionless on the canvas. Rivers sunk to one knee, clutching his groin with agony on his bloody face. The referee started to count, as both men were down. Then, incredibly, he helped Wolgast to his feet with his left arm and, holding him up, continued to count over Rivers with his right. At ten he dumped Wolgast back to his stool, pointed at him as the winner and fled before the riot started.

In his previous defense, in San Francisco, Wolgast had knocked out the unlucky Birmingham-born Owen Moran, who had previously knocked out Nelson and twice drawn with featherweight champion Abe Attell. Moran was left writhing on the canvas from a low blow in the thirteenth round while Jack Welch counted him out.

Retribution was waiting for Wolgast, however. His next defense, at Daly City, California, was without referee Welch. In the sixteenth Wolgast was put down by a right to the jaw from challenger Willie Ritchie, and he rushed back to throw two left hooks below the belt. He was promptly disqualified. Ritchie's first defense was fittingly against the unlucky Joe Rivers, on the first anniversary of the fight talked about as the 'double knockout.' This time Rivers was clearly beaten by the polished Ritchie and knocked out in the sixteenth round.

Tex Rickard, the promoter whose flair had put the lightweights, as well as Goldfield, Nevada, on the map, went on to promote the Johnson versus Jeffries heavyweight battle already described, and bigger successes were to come his way.

The Assassinated Champion

The middleweight division has always produced great champions – it is the division where the speed of the lighter men is sometimes combined with the destructiveness of the heavyweights to produce the most exciting battles of all.

One such was a man born at Grand Rapids, Michigan, on 14 September 1886, the son of a Polish immigrant farmer. His name was Stanislaus Kiecal. As a boy he wanted to be a cowboy and at 15 rode the rails to Montana. He began his fistic activities by trying his luck at a boxing booth and knocking out the star of the show. When he started professional boxing at the age of 16, a promoter gave him the name of Stanley Ketchel. Nobody taught him to box. He was a natural and he dealt destruction with both hands.

The middleweight championship after Fitzsimmons moved up to the heavyweights was a confused affair, with Kid McCoy and Tommy Ryan generally regarded as champions before Ketchel arrived on the boxing scene.

McCoy's claim was based on a victory over Dan Creedon in 1897, but he did not defend his title and, like Fitzsimmons, moved up to campaign with heavyweights. McCoy was an extraordinary boxer who was something of a confidence trickster. When he tried he was excellent, but occasionally he did not and the public never knew whether they were going to see the 'real McCoy.' He beat Tommy Ryan, then the welterweight champion, with a ruse in 1896. He told Ryan he was dying of consumption and wanted the fight to pay for doctor's bills. Ryan, going through the motions as an act of charity, was knocked out by what was undoubtedly the real McCoy.

Later, as a heavyweight in 1900, McCoy 'threw' a fight with James J Corbett in such a blatant manner that it led to the Horton Law being repealed and public bouts in New York being banned for 20 years. He acted in films in later life, before committing suicide in 1940.

Tommy Ryan, a New Yorker, moved up to the middleweight

Ketchel.   Welsh.   Johnson.   Little.

LEFT: *Stanley Ketchel (left) posing before his fight with Billy Papke on 4 June 1908. The referee standing between them is Jack Welsh, and Ketchel's manager, Willus Britt, is behind Ketchel.*

ABOVE: *Ketchel in similar pose before taking on heavyweight champion Jack Johnson. Johnson's manager, George Little, is on the right behind Johnson. The 'Michigan Assassin' lost several teeth and the fight.*

ranks after ruling the welters. He is regarded as having held the championship from 1898 to 1902, the year in which he retired. He lost only three contests, and is one of fewer than 20 boxers ever to hold undisputed championships at two weights.

After Ryan there was no acknowledged wearer of the middleweight crown until Ketchel knocked out Joe Thomas in the thirty-second round at San Francisco, on 2 September 1907, having previously drawn with Thomas, who was claiming the title. Ketchel knocked out the Sullivan twins from Cambridge, Massachusetts, who boxed under the names of Mike Twin Sullivan and Jack Twin Sullivan, he outpointed Billy Papke, and he then quickly disposed of Hugo Kelly, who had himself pretended to the throne after Ryan's retirement. Hugo Kelly, despite his name, was Italian. A return with Joe Thomas lasted only two rounds. Ketchel was proving to be a most destructive and exciting fighter and was known to his fans in the boxing world as 'The Michigan Assassin.'

The second best middleweight of the time was probably Billy Papke, from Spring Valley, Illinois, who was born three days after Ketchel. Papke, known as 'The Illinois Thunderbolt,' was also strong and very aggressive and his second challenge to Ketchel, on 7 September 1908 at Los Angeles, was a bloody affair. Papke had taken a beating on their first encounter and this time he had a plan. At the bell, when Ketchel advanced and extended his glove for the customary shake, Papke smashed him in the throat and followed up so rapidly and mercilessly that by the end of the round Ketchel was half-blinded from blows to the eyes. The tough champion fought on but never recovered. The referee intervened in the twelfth and the championship had changed hands.

At the fight was the promoter James Coffroth, known as 'Sunny Jim' because of his extraordinary luck with the weather for his open-air promotions. He saw instantly the attraction of the return fight, which would be a 'grudge' fight of the first order, and less than three months later the two were climbing into his San Francisco ring. Ketchel quickly got the upper hand and took full revenge on Papke by giving him a systematic beating until, by the eleventh, Papke could take no more.

Ketchel now took on the light-heavyweight champion, 'Philadelphia' Jack O'Brien, at the Pioneer Athletic Club in New

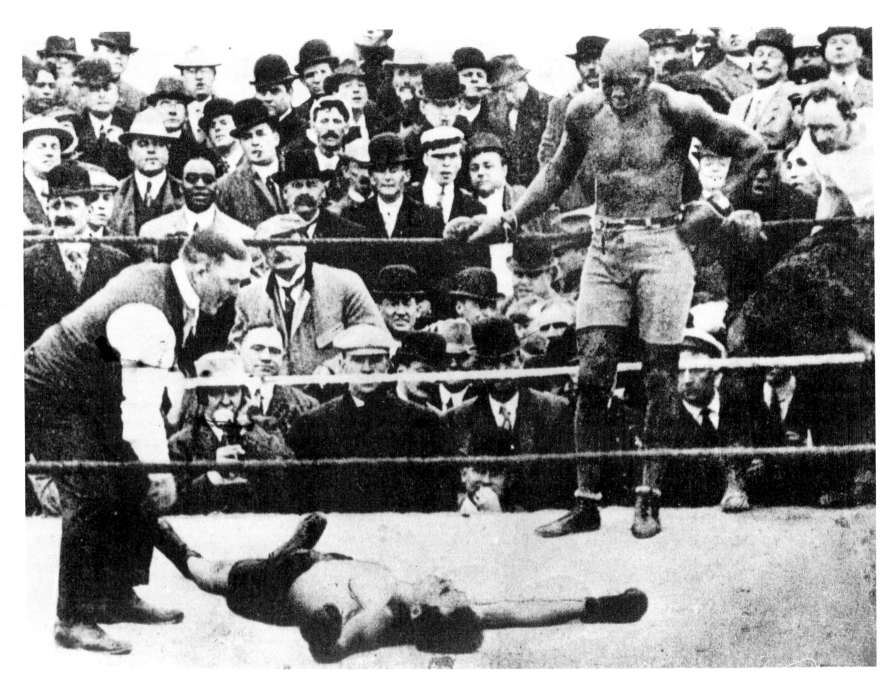

York, where the match had to be a 10-round no-decision bout. It was a good, even fight, but right at the end Ketchel caught O'Brien with a savage right on the jaw. O'Brien was knocked completely out, his head resting in the resin box in his own corner. But the bell ended the contest with the count at eight, so it was entered as yet another 'no decision' contest and Ketchel could not claim the light-heavyweight title. Strangely enough, Ketchel did knock out O'Brien in a return a few months later, but he was never credited with the dual championship. It seems that the light-heavyweight title had more or less been forgotten. O'Brien never officially defended it, although in some record books he is listed as champion from 1905 to 1912.

Sunny Jim Coffroth then put another proposition to Ketchel: it was to fight Papke for a fourth money-spinning time at his Colma arena, victory to be followed by a match for the heavyweight championship with the awesome Jack Johnson. Stanley agreed, and on 5 July 1909 took on 'The Illinois Thunderbolt' again.

The two men tore into each other, with Ketchel again pummeling Papke and causing him to bleed from nose and mouth. But Papke had trained hard for his chance of revenge and Ketchel had perhaps underestimated his challenger. The champion began to tire and toward the end of the 20 rounds took a lot of the punishment he had so readily handed out. However, like a true champion, he put in a grandstand finish and just managed to get the decision.

Ketchel's battle with Jack Johnson three months later, in which he lost several teeth, has already been described. The fight increased Ketchel's prestige. A middleweight who could

ABOVE: *The end of the Johnson-Ketchel bout. Stanley is knocked out with at least one of his teeth, so far undiscovered, embedded in Johnson's* *glove. Ketchel stood no real chance with Johnson, and should not have floored the big man; the fierce retaliation proved Ketchel's undoing.*

knock down Johnson was practically superhuman. But it was another eight months before Ketchel defended his championship again. He resumed with two quick knockout victories to show that his talent hadn't been impaired.

There was talk of a return with Johnson and meanwhile Stanley went off to the ranch of one of his supporters, Pete Dickerson, at Conway, Missouri, for a holiday. Enjoying the riding and swimming in the relaxing sunshine, Ketchel found himself attracted to Goldie Smith, a blond housekeeper who cooked his meals. Like Jack Johnson he had always liked the ladies and because of his good looks, perfect physique and a line in throwaway humor, many found him irresistible in return. Goldie Smith was one of them. The two enjoyed a very visible flirtation, to the annoyance of her regular boyfriend, the ranch foreman, Walter Dipley.

One day Stanley sat down for a late breakfast and enjoyed a little dalliance with Goldie who brought it. As he began to eat Dipley poked his double-barreled shotgun through the window and shot him in the back. Stanley was rushed to hospital but was dead within hours, despite the advice of a boxing reporter, 'Start counting over him and he'll get up.'

Dipley served 23 years in prison, the length of Ketchel's life. In that short time 'The Michigan Assassin' had made himself one of the greatest middleweights in boxing history.

Three Great Welshmen

Among the small men before the First World War, one of the earliest to make a big impression was 'Terrible' Terry McGovern who fought as a bantam and featherweight and was one of the men to hold world titles at two weights.

McGovern, of Irish parentage, was born in Johnstown, Pennsylvania in 1880. As a boy he was taken to Brooklyn. There he learned to use his fists guarding a newspaper pitch. He began a professional career at 17 and built up such a string of impressive knockout victories that he became known as 'Terrible' Terry McGovern. Because of his record he began claiming the world bantamweight championship, but unfortunately, in England, 'Pedlar' Palmer, a clever boxer known as 'The Box O'Tricks,' had a much better claim to it. On 22 September 1899 a confident Palmer came to America to put McGovern in his place. They met at Tuckerhoe, New York, and McGovern won in a very unsatisfactory manner. Shortly after the first round the timekeeper accidentally struck the bell a second time. The referee sent both men to their corners and then asked them to resume boxing. On the second start Palmer extended his glove for the handshake, but McGovern ignored it and smashed over a right. The fight was all over in 75 seconds. Papke, as previously related, used this ploy against Ketchel.

McGovern defended only once, moving the weight limit up 4 pounds, before retiring from the bantamweights and taking the featherweight title from George Dixon in January 1900. For nearly two years Terry ruled this division, knocking out all comers. However, there were blots on his record. A 'victory' over Joe Gans, the 'Old Master,' was one. The fight was so obviously 'fixed' that boxing was immediately banned in Chicago for many years. A knockout of Oscar Gardner was another. McGovern was flattened in the first round but the referee was Terry's own and was so slow to take up the count that the champion had twice the stipulated time to recover.

McGovern's reign ended on 28 November 1901 when Young Corbett II knocked him out after arousing his Irish temper with remarks about his wife and mother. Corbett also won a return and McGovern's short spectacular career was over.

Corbett lost the featherweight title to one of the ring's greats, Abe Attell, from San Francisco. Attell reigned for just over eight years, from 1904 to 1912, and was a very busy boxer. He was finally outpointed by Johnny Kilbane, another great boxer who reigned for eight years.

Attell's toughest opponents came from the other side of the Atlantic. In 1908 he drew over 25 rounds in San Francisco with Owen Moran when most thought Moran had won. Attell

BELOW: *Freddie Welsh (left) boxing Jim Driscoll in 1910. It was an unfortunate fight. The two men were among the cleverest boxers of all time; Welsh was to be world lightweight champion and Driscoll was featherweight champion in all but name. Driscoll fought Welsh against his wishes, the fight developed needle and the normally gentlemanly Driscoll was ruled out for butting.*

LEFT: *'Peerless' Jim Driscoll, wearing an early version of a Lonsdale Belt. He learned his boxing skills in the boxing booths, and remained unbeaten, except for a disqualification, until he made a comeback after the First World War – and by then he was already ill. In 1909 he outclassed Abe Attell, the world featherweight champion, but as it was a 'no-decision' bout, he was not able to claim the title.*

RIGHT: *Freddie Welsh (left) meets Jack Dempsey in 1921; at the time the heavyweight champion was at the height of his powers. Welsh had retired four years earlier when he lost his world lightweight title to Benny Leonard, but he was making a brief comeback. He lost only four fights in a long career.*

wanted the return later that year to be over 20 rounds, Moran wanted 25 and the unique compromise of 23 rounds was agreed. Again Moran was awarded a draw after appearing to win. In 1909 Attell fought the British champion, Jim Driscoll, in New York in a no-decision bout. Even the New York papers agreed that Driscoll had outpointed Attell in every single round and when Attell then refused to meet Driscoll again, recognition was withdrawn from him in Britain and Europe and Driscoll was regarded as champion.

Driscoll, born in Cardiff of Irish parents on 15 December 1881, was one of the greatest of all boxers, a stylish artist who nevertheless won half his bouts by the knockout route. He was so superb that he was called 'Peerless' Jim Driscoll. He was a printing apprentice as a boy and took to boxing his fellows with old newspapers wrapped round their fists as gloves. Soon he was attracted to the boxing booths and traveled with one as a resident champion, having hundreds of fights. He became a

leading attraction at the National Sporting Club and won the British featherweight title in 1906 by outpointing Joe Bowker. In 1909 came his bout with Abe Attell and he was subsequently recognized as world champion outside America. He defended his world title and added the European when knocking out Jean Posey of France in 1912. After boxing a draw with the luckless Owen Moran in 1913, Driscoll retired unbeaten. The only fight he lost before the First World War was on a disqualification – to his great Welsh rival Freddie Welsh. Alas he was persuaded to make a comeback challenge for the European bantamweight title in 1919 and was forced to admit defeat against Frenchman Charles Ledoux who was 11 years younger, and this spoiled his great record. He was already ill with chest problems and died six years later of pneumonia.

Freddie Welsh was born at Pontypridd, Wales, on 5 March 1886. His name was Frederick Hall Thomas and at 16 he came to America to seek fame and fortune. He worked in a sports shop and began boxing, but to prevent his mother finding out, he took a pseudonym based on his origin – Freddie Welsh. He was not particularly strong and developed an evasive technique, which, coupled with destructive infighting, enabled him to run up many impressive victories.

Welsh returned to Britain in 1907 and became British lightweight champion. He fought his friend Driscoll, the featherweight champion, in a mistaken fight – Driscoll was eventually disqualified. He lost his title to Matt Wells who, though utterly outboxed, was given the verdict on aggression. But Wells regained it and then beat all comers for six years. He beat all the leading contenders for the world title in America but first Battling Nelson and then Ad Wolgast avoided him. In Britain he was regarded as uncrowned king.

In 1914 promoter C B Cochran paid an enormous fee to the new world champion, Willie Ritchie, to defend at Olympia in London. Welsh got the narrow decision after a sparkling 20-round bout. It was his last fight in Britain for he returned to the States where he fought in New York, mostly no-decision contests. He remained world champion for about three years, when he lost the title to Benny Leonard. Welsh was then past 30 and he retired, making a brief comeback 3½ years later. Although many of his 167 bouts were no-decision contests he lost only four times. He was so skillful that the cruder lightweights of the era could not lay a glove on him. Unfortunately he lost his money on a health farm venture, and was poor when he died at only 41.

The third of the great Welsh triumvirate of friends and world champions was flyweight Jimmy Wilde. Born at Tylorstown on 15 May 1892, Wilde was a physical freak. Fully grown he only reached 5 feet 2½ inches and he never weighed more than 108 pounds. His legs and arms were skinny. But having worked in the mines from the age of 14, often hewing coal while lying in seams too small for anybody else, he built up tremendous

power in the muscles of his back and shoulders. He loved fighting and became a regular in the boxing booths that were popular around the coal-mining towns of the day.

When Wilde first boxed in London, at the famous Blackfriars Ring, the proprietor's wife thought the new arrival was a child and was most reluctant to let him box lest he should be killed. But he won by a knockout. Wilde's progress received a setback when he lost to Tancy Lee for the British flyweight title at the National Sporting Club, but soon he had won this title and avenged his defeat.

Wilde won the world flyweight championship when Joe Symonds was forced to retire at the NSC on 14 February 1916. Two months later Wilde stopped Johnny Rosner of New York in 11 rounds at Liverpool. There arose another American pretender to the title, Young Zulu Kid, who was, in fact, an Italian named Giuseppe de Melfi, boxing out of New York. Wilde knocked him out in London in 1916 and was indisputedly the best in the world.

Many regard Wilde as the greatest flyweight of all time. He acquired a number of nicknames: 'The Tylorstown Terror,' 'The Mighty Atom' and, perhaps the best, 'The Ghost with a Hammer in his Hand.' Over a hundred of his victims were knocked out. His style was his own. He carried his hands very low, level with his hips, and would almost always attack from the bell, swaying and weaving as he came forward. Wilde was often forced to take on boxers of a higher weight class, even beating featherweights, and in 1919 he scored splendid victories over two American bantamweights, Joe Lynch and Pal Moore, the former soon to be world champion.

In 1920 he toured the United States, remaining unbeaten in 12 contests, five won by the short route. However, in 1921 he lost to Pete Herman in unhappy circumstances. The fight was meant to be for Herman's world bantamweight title, but in his previous fight Herman lost it temporarily to Joe Lynch. He was also over the bantam limit against Wilde and refused to weigh in. Wilde declined to fight but was persuaded to do so because the Prince of Wales was in the audience. The referee stopped the fight in the seventeenth round.

Wilde, 29 years old, retired after this as undefeated flyweight champion, but, unfortunately, two-and-a-half years later was persuaded by Tex Rickard and $65,000 to come back to defend against Pancho Villa in New York on 18 June 1923. Wilde was no match for the younger man but fought with tremendous courage before being knocked out in the seventh.

Unlike Driscoll and Welsh, Wilde enjoyed a long retirement, working as a boxing manager, referee and newspaper columnist before his death in 1969. The dozen defeats suffered by these three great boxers in around 400 fights all came at the beginnings or ends of their careers. All could claim to be unbeatable in their prime. It was remarkable that all should come from Wales in the space of 11 years.

FAR LEFT: *Jimmy Wilde (left) before a fight with Mickie Russell in 1920. Wilde, who was approaching the end of a great career, won by a knockout.*

BELOW LEFT: *Jimmy Wilde, who earned the nicknames 'The Ghost with a Hammer in His Hand' and 'The Mighty Atom,' sporting a black eye.*

BELOW: *Pete Herman, bantamweight champion, who beat Wilde in 1921.*

The Cowboy
and the Mauler

When the Second World War started the heavyweight champion, Jack Johnson, was in South America and had agreed to fight Jess Willard. The match was originally intended for Mexico but at Johnson's suggestion it actually took place on the racetrack at Havana, Cuba, where a ring was erected before the grandstand. The date was 5 April 1915.

Willard was 6 feet 6¼ inches and weighed around 230 pounds, so dwarfed even Johnson. He was born on 29 December 1881 at Pottawatomie, Kansas. He was not a good boxer but obviously possessed a long reach. Most of his victims were knocked out but he was not a natural fighting man and often appeared moody. He worked on a ranch and liked to dress in western style, so he became known as 'The Giant Cowboy.'

The controversy surrounding this fight has never been resolved. Johnson always claimed to have lost deliberately. It will be recalled that Johnson maintained that an arrangement

had been made that he should lose and that he would then be excused the prison sentence which was hanging over him. According to Johnson, half his fee was to come from the takings and was to be handed to his wife at the ringside after the tenth round. It was arranged that she should give him a signal and leave, and shortly afterward he would allow himself to be 'knocked out.' According to Johnson this signal was not received until the twenty-fifth round. Johnson was knocked out in the twenty-sixth and cited a famous photograph of the count (see page 57), in which he has his arms above his face as if shielding his eyes from the sun, as evidence that he was in control of his senses.

Others saw the fight quite differently. Johnson outclassed Willard at first and by the tenth round Willard was bleeding from mouth and cheek. Johnson was behaving in his usual arrogant manner. But as the fight went on in the blistering heat

FAR LEFT: *Jack Johnson gets a right to the face of Jess Willard in their title fight at Havana in 1915. Johnson had the upper hand in the early stages. The referee is Jack Welsh.*

ABOVE: *A famous photograph: Johnson claimed this shot showed him shading his eyes from the sun, and not truly knocked out. However, Johnson was 37 and had probably had enough action for the day. His defeat was no disgrace.*

LEFT: *Jess Willard, 'The Giant Cowboy.' Willard stood 6 feet 6¼ inches and had an 83-inch reach.*

of over 100 degrees Fahrenheit, the 37-year-old Johnson began to wilt. He could not dispatch this giant and was almost exhausted when Willard knocked him out. It has been suggested that the fight was originally arranged for 45 rounds for this very reason: that Johnson could not last this long.

Maybe the truth is inbetween. Johnson badly wanted to return to the United States to see his ailing mother. It is conceivable that he decided that his best chance of being allowed back was to lose. And in a 37-year-old exile who had been living easily, thoughts like these are soon translated into defeat, either deliberately or subconsciously.

In any case it was the end of Johnson's career as a champion. He returned to the United States but was forced to serve his prison sentence there.

Willard more or less put the title in storage. He amused himself by traveling with a circus. He made one defense, against a veteran Frank Moran, in 1916, before agreeing to meet Jack Dempsey, an up-and-coming boxer with a string of quick wins to his credit, on 4 July 1919.

Tex Rickard secured the fight by offering Willard a $100,000 guarantee. Dempsey was paid considerably less but aimed to clear $100,000 himself in another way: by betting $10,000 of his purse at 10 to 1 that he would knock out Willard in the first round. This confidence arose from the fact that he had achieved five one-round knockouts in a row and had knocked out a 6-foot 5-inch boxer, Fred Fulton, in 18 seconds. In the

title fight Dempsey was asked to concede 5½ inches and no less than 58 pounds in weight.

The contest was in a ring Rickard built specially at Bay View Park, Toledo. Again it was a blazing hot day and the 20,000 spectators sat in shirt sleeves. Willard objected to the canvas, which was bloodstained from a previous fight, so there was a delay while a new one was fitted. The new canvas muted the bell, so a whistle was used instead, a fact which was to have a bearing on Dempsey's bet.

Few 'feeling-out' blows were struck in this fight. Soon Dempsey leaped in with a left to the body and a right to the jaw, and as Willard gasped he repeated the combination and Willard collapsed on the canvas. He scrambled up but his senses were gone. Willard offered little resistance as Dempsey smashed him to the floor seven times in the first round but he showed extraordinary bravery in rising each time. However, finally he could not summon up the stamina to rise again and referee Ollie Pecord counted him out.

Dempsey leaped into the air in joy and left the ring with, apparently, the title and $100,000 to his name. But soon he was called back. It appeared that the round had ended before the

ABOVE: *Willard being counted out in his fight with Dempsey in Toledo in 1919. Nobody had heard the timekeeper signal the end of the round, so Willard was forced to face two more rounds of severe punishment. At the end he suffered broken ribs and a broken jaw and had to be helped from the ring.*

RIGHT: *Willard (left) before a fight with Luis Firpo on 12 July 1923, which Firpo won by a knockout. These two men took part in two of Jack Dempsey's best-remembered fights. Neither fight lasted more than three rounds, but Dempsey meted out tremendous punishment on each occasion.*

knockout, but nobody had heard the sound of the whistle.

Dempsey was forced to fight two more full rounds before the title was his. Willard was given one of the biggest beatings any fighter suffered. His jaw and two ribs were broken, his eye was closed and he never recovered his full hearing. He retired at the end of the third round having shown amazing, if useless, courage. In truth the fight should have been stopped much earlier, before too much suffering had been inflicted.

Willard always believed that Dempsey had something in his glove that day but Dempsey was to prove that he could hit hard enough without aids. A fortune lay before him and Tex Rickard was at his side to make sure no opportunities were lost of turning over an honest million or two.

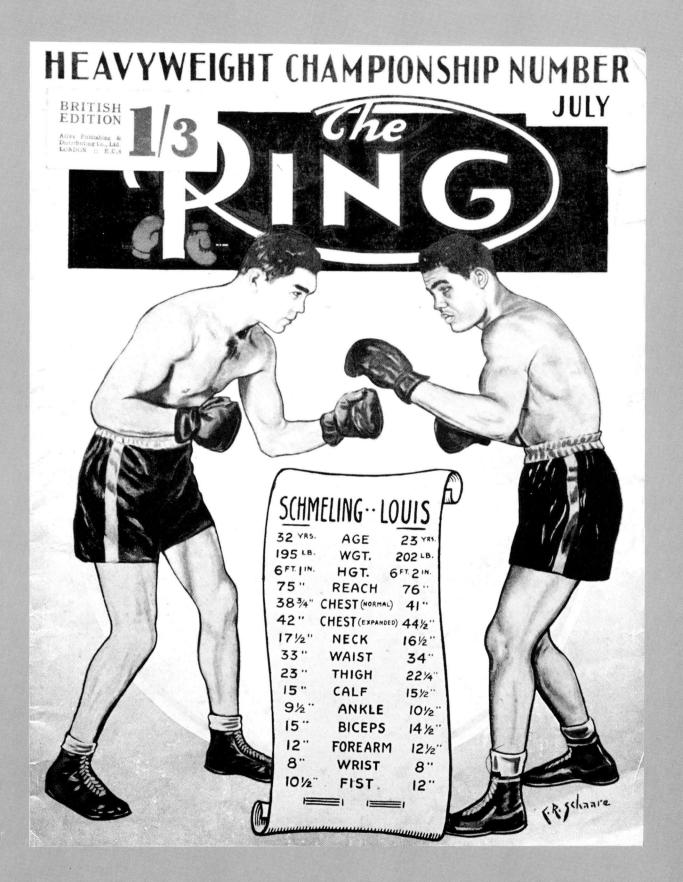

ABOVE: *The cover of* The Ring *magazine for July 1938 giving the vital statistics of the protagonists in the world title fight of 22 June 1938, champion Joe Louis (right) and challenger Max Schmeling.*

PART II

The Golden Boom Days

The $1,000,000 Fight

In 1920 Jack Dempsey first defended his title against a friend, Billy Miske, who was terminally ill and needed the money – the knockout came in the third round. Dempsey then knocked out Bill Brennan in the twelfth, after being behind on points.

A wartime publicity photograph then rebounded on the champion. It purported to show him helping the war effort by working in a New York shipyard. Unfortunately, inattention to detail had allowed Dempsey to pose wearing patent leather shoes. This picture was now republished in an attack on Dempsey, who was rapidly granted the reputation of cheat and draft dodger. He was even indicted but was acquitted.

However, this adverse publicity proved to be about the best thing that could have happened to Dempsey. Rickard, casting round for a likely money-spinning opponent, hit upon a man whose reputation was in direct contrast to Dempsey's new one: Georges Carpentier.

Carpentier was an extraordinary boxer. He was born in Lens, France on 12 January 1894 and first appeared in a ring when he was only 12, but the boxing he practiced was *savate*, the French form of combat in which the feet were used. Two years later Georges had his first experience of *la boxe anglaise* and won. He was taken over by an astute manager, Francois Descamps,

an acrobat, hypnotist and showman. The clever Frenchman continued winning and at 17 was welterweight champion of France. At the same age he was European champion (still the youngest ever). Soon after he turned 18 he became European middleweight champion and when he was 19 he first knocked out Bandsman Rice to become European light-heavyweight champion, and he then knocked out the British heavyweight champion, Bombardier Billy Wells, to become European heavyweight champion. Georges won the return with Wells at the National Sporting Club with a knockout in 73 seconds. Carpentier's last act before the First World War was to challenge the holder of the 'white heavyweight championship of the world,' a competition which had been dreamed up while Jack Johnson was the real world champ. The holder was Ed 'Gunboat' Smith, and Georges took the title on a disqualification,

BELOW: *The signing of the fight which was the first to top $1 million. From left, seated: Jack Dempsey, William A Brady, Charles Cochran, Tex Rickard, Georges Carpentier, Francois Descamps (Carpentier's manager). Behind Brady is Jack 'Doc' Kearns.*

RIGHT: *The young Jack Dempsey grinning at the camera while squinting against the sun. Dempsey's reputation as a 'draft-dodger' set up the publicity for the 1921 fight with handsome war-hero Georges Carpentier, and earned everybody concerned a fortune.*

ABOVE: *Dempsey on his way to knocking out Carpentier in Jersey City on 2 July 1921. Dempsey was too strong for the lighter Carpentier, whose famous knockout right-hand punch let him down when it broke his own thumb instead of hurting Dempsey's head. From then on Carpentier was doomed, and he was beaten in the fourth round.*

LEFT: *Carpentier carefully poses for a training shot. Carpentier was the youngest-ever European champion, and won national and European titles at many weights as he grew bigger. But he was never quite a heavyweight, and had to be content with the light-heavy title.*

RIGHT: *The sort of picture that boosted Carpentier's publicity for the big fight with Dempsey – the aviator, with his medal for gallantry and his fast car.*

65

ABOVE: *The two men most responsible for the million-dollar gates of the 1920s. Jack Dempsey (left) and Tex Rickard (right), the heavyweight champion and the promoter, outside the Hotel Belmont, New York, where they were negotiating for Dempsey's fight with Jack Sharkey that took place in 1927. By this time Rickard was also acting as Dempsey's manager.*

although Smith was unlucky, having cuffed Georges when the Frenchman slipped onto one knee in the sixth.

Georges was still only 20, and if all these titles weren't enough, he was also so handsome that there was a marked increase in the interest of women in boxing, reflected in their growing numbers in the ringside seats. Carpentier became known as 'Gorgeous Georges,' or to those with more conservative tastes, 'The Orchid Man.' Georges was taken up by society, was a friend of Mistinguett the music hall star, boxed with Maurice Chevalier and was often in the company of the Prince of Wales. When he arrived in London for the Gunboat Smith fight, 80,000 blocked the traffic; his open car was ceremoniously pulled by ropes to his hotel, while he waved as though he were a member of royalty.

During the war Carpentier became a hero. In those pioneering days of air warfare he became an officer in the air force and was awarded the *Croix de Guerre* and *Médaille Militaire* for gallantry. In 1919, back in the ring, he knocked out the new British heavyweight champion, Joe Beckett, in 74 seconds at the NSC.

Rickard, ace promoter, realized that a contest between this war hero, this paragon of all the virtues and the crude lumbering Dempsey, newly exposed as a 'slacker,' was a suitable case for the hype treatment. First the qualifications of Carpentier had to be revealed to the American public. So Georges, who was never more than a light-heavyweight, was brought to America and took on the world champion, Battling Levinsky, at Jersey City on 12 October 1920. The fight was over soon, and Carpentier became the new champion when he achieved a fourth-round knockout.

Rickard could now go ahead with the first 'Battle of the Century.' Every angle was exploited in the publicity. Every

contrast between the two men was highlighted. Not only were the possibilities of the outcome hotly debated, but popular sentiment became polarized. The fight generated an enormous amount of interest.

Rickard built a huge open-air wooden bowl of an arena on Boyle's Thirty Acres at Jersey City, capable of accommodating over 80,000 spectators, and all the seats were sold. For the first time the gate receipts for a match topped a million dollars by a long way – the gate was $1,789,238. The fight was the first world title fight to be broadcast, and there were 700 press men to relate the story in print. In Paris an estimated one million fans turned out into the streets to await the result. Luminous signs and loudspeakers were to be used, but for those out of earshot it was arranged that rockets would be fired into the sky – red for victory and white for defeat.

Neither man was big for a heavyweight by today's standards, but of course Carpentier was not even a heavyweight. He conceded Dempsey 16 pounds. It was noticeable that the crowd's cheers were with Carpentier, introduced as a 'soldier of France,' rather than with their countryman. Dempsey had the best of the first round but Carpentier won the second and staggered Dempsey with his famous lightning right, which connected on his cheekbone. But Dempsey held on and a follow-up punch was the end for Carpentier, for he broke his thumb on Dempsey's hard head. With his right hand useless, Carpentier was pummeled throughout the third round and was knocked out with a right to the body in the fourth. Even without his injury, it is doubtful if he could have withstood the body punching of the heavier and stronger Dempsey for any length of time.

Carpentier's days of triumph following hard on triumph were over – at least in the ring. He did enjoy one more glorious day on his return to Paris three weeks later, however, when several thousand welcomed him at the railway station. For Jack Dempsey and Tex Rickard, on the other hand, the golden era of boxing had only just begun.

Jack Dempsey,
The Manassa Mauler

Jack Dempsey was born in Manassa, Colorado, on 24 June 1895. His real name was William Harrison Dempsey and he was the ninth of 11 children. It was a poor family. His father Hiram was frequently out of work and his mother Celia had a hard time of it.

As soon as he was old enough, Harry, as he was known, worked in the timber and mining camps, and at 16 he started training to be a boxer in Young Peter Jackson's gym in Salt Lake City. His older brothers Bernie and Johnny were also fighters and naturally, because of the family name, their collective hero was the old middleweight champion, Jack Dempsey 'the Nonpareil.' Bernie thus fought under the name 'Jack' Dempsey and Harry took the name 'Young' Dempsey, but when he turned professional in 1914 he called himself Kid Blackie. The proliferation of names was resolved a couple of years later when Bernie retired, and the future heavyweight champion was able to take over the name 'Jack Dempsey.'

Dempsey's village of Manassa was named by Mormons and his early fights were in states associated with this religion – Utah and Nevada. Damon Runyan spotted him as a likely champion but his record was not impressive. In 1917 he was knocked out in one round by 'Fireman' Jim Flynn. He 'rode the rods' to find work and fights, went to New York, had his ribs

LEFT: *Dempsey, the film star and married man. He is with the beautiful film actress Estelle Taylor whom he met while filming at Hollywood and married. One union led to the break-up of another, that between Dempsey and manager 'Doc' Kearns – Estelle persuaded Jack to ditch Kearns when she discovered that he was deducting more than half of Jack's earnings for expenses.*

ABOVE: *Dempsey, the fighting man. Dempsey was lacking in science, but rose from an unpromising start to become one of the most destructive punchers of all time – once he had his man hurt he was invincible. For a couple of generations he was the epitome of toughness in the ring, a 6-foot 1-inch out-and-out heavyweight slugger who at the peak of his career was capable of knocking out anyone in the world.*

ABOVE: *Dempsey (right) with the man who molded him into a star. Jack 'Doc' Kearns organized the career of the flagging Dempsey so well that this picture was captioned 'A Million-Dollar Smile.' Dempsey was training at Saratoga Lake for his fight with Firpo.*

broken, was estranged from the café pianist he had married at 21 (they divorced in 1918) and almost decided to give up the unremunerative boxing game.

Then in a San Francisco bar in 1917 he met Jack Kearns, an exfighter and now gambler and small-time manager. Because he carried his cuts equipment in a small black bag, Kearns was called 'Doc.' He and Dempsey decided to try their luck together and Dempsey went to live with Doc and his mother in Oakland. He ate well, trained hard, and began to win his fights consistently. Doc chose his opponents carefully and built up his fighter, both in physical competence and in the public's awareness of him.

It was Kearns who persuaded Tex Rickard to match Dempsey with Willard, and although they lost their bet in that fight, the championship began to bring them riches. The Carpentier fight made them a small fortune. Although Kearns and Rickard were hardly friendly the partnership of the two of them and Dempsey became 'The Golden Triangle' which made millions from boxing in the 1920s.

Not everybody made money from 'The Manassa Mauler,' as Dempsey was now known. His next defense was against Tommy Gibbons in Shelby, Montana, on 4 July 1923. Shelby was a small town where oil had recently been discovered. The citizens decided that to publicize the town they would stage the next championship, in much the same way Goldfield had staged Rickard's first promotion 17 years before. Dempsey was guaranteed $300,000, two-thirds of which was paid in advance. Gibbons chose a percentage of the gate rather than take a guaranteed $50,000. Gibbons, only a light-heavyweight, put up a good show losing only on a 15-round decision. However, there was a singular lack of interest, only 7000 attending. When Dempsey had been paid, Gibbons and the contractors associated with the fight received nothing, the banks failed and the town was broke. Kearns was lucky to get out of it on a special train with the money.

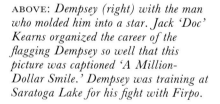

RIGHT: *Dempsey (facing camera) in his fight with Tommy Gibbons at Shelby, Montana, in 1923. No $1 million smiles here – at least, not for the citizens of Shelby. The fight was a flop and the town was bankrupted.*

The next defense was a different story. The opponent was a taciturn Argentinian, Luis Angel Firpo. He was not a particularly good fighter – in fact he was raw and crude – but at 6 feet 3 inches and around 220 pounds he was bigger and stronger than Dempsey, which made a change from the champion's recent opponents. In Firpo's first six contests in the United States he scored six knockout victories, including one over Jess Willard. He was called 'The Wild Bull of the Pampas.' Rickard could see the possibilities of another big hype. He was right. The two met at Polo Grounds, New York, on 14 September 1923. One hundred and twenty-five thousand packed in and it was the second $1,000,000 gate for the three moneymakers.

The fans got their money's worth. The two men charged out at the bell, Dempsey missed and Firpo's right knocked him to the deck. Dempsey scrambled up, clinched, the ref called for

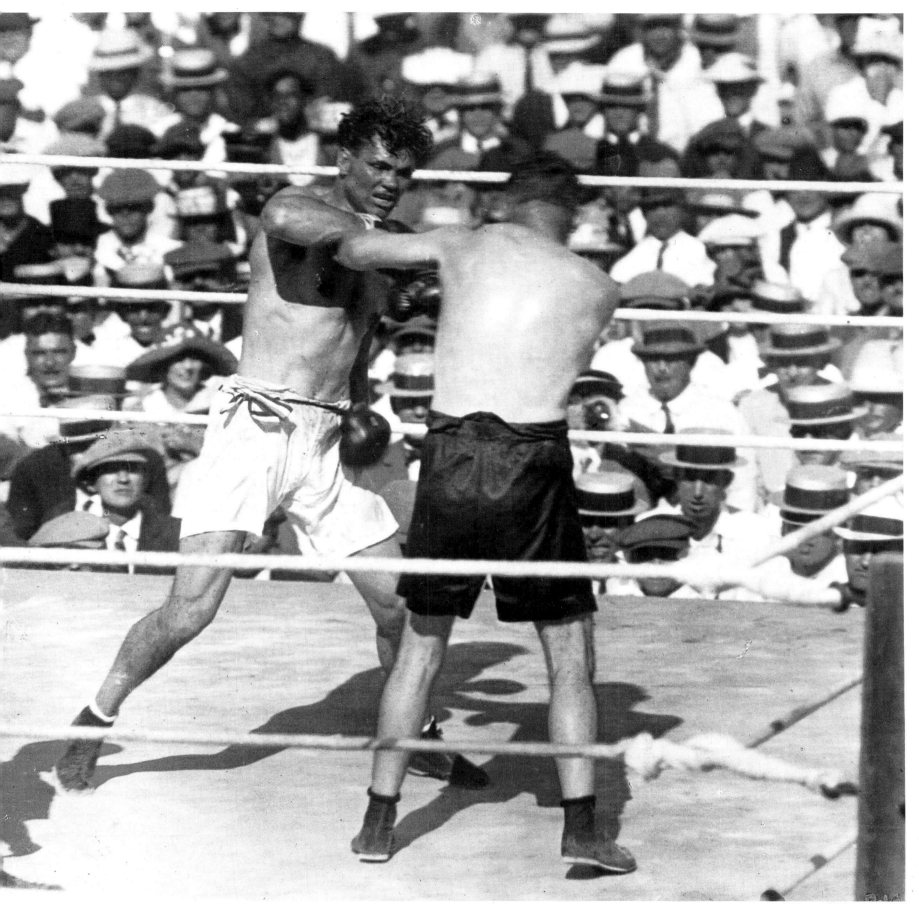

the break and Dempsey flashed over two left hooks which floored the challenger. Within 25 seconds both men had been on the floor. Seven times Firpo was down in that opening round and each time Dempsey stood over him ready to smash him down again when he rose. Finally the enraged Firpo got up, fought Dempsey off and sent over a tremendous right which threw Dempsey clean through the ropes onto the press typewriters, his legs pointing upward into the air. That should have been the end for Dempsey. It is against the rules for a boxer to be helped to regain his feet but those reporters pushed Dempsey back through the ropes before the count reached ten. Dempsey was nearly unconscious but the bell rang before the inexperienced Firpo could nail him again.

Both men were in a bad way at the start of the second round, but Dempsey had the experience and the fighter's instinct to get his left hooks in first. On the third knockdown Firpo could not rise again. This amazing fight lasted only four minutes, but none of the excited fans felt cheated. Firpo might have. In standing over him Dempsey had broken the rules, as had those who helped Dempsey back. Dempsey was lucky that he was still champion.

Doc and Dempsey now decided the champ should have a holiday but Doc combined it with business by arranging for Dempsey to make a film in Hollywood called *Daredevil Jack*. It was a success, was followed by another and then a feature film, *Manhattan Madness*, in which Jack starred with a beautiful young actress called Estelle Taylor. Romance blossomed. Gossip writers gossiped and wrote. It didn't take long before the Doc rushed to Los Angeles.

Doc told Dempsey to give up his foolishness. Dempsey said

he would marry Estelle. The Doc tried to get Dempsey away, but Jack was tied to Hollywood by a contract Doc had signed. Kearns knew that without complications he and Dempsey could make a huge fortune. This actress could spoil it all. The Doc and the actress declared war on each other and Estelle appeared to play a winning card by marrying Dempsey when his Hollywood contract ended. It came as no surprise that Kearns wasn't asked to the wedding.

Jack's holiday was extended when Rickard was reluctant to match him with Harry Wills, the natural challenger. Wills was black and Rickard remembered his vow at the time of Johnson's win over Jeffries. Jack and his wife went to Europe then returned to star in a Broadway play, *The Big Fight*. It was a flop. Estelle was able to act a little better than Jack – but then Jack couldn't act at all.

Estelle's career began to flounder and she got fed up with being referred to as 'Mrs Jack Dempsey.' The marriage began to feel strains, including financial ones, with Jack not having fought for three years. Estelle was horrified to discover that Kearns and Dempsey had been splitting receipts down the middle, after 'expenses.' She persuaded Dempsey to drop Kearns and the two went to Rickard and put Jack's boxing affairs in his hands.

Rickard was delighted, but Kearns was bitter. He dug out documents that he had asked Dempsey to sign and issued writs against him. The affair strained the Dempsey marriage further, especially when Estelle's car was taken on a writ of attachment. Dempsey developed a disease of the nerves. Meanwhile Rickard had fixed up the champion's first fight for three years. It was to be with Gene Tunney, an ex-Marine light-heavyweight with whom it was thought 'the Mauler' would have little trouble. . . .

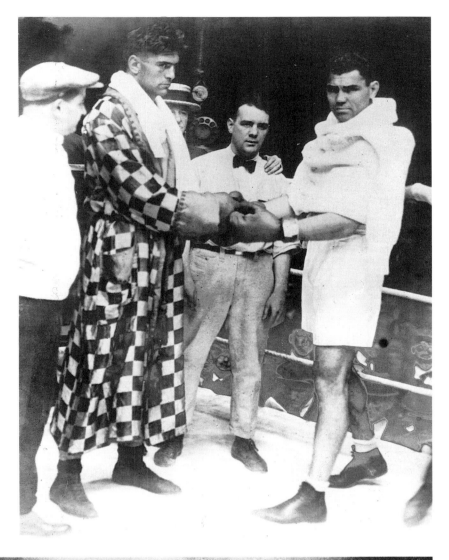

LEFT: *Luis Firpo, a big-hitting Argentinian called 'The Wild Bull of the Pampas,' poses before his fight with Dempsey. He was knocked down seven times in the first round of a fight that lasted only four minutes.*

ABOVE RIGHT: *Firpo (left) and Dempsey shake hands before the big fight at New York City on 14 September 1923. It was another million-dollar gate, and most thought it value for money.*

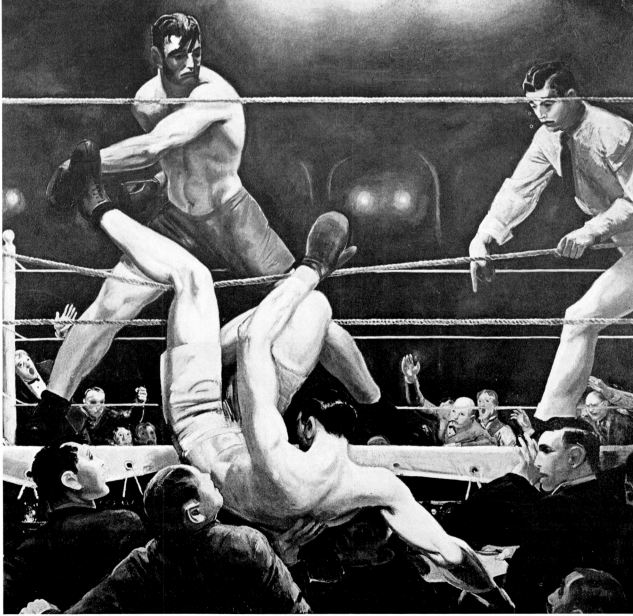

RIGHT: *A detail from a painting by George Bellows showing Dempsey being knocked out of the ring by Firpo in the 1923 fight in New York City. Dempsey was illegally helped back, but even so Firpo might have won had he remained cool enough to capitalize. As it turned out, Dempsey recovered to win.*

The Britton/Lewis and Greb/Walker Shows

Dempsey was not Doc Kearns's only world champion – in fact his 'favorite' fighter was Mickey Walker, one of the few boxers to hold an undisputed title at two weights. But before his long nine-year reign as a world champion, boxing had seen the longest series of fights between world champions: the Britton/Lewis show.

Jack Britton was born as William J Breslin in Clinton, New York, on 14 October 1885. He was not a knockout specialist but a brilliant boxer with a classical upright stance. He won the world welterweight championship on 22 June 1915 by outpointing Mike Glover in Boston. Ten weeks later, on 31 August, Britton lost his title when losing the decision to Ted Kid Lewis, also in Boston.

Lewis was the opposite in style to Britton. He was an all-action fighter known as 'The Crashing, Dashing Kid.' He was nine years younger than Britton, being born as Gershon Mendeloff in Aldgate, London, on 24 October 1894.

Britton and Lewis held the title between them for seven busy years. As well as beating off all other challengers they fought each other no fewer than 20 times, always in scintillating bouts, with Britton being the only one to score a knockout. Britton won the series 4-3 by gaining a decision in 1921 when Lewis returned to campaign in Britain. One bout was a 20-round draw, and the other 12 contests were of the no-decision kind. In fact Lewis and Britton totaled over 600 fights in their careers, of which nearly half were of the no-decision variety.

Lewis held a record nine national and international titles during his career: the British and European titles at feather, welter and middleweight, the British Empire title at middle and welterweight and, of course, the world welterweight title. He challenged Georges Carpentier (second with eight titles) for the world light-heavyweight championship in 1922, but when the referee spoke to him in the first round he turned his head and Carpentier promptly struck his unguarded chin and knocked him out.

Meanwhile with his main challenger gone home, Britton held on to the welterweight title for five more defenses before, as a 37-year-old veteran, he was outpointed in an outstanding battle by Mickey Walker, then 21 years old.

Mickey Walker was born in Elizabeth, New Jersey, of Irish ancestry, on 13 July 1901. He trained as an architect, but quickly showed great skill as a boxer. In his nineteenth bout he drew with Jack Britton before taking his title 18 months later. He was a brilliant boxer but he also carried a knockout punch and his nonstop aggression earned him the nickname 'The Toy Bulldog.'

Walker made four defenses of his title and then tried to add the middleweight crown by challenging Harry Greb on 2 July 1925 in New York.

Greb was a fistic phenomenon. He was the best middleweight title-holder since Stanley Ketchel – although there were some good ones inbetween, notably Les Darcy, an Australian, who came to a sad end. In the days before the First World War (and sometimes since) it was almost impossible to be recognized as world champion without coming to America to prove the claim. Darcy, anxious to do just this, jumped a ship for America at the invitation of Tex Rickard, ignoring the fact that his country was at war. The Governor of New York refused him a license, and in 1917 he died there, officially of pneumonia, but some thought partly of shame.

Greb won the championship by beating Johnny Wilson, a character who owed his title as much to his underworld connections as to his undoubted ability. When he retired, his Silver Slipper nightclub in New York was a haunt of gangsters like Legs Diamond – the sort of place made familiar by Edward G Robinson movies of the 1930s.

Greb himself was a character at home in speakeasies. He loved the illicit bars and the women who attended them much more than the rigors of training. He must have been immensely strong to perform as he did, for he boxed without much regard for the rules. He just 'mixed it' nonstop and was known as 'The Human Windmill.' The year before he took the middleweight crown he had inflicted the only defeat of his career on Gene Tunney, who later became the heavyweight champion. They fought as light-heavyweights and Greb gave Tunney a 12-pound advantage and a beating that put him in bed for a week.

Harry Greb was born 6 June 1894 in Pittsburgh, Pennsylvania. He began professional boxing at 19 and had nearly 300 fights, many of them against men bigger than himself,

RIGHT: *This photograph was labeled 'Three US boxers trim foreign opponents in London.' At the Royal Albert Hall in London in December 1919 Johnny Griffiths (left) beat Francis Charles, Pal Moore (center) beat Charles Ledoux and Ted 'Kid' Lewis (right) beat Matt Wells. Lewis was, of course, English, although he had been campaigning in New York for a few years.*

BELOW LEFT: *Mickey Walker, 'The Toy Bulldog,' one of the all-time greats as welter and middleweight champion.*

BELOW: *Jack Britton, welterweight champion with Lewis for six years. His career lasted 22 years and he fought 299 times.*

BELOW RIGHT: *Britton's great rival, Ted 'Kid' Lewis, had 280 fights, from feather to light-heavy.*

including heavyweights. The astounding thing about Greb is that from 1921 he was blind in one eye.

The fight between him and Walker for the middleweight crown is famous for the fight which followed it. Greb won the official contest on points after 15 magnificent rounds at the Polo Grounds, New York. In the early hours the two met in a night-club with their girls. Afterward on the pavement outside where they got to chatting about the fight, as naturally they would, the two men differed in their interpretations of it and removed their coats for an impromptu and unpaid return. The police soon broke it up, and years later Walker claimed to have won. But by then Greb was dead. A month after fighting a return with Tiger Flowers, who had taken his title from him, Greb had

had his useless eye replaced with a glass one and a month after that he had entered hospital again for a minor operation to his nose – he died after a heart attack during the operation.

Walker, meanwhile, had been having difficulty keeping his weight within the welter limits and had lost his title to Pete Latzo. But he merely moved up to the middleweights and took Flowers' title. Flowers, whose first name was Theodore, was a church deacon and the first black middleweight champion.

'The Toy Bulldog' was by now managed by Doc Kearns and his first defense was in London against the British champion, Tommy Milligan. Finding Milligan favorite, Kearns and Walker bet all of C B Cochran's huge purse of £20,000 on a victory and collected on the tenth round knockout.

Walker lost a challenge to Tommy Loughran for the light-heavyweight title and soon gave up the middleweight title (he held it for four years) to fight bigger men. He drew with Maxie Rosenbloom in another attempt on the light-heavyweight title and then surprised everybody by boxing a draw with Jack Sharkey, who was soon to be heavyweight champion. The next year he took on Max Schmeling, the newly deposed heavy-weight king, but Schmeling gave him a terrible beating, as befits a man 6 inches taller and 28 pounds heavier. Schmeling had to plead with the referee to stop the slaughter. Walker was now past 30 and his championship hopes were over. He retired and took up painting but he was always considered to be both a great character and a champion.

ABOVE LEFT: *Johnny Wilson (left) and Harry Greb before their title fight on 31 August 1923. Greb was the winner and was one of the most remarkable of world champions. He fought with only one eye for much of his great career. With the hat is announcer Joe Humphries.*

ABOVE: *'Battling' Siki, training in a gymnasium in the 1920s. Brought from Senegal as a boy by a German dancer who abandoned him in Paris, he joined the army, won the* Croix de Guerre *for bravery and beat his idol, Carpentier, for the light-heavyweight crown.*

Before Rosenbloom, who became a film actor, the light-heavyweight had seen an outstanding champion in Tommy Loughran, and a colorful one in 'Battling' Siki from Senegal, who had surprisingly taken the title from Carpentier. He found difficulty handling the fame. He walked the streets with a lion on a lead and ended up murdered in Harlem when only 28.

Among the smaller men who graced boxing after the First World War, the greatest was the lightweight Benny Leonard, one of the best of all time. He was born Benjamin Leiner on 7 April 1896 in New York. He was only 15 when he started boxing for money and after a couple of reverses he went nine years without defeat. He was a brilliant stylist who studied the techniques of boxing and learned to deliver a punch with knockout power. Most of his fights were of the no-decision kind and he had twice been on the receiving end in such contests with light-weight champion Freddie Welsh before; on the third attempt, he knocked Welsh out and became champion. In the next six years Leonard made eight successful defenses, fighting the best challengers. Nearly 60,000 watched his great battle with Lew Tendler at the Yankee Stadium in 1923. Three times in these fights Leonard seemed on the point of losing but his fighting brain turned potential defeat into victory. He tried to become a dual champion in 1922 by challenging Jack Britton for the welterweight crown but, having dropped Britton to one knee in the thirteenth, he cuffed him and was disqualified. He retired as undefeated champion after the Tendler fight but lost his money in the Wall Street Crash of 1929 and came back at 35, winning 19 more fights, before Jimmy McLarnin knocked him out. He later became a referee, and sadly died of a heart attack while refereeing a fight in New York in 1947.

Of the really small men, the most interesting of the era was flyweight Fidel La Barba of New York, who won an Olympic gold medal in 1924 and became world champion in 1927 by beating Elky Clark, the British and European champion, in New York. He did not defend the title but retired to go to university, a unique occurrence in boxing history. He came back a year later, but never could recapture a world crown.

BELOW: *Benny Leonard (right) was one of the greatest lightweight champions, a brilliant stylist who could deliver a punch with tremendous knockout power. He is seen shaking hands with Lew Tendler before their title fight on 24 July 1923, which Leonard won on points.*

RIGHT: *Fidel La Barba, regarded in America as world flyweight champion since 1925, in training for his fight with the European champion, England's Elky Clark on 21 January 1927. La Barba won on points in New York to become undisputed champion.*

The Battle of the Long Count

The heavyweight champion, Dempsey, made his long-awaited return to the ring at the Sesquicentennial Stadium, Philadelphia, on 23 September 1926. The choice of Philadelphia was a shrewd one by Rickard for the law there allowed matches to be no longer than ten rounds and the probability was that after a three-year layoff Dempsey would not be fully fit.

The 120,757 fans who turned up to see the fight were forced to watch it in pouring rain. They did not see what they expected. Tunney fought a masterful battle, moving easily around the champion on the wet surface and catching him with a variety of punches, while Dempsey's lumbering attacks were easily avoided. Only once did Dempsey connect solidly and Tunney boxed himself out of trouble. There was no doubt about the winner and the world had a new heavyweight champion. The fans were silent at the verdict. Tunney did not possess the color or excitement of Dempsey in the ring. Dempsey's legendary popularity in his retirement began with this defeat. Unpopular when beating Carpentier, he now had the esteem but not the crown.

James Joseph Tunney was born in Greenwich Village, New York, on 25 May 1897. He came from a well-off family, and unlike most boxers he did not learn by scrapping in the streets. He actually made an early career decision – he asked for boxing gloves as a tenth birthday present. Far from learning to fight

BELOW: *Gene Tunney as heavyweight champion of the world in 1926, between his two fights with Dempsey. Tunney was a throwback to Corbett in the way be studied boxing scientifically in his desire to master the sport.*

through necessity, as men like Dempsey did, he studied it in manuals. After turning professional he served in the Marines and became a services champion.

When he resumed his professional career he was beaten by the middleweight Harry Greb, as related, but it was to be his only defeat and he subsequently beat Greb four times (half of Greb's total career defeats). Tunney beat the heavyweight contenders, but Rickard no doubt had not regarded him as a real threat when fixing his title contest with Dempsey.

Dempsey's immediate task was to establish himself quickly for a return. He took on Jack Sharkey on 21 July 1927. He won, but only with the help of a blow in the seventh round which Sharkey, seemingly with justice, claimed was low. Nevertheless, the fans wanted to see a rematch with Tunney and this win was considered adequate grounds for it.

The second Dempsey versus Tunney fight is probably the most famous of all fights. It took place at Soldiers' Field, Chicago, on 22 September 1927 and was the greatest of the Tex Rickard promotions. The attendance was 104,943, the takings a record $2,658,660. Tunney's share was an extraordinary $990,658 and he gave Rickard a check for the 'change' from $1 million so that Rickard could give him a check for that amount.

The reason for that fight's fame is the count that Tunney took in the seventh round. The story has gone into boxing history as 'The Battle of the Long Count.' For six rounds Tunney had outboxed Dempsey as before, but in the seventh Dempsey caught Tunney near the ropes with some fierce two-handed punching and Tunney sank to the floor, his left glove grasping the second rope.

Throughout his career Dempsey, until this fight, had persistently flouted the rule which requires a boxer to retire to a neutral corner when an opponent is floored. Before this contest referee Dave Barry had informed both men that he would insist on this rule being honored. Now, at the prospect of triumph,

Dempsey forgot and stood over Tunney. The referee tried to push him away, Dempsey moved toward the wrong corner, the referee hesitated in his counting and pointed and pushed Dempsey toward the neutral corner and then took up the count. Tunney had already been down for five seconds and, taking the maximum rest, did not resume boxing until at least 14 seconds had passed since the blow.

The long count caused tremendous controversy at the time and has been the subject of speculation for 60 years. Would Tunney have won without it? In his autobiography he claimed he was in control and would have risen at 'nine' no matter when the referee had started, and Dempsey, in a subsequent interview years later, admitted as much himself. There is no reason to doubt them. Tunney dropped Dempsey briefly in the next round and boxed his way to a clear points win.

That was the end of Dempsey as a title contender. In private life Estelle Taylor, to whom he remarked after his first Tunney defeat: 'Honey, I forgot to duck' (the expression has since used by President Reagan), left him in an expensive divorce. He married twice subsequently and opened a famous restaurant in New York. His popularity increased with the years and he was a legend by the time of his death on 31 May 1983.

Tunney defended his championship once. He knocked out Tom Heeney of New Zealand in the eleventh round 10 months later and then retired. This fight was Tex Rickard's last promotion. He died six months later. Tunney married an heiress, Polly Lauder, and their son became a US senator. Tunney himself became a successful businessman and resisted all attempts to persuade him to make a comeback. Like Corbett, who 35 years before had toppled the swashbuckling hero Sullivan, he lacked popularity because his more thoughtful style suffered in comparison with that of his predecessor. Both men were underrated and deserve a place in the front rank. Tunney died a rich man after a full and happy life, on 7 November 1978.

LEFT: *Dempsey, in training for the second Tunney fight in 1927, takes time off during a rain storm to play poker and to pose for the photographer with the best of all poker hands, a royal straight flush. If this was a hint that he required some luck from on high, he didn't get it in the fight.*

RIGHT ABOVE: *The famous knockdown in the second Tunney-Dempsey fight. Dempsey, as was his habit, remained standing over his opponent Tunney instead of retiring, and the referee's count was delayed while he maneuvered Dempsey to a neutral corner.*

RIGHT: *Dempsey rushes in as the referee nears the end of his count and Tunney begins to rise. Tunney had been down for at least 14 seconds, and recovered to win. The episode was the subject of debate for many years afterward and is one of the most famous incidents in the history of boxing.*

The Heavyweight Succession of the 1930s

With the death of Rickard and the retirement of Tunney, boxing's golden era ended. Not since Jeffries had retired in 1905 had there been such a hiatus in the heavyweight progression. It is often said that boxing is as good as the heavyweight champion, so there was anxiety to crown a new king, but the manner of the crowning was very inauspicious.

Jack Sharkey, Young Stribling, Johnny Risko, Max Schmeling, Paolino Uzcudun, Tommy Loughran and Phil Scott engaged in various eliminating contests. Finally Sharkey beat Scott in a bout in which the British champion several times claimed to have been hit below the belt. He refused to carry on, was persuaded to, and then was left writhing on the canvas with another blow he claimed was low.

This allowed Sharkey to face Schmeling on 12 June 1930 for the vacant title. The gate of nearly 80,000 and takings of $749,935 were large but nevertheless a decline from the heady days of the 1920s. Schmeling won on a disqualification in the fourth round, the only man to win the top prize in sport in such a manner. It seemed that the referee and one judge had not seen the undoubted low blow and were almost bullied into the decision by Schmeling's manager, Joe Jacobs, and a powerful ringside newspaperman, Arthur Brisbane, who threatened to have the Walker Law repealed if the fight was not awarded to the German boxer.

Max Schmeling was born on 28 November 1905 in Brandenburg. He became a professional in 1924 and won the European championship in 1927. On Tunney's retirement he came to America. His first defense was a last-round knockout of Young Stribling a year later and then on 21 June 1932 at Long Island, New York, he bowed to the pressure of the American public and gave a return to Jack Sharkey.

This time Sharkey was given the fight on a split decision, a result which left the Schmeling camp extremely dissatisfied and led Joe Jacobs to mangle the language with the famous phrases: 'We wuz robbed. We shoulda stood in bed.'

Sharkey was a very temperamental fighter of Lithuanian ancestry, who was born Josef Paul Cukoschay on 26 October 1902 in New York. He served in the navy and was known as 'The Boston Gob.' He was an emotional performer who was not unknown to cry when things went wrong. Sharkey held the title for a year and then lost it on his first defense. He was

BELOW: *Photographers crowd into the ring to get their pictures of Max Schmeling and Jack Sharkey who are about to fight for the vacant heavyweight championship of the world after the retirement of Gene Tunney, on 12 June 1930 at Yankee Stadium, New York City.*

RIGHT: *Schmeling demonstrating his reach at his training camp at Endlicott, New York, where he was preparing for his title fight with Sharkey in June 1934. Schmeling won the title on a disqualification and remains the only man to have done so.*

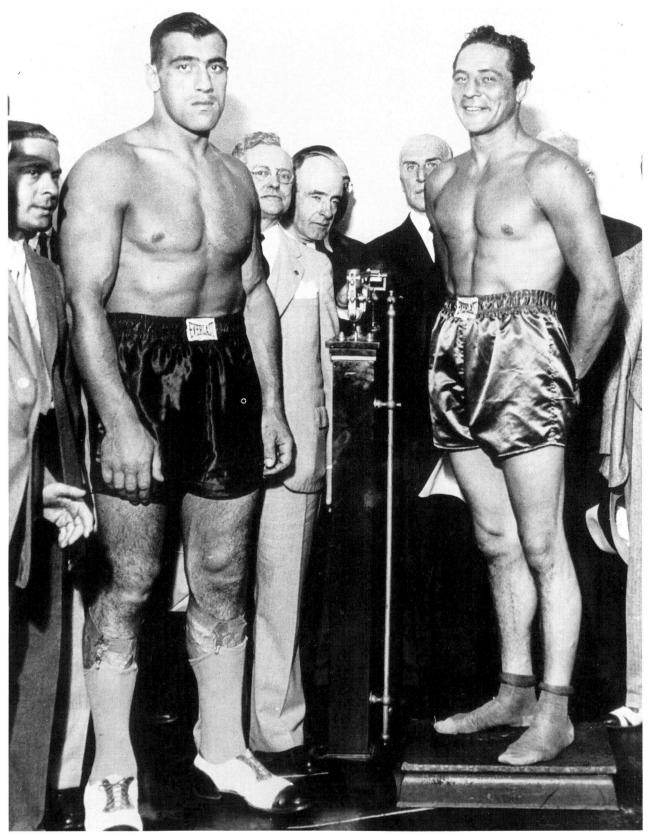

LEFT: *Primo Carnera (left) was champion in 1934, having taken the title from Jack Sharkey, when he was challenged by Max Baer (right). The photograph of the weigh-in emphasizes Carnera's great size and both men's lamentable inelegance in the footwear department. Baer's rolled down socks lose on points to Carnera's extraordinary two-tone shoes and old-fashioned sock suspenders.*

RIGHT: *Baer (left) in a training run with a colleague. Baer's problem was that he enjoyed life too much to tolerate the strictness of a boxer's way of life. He was called a clown and a playboy and lost his title in a big upset to Braddock.*

BELOW: *Jack Sharkey, who won the championship from Schmeling in a return on 21 June 1932, a decision that was by no means greeted with universal agreement, but soon lost it to Primo Carnera a year later.*

BELOW RIGHT: *The referee interposes in the title fight which Baer won easily. He was the better boxer, but also imposed his personality on the likeable Carnera – on one occasion he wiped his shoes in Carnera's resin box, while the champion looked on flabbergasted.*

knocked out in the sixth round on 29 June 1933 in New York by Primo Carnera, one of the division's unlikeliest champions.

Primo Carnera was born in Sequals, Italy on 26 October 1906. He stood 6 feet 5¾ inches and weighed around 260 pounds. He was a magnificent physical specimen who began as a laborer, but became a wrestler and strongman in a circus, before a boxing manager saw him and decided to groom him for honors. Unfortunately Carnera was not a natural fighting man and could not use his physical strength in the most effective ways. He was called 'The Ambling Alp.' In fact he was rather good-natured and became the tool of the gangsters who had a big influence on boxing in the 1930s. They manipulated his career and eased his way to the title shot with shady deals and arranged fights. Not everything was fixed and several boxers beat him easily enough, including the classy black Canadian, Larry Gains, who was never given a title chance because of the color of skin.

Carnera, unskilled boxer though he was, did make two successful defenses, against Paolino Uzcudun and light-heavy-

weight Tommy Loughran (conceding 86 pounds), before losing his crown to Max Baer.

Baer had the potential to be a great champion. He was born in Omaha, Nebraska, on 11 February 1909. He had a tremendous right hand which sent most of his opponents to sleep, and perhaps because of this he did not bother to train very much. He preferred to clown and joke and keep the fans amused by his antics. Before their match Baer made a film with Carnera called *Every Woman's Man* and during shooting the quick-witted extrovert estabished a great psychological advantage over the slow amiable Carnera. In the title fight on 14 June 1934 at New York, Baer had Carnera on the canvas 11 times, including one occasion when both men slipped to the floor, Baer telling Carnera, 'Last one up is a sissy.' He even plucked the hair on the bemused Italian's chest in his clowning before the referee ended the fight in his favor in the eleventh round.

Baer led the easy life with even more dedication as champion. Confining himself to exhibition boxing he appeared on stage and screen and had a popular radio show. It was with an

LEFT: *James J Braddock (left) swapping punches with Baer in the title fight in 1935. Braddock, who had virtually given up boxing a couple of years earlier, won on points. His rags-to-riches story earned him the name 'The Cinderella Man.'*

BELOW LEFT: *If Braddock's victory was astounding, the defeat of the up-and-coming Joe Louis by ex-champ Max Schmeling was sensational. Louis was regarded as almost unbeatable but Schmeling knocked him out on 19 June 1936 in New York. The referee is motioning Schmeling away as Louis is about to let go of the rope and slide to the canvas for the count.*

BELOW RIGHT: *Before his defeat by Schmeling, Louis had made a habit of knocking out previous heavyweight champions. This is Primo Carnera subsiding to a sixth-round defeat on 25 June 1935 at the Yankee Stadium, New York City.*

air of resigned reluctance that he interrupted his 'career' to take on James J Braddock at the Long Island Bowl in New York on 13 June 1935.

James Joseph Braddock must have rubbed his eyes to find himself fighting for the world heavyweight championship. Born in New York on 7 June 1906, he had become a professional boxer 20 years later but his had not been a glittering career. An unsuccessful challenge to Tommy Loughran for the light-heavyweight crown had been the previous highlight and only the year before meeting Baer he had been in the bread-line after losing a job as a dock hand. Braddock had won only four of his previous 11 fights before stepping into the ring for his big night. It was said that an ambulance was waiting outside the arena to take him away after the fight. So strange was it that he should even be there that he was called 'The Cinderella Man.' The betting odds were 10 to 1 on Baer.

In the event of course, the talented but carefree Baer was methodically outpointed by the journeyman Braddock in probably the biggest upset in heavyweight boxing. Braddock became the fourth of the 14 champions till then to have the christian names of 'James J' – Corbett, Jeffries and Tunney being the others.

Braddock's logical challenger was the old champion Max Schmeling. Max knocked out an impressive up-and-coming youngster called Joe Louis in 1936 to establish his claim, and signed to meet Braddock. But war was impending in Europe and Americans were apprehensive that the heavyweight championship might leave their shores for a long time. Louis' manager cooked up an elaborate deal with Braddock's manager and Schmeling was side-stepped. Louis got the title fight instead and the years of heavyweight mediocrity without any truly great boxers were soon to come to an end.

The Brown Bomber Era

Joseph Louis Barrow was born in Lafayette, Alabama, on 13 May 1914, the son of parents who had been slaves. When Joe was four his father had a mental breakdown, his mother married a family friend and a few years later the family moved to Detroit. The young Joseph was given money by his mother for violin lessons but he spent the money on boxing lessons and gym training, embarking on a reasonably successful amateur career. He lost in the finals of the national amateur championships but won a Golden Gloves title and turned professional in 1934. His manager was a local businessman, John Roxborough, who found him a job and decided to shorten his name to Joe Louis.

He started to build up an impressive professional record, winning 12 fights in his first year. Then in 1935 he demolished former champions Primo Carnera in six rounds and Max Baer in four rounds. Louis' fists, which seemed capable of knocking out any opponent, earned him the nickname 'The Brown Bomber.' He was trained by Joe Blackburn and developed the technique of shuffling forward behind a straight left, watching for an opening. Nobody could destroy an opponent more quickly than Louis, once he gained the upper hand.

His cool fighting brain was a natural gift, of course, but his position in society was something that had to be learned. His handlers, the principal of whom was Mike Jacobs, a ticket speculator, who used Louis to gain control of heavyweight boxing, impressed upon him the need to keep a poker face and not to show any emotion at winning. There was to be no stirring of the old Jack Johnson animosity. In fact, when Johnson visited his camp he was discouraged from meeting him. Louis had to put up with much patronizing attention in the papers, where he was presented as 'a good ambassador for his race,' that is, a black man who knew his place. But it was his exciting boxing which was to win him the support of Americans of all colors.

Louis was being spoken of as a future champion when he suffered the only defeat he was handed in his prime. Max Schmeling, another ex-champion, floored Louis in the fourth round and knocked him out in the twelfth.

Louis rehabilitated himself with seven more wins, including a three-round destruction of another former champion in Jack Sharkey. It was then that Mike Jacobs and Braddock's manager, Joe Gould, cooked up their deal. Braddock was given a guarantee of $300,000 for the title fight plus, should Louis win, ten percent of the net profits from Jacobs' heavyweight promotions for the next ten years. It was a marvelous deal for Braddock who could hardly expect to remain champion for long and who stood to earn far more than he was likely to by his own fists. The deal, of course, was reprehensible and Jacobs was not above playing on the feelings of the public by stating that the title was best kept in the States rather than risked against a German. This argument also disarmed some of those still doubtful of allowing a black man a chance of the title. Thus was Schmeling deprived of his rights.

In the fight itself, on 22 June 1937 in Comiskey Park, Chicago, Braddock put up a surprisingly good and game show.

ABOVE: *The beginning of the end for Baer in his encounter with Louis. He goes down for the first time in the third round, as referee Arthur Donovan motions Louis away. Surprised at the power of Louis' punches, Baer put up only token resistance and was knocked out in the following round.*

LEFT: *The world heavyweight champion, James J Braddock (left), shaking hands with the future champion, Joe Louis, before Louis' fight with Max Baer on 24 September 1935. Their two managers were to come to an arrangement whereby, if he lost his title to Louis, Braddock was paid a percentage of the earnings from the championship.*

RIGHT: *Joe Louis in his prime defended about four times a year for five years, and was regarded as one of the best champions of all time.*

He dropped Louis in the first round but by the eighth his face was a mess of blood, his eyes and mouth so badly cut that when Louis finally knocked him unconscious, face down on the bloody canvas, he was removed for 23 facial stitches.

The black population of America celebrated Louis' victory. He was the second black man to hold the heavyweight championship, the first for 22 years. But there was no repetition of the riots of the earlier years.

Louis' first defense was to be one of his hardest. It was against Welshman Tommy Farr, a fine boxer who did not possess an outstanding punch and so was considered 'safe.' But Farr put up such a good show that many thought he'd won, although Louis got the decision. Farr was one of only three challengers to go the distance in title fights with Louis and the other two were subsequently knocked out.

Louis' fourth defense, on 22 June 1938 in New York, was the one the public had been waiting for, the return with Schmeling. The prefight publicity for this fight was appalling, with Louis built up as the hero of the 'good ole USA' against the villain of the Nazi Third Reich. Louis was by now in his prime and much more of a fighting machine than in their first encounter, while Schmeling was now a veteran of 32. Louis' destruction of 'The Black Uhlan' was awesome. In 124 seconds Louis put Schmeling down four times and broke two of the vertebrae in his back. Schmeling's cry of pain when this happened was clearly heard

LEFT: *An early defense of Louis' title was a return with Max Schmeling on 22 June 1938. They are seen here early on in the fight, with Schmeling (right) looking confident about his prospects.*

BELOW: *The same fight: Schmeling took a terrible one-round battering and is seen here defenseless on the ropes as Louis powers in.*

RIGHT: *Billy Conn, the former light-heavyweight champion, put on a superb display against Louis on 18 June 1941 and was winning on points until Louis caught him in the thirteenth round.*

BELOW RIGHT: *Louis' first defense was a close match with Tommy Farr, who gave Louis plenty of problems over the 15 rounds and did not lose by much.*

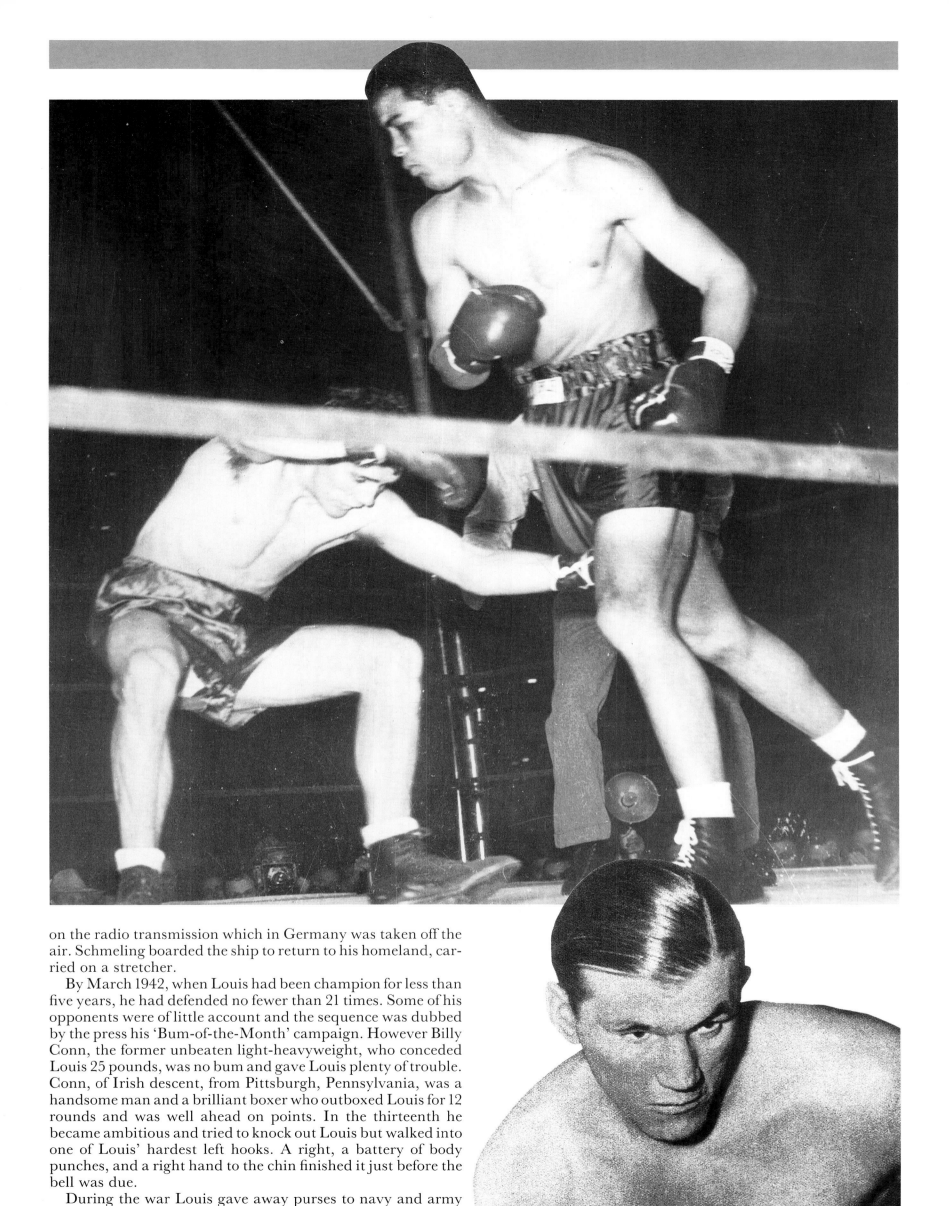

on the radio transmission which in Germany was taken off the air. Schmeling boarded the ship to return to his homeland, carried on a stretcher.

By March 1942, when Louis had been champion for less than five years, he had defended no fewer than 21 times. Some of his opponents were of little account and the sequence was dubbed by the press his 'Bum-of-the-Month' campaign. However Billy Conn, the former unbeaten light-heavyweight, who conceded Louis 25 pounds, was no bum and gave Louis plenty of trouble. Conn, of Irish descent, from Pittsburgh, Pennsylvania, was a handsome man and a brilliant boxer who outboxed Louis for 12 rounds and was well ahead on points. In the thirteenth he became ambitious and tried to knock out Louis but walked into one of Louis' hardest left hooks. A right, a battery of body punches, and a right hand to the chin finished it just before the bell was due.

During the war Louis gave away purses to navy and army relief and served as a sergeant-instructor. Between 1942 and 1946 he had a four-year break from boxing. At the age of 32 he decided to resume his boxing career.

Homicide Hank and the Prewar Champions

There were outstanding champions in the 1930s from flyweight to welterweight. Just as Louis in the heavyweights fought his way through the late 1930s to be supreme at the outbreak of war, so among the smaller men Henry Armstrong worked through the weights until for a time in 1938 he was the undisputed world champion at three weights simultaneously, a unique distinction.

To put the achievement of Armstrong and the other champions into proper perspective, let us work up from the smallest of all, the flyweights.

As the 1930s started, Frankie Genaro, a New Yorker, had the best claim to the title but he lost it to Young Perez, a Tunisian, in Paris, and he in turn gave it up to Jackie Brown in the latter's home town of Manchester. This was in 1932 and the United Kingdom was to hold on to this title for nearly 20 years. The best prewar champion was the brilliant Scot Benny Lynch, who took over the title from Brown and did not lose it in the ring. All of Lynch's championship fights were outstanding in one way or another. He beat Brown in a terrific display of power, flooring him 11 times in the two rounds the fight lasted.

He knocked out Pat Palmer of London in Glasgow in eight rounds, and then, when Small Montana of the Philippines, the holder of the New York version of the title, came to challenge Lynch at Wembley in 1937, the two put on a dazzling display regarded as one of the most skillful bouts ever seen. Lynch won a clear decision.

Lynch then faced the 19-year-old blacksmith Peter Kane from Golborne, Lancashire, unbeaten in 41 bouts, in a fight that drew a record Scottish attendance to Shawfield Park, Glasgow. Lynch had Kane down almost with the first punch but Kane fought back so well that the contest was another classic, with Lynch eventually winning by a thirteenth-round knockout in front of his delirious fans.

Alas that was the end of Lynch. He was already drinking heavily and lost his titles when disgracefully failing to make the weight for a match with Jackie Jurich of California. He knocked out Jurich in the catchweight contest and Kane later beat Jurich for the vacant title, holding it until after the war.

Tragically Lynch sank rapidly downhill under the influence of alcohol and died a wreck, aged 33.

RIGHT: *One of the most famous of the fights that took place before the Second World War in Britain was the British lightweight title fight on 23 February 1939. Champion Eric Boon (left) was a 19-year-old puncher, while Arthur Danahar (right) was a classical boxer, an ABA champion. The fight drew a capacity crowd of 12,000, and for the first time in boxing history a fight was televised live to an overflow audience in a theater. Boon won when the referee stopped the fight in the fourteenth round.*

FAR LEFT: *Benny Lynch, the great Scottish flyweight who was world champion from 1935 to 1938, but who destroyed himself with drink.*

LEFT: *One of Lynch's greatest defenses was against the 19-year-old blacksmith with the staring eyes, Peter Kane. Kane became champion when Lynch's career came to a premature end.*

The bantamweight division had one of its greatest exponents in the lanky 'Panama' Al Brown, an extraordinary 5 feet 11 inches for the 118-pound brigade. He was a linguist who defended in the United States, Canada, Denmark, France, Italy and Tunisia, speaking the language in most of the countries he fought. He held the title more or less from 1929 to 1935, losing it eventually in Valencia to Spain's first world champion, Baltazar Sangchili.

The featherweight division was that in which Armstrong won his first title. Battling Battalino of Hartford, Connecticut, held the title as the 1930s began, but he forfeited the title after failing to make the weight for a defense against Freddie Miller of Cincinnati, and the championship became disputed for a while. Freddie Miller was an outstanding champion and Kid Chocolate and Petey Sarron were the best of the others. Armstrong took the undisputed title after beating Sarron in 1937.

Kid Chocolate also won the super-featherweight championship in the 1930s. This division had been started in 1921 when Johnny Dundee was the first champion, but it fell into disuse in 1933 and was not revived until after World War II ended.

The lightweight division was very strong in the 1930s. Tony Canzoneri was the head man as the decade began. He had previously held the featherweight title, in 1927 and 1928, and in 1931 he added the light-welterweight title when he knocked out the holder, Jack Kid Berg of London, in a match at Chicago in which both men's world titles were at stake. Canzoneri in turn lost both titles to Barney Ross but regained the lightweight title when Ross moved up to welterweight. Canzoneri in turn lost both titles to Barney Ross but regained the lightweight title when Ross moved up to welterweight. Canzoneri lost the title for good to Lou Ambers from Herkimer, New York, and Ambers lost and regained the title in matches with Henry Armstrong, whose third world title it was.

Barney Ross, when he relinquished the lightweight title in 1933, retained the light-welterweight title until 1935, when he gave that up, the championship then falling into disuse until after the war. Ross meanwhile had won the welterweight championship from Jimmy McLarnin, with whom he had

LEFT: *Barney Ross (left) and Tony Canzoneri before their lightweight championship fight on 12 September 1933. Ross ended Canzoneri's three-year reign with a points win.*

BELOW: *Canzoneri (left) and 'Baby-Face' Jimmy McLarnin. With Ross and Armstrong, these fighters dominated the weights from feather to welter in the 1930s, all becoming world champions.*

ABOVE: *Henry Armstrong ducking below an attack from Beau Jack on 2 April 1944. Both men were ex-world champions at the time, Jack having the month before lost the lightweight title. Armstrong's last world title fight took place in 1941.*

three tremendous battles, which packed the stadiums, before he lost this championship in 1938 to Armstrong.

The swapping of titles in the 1930s arises from the fact that there were five divisions from featherweight to welterweight, and that Armstrong campaigned at both ends of the scale and other great boxers like Berg, Canzoneri and Ross fought in two or three divisions. Canzoneri, born in 1908 in Slidell, Louisiana, was at times during the years from 1928 to 1936 the featherweight, lightweight and light-welterweight champion. Ross, born in New York at the end of 1909, succeeded Canzoneri, winning the lightweight, light-welterweight and welterweight titles. Armstrong, born in Columbus, Mississippi, in 1912, succeeded Ross and won the featherweight, lightweight and welterweight championships.

Of these great battlers, Armstrong was exceptional in that his three titles did not include any of the 'inbetween' titles (what the WBA and IBF today call 'junior' titles). Armstrong's championships were in three of the classic eight divisions set out earlier in this book. In the whole history of boxing only Bob Fitzsimmons and Henry Armstrong have held undisputed world titles at three of these weights. Armstrong is unique in that for a short time he could pride himself on holding his three titles simultaneously.

He was born Henry Jackson on 12 December 1912, the eleventh of 15 children. His paternal grandfather was white, his grandmother a black slave, his mother a half-Cherokee Indian. After boxing as an amateur and professional, living rough and riding the rails, he took the name Henry Armstrong, after his

RIGHT: *Henry Armstrong, facing camera, advancing on Barney Ross in the welterweight championship fight on 31 May 1938. Armstrong got the decision, to win his second world title.*

BELOW: *Armstrong, the all-action fighter with the slow heart-beat who battered his way to the top in three divisions. This picture dates from May 1939, a few months after Armstrong became the only boxer in history to hold world titles at three weights simultaneously.*

trainer. Al Jolson, the singer, took an interest in his career, buying his contract from a former manager and setting him on a progressive ladder upward. Eventually, on 29 October 1937, he fought Petey Sarron for the featherweight title in New York and won by a knockout in the sixth round. On 31 May 1938, also in New York, Armstrong won a decision over Barney Ross for the welterweight crown in a tremendous battle which spelled the end of Ross's great career. With these titles in his possession, Armstrong challenged the tough Lou Ambers for the lightweight title on 17 August 1938 and, by outpointing him, won his third world title, all in New York.

Armstrong's secret was a very slow heartbeat, which allowed him to fight 15 rounds at top speed – in fact he needed to warm up before a bout. His nonstop aggression and destructiveness overwhelmed most of his opponents inside the scheduled distance and earned him the nickname 'Homicide Hank.'

Difficulty in making the weight caused him to give up his featherweight title and he lost the lightweight title back to Lou Ambers. He concentrated on the welterweight division, making 19 successful defenses in less than two years, before he finally lost this title to Fritzie Zivic on 4 October 1940. Only four of these opponents took him the distance, one being Ernie Roderick, the British champion.

During this run, on 1 March 1940, Armstrong tried to win a fourth title, the middleweight, by challenging Ceferino Garcia, a man whom he had beaten as a welterweight. But he just failed, the verdict being a draw. He retired from the sport in 1945 with his place in boxing history secure for all time.

The Golden Age of the Middleweights

The middleweight situation during the 1930s was confused, with different bodies naming their champions. The best claims in the early part of the decade were held by Marcel Thil, an extremely tough character from Saint-Dizier France, who was 21 before his first bout, and at the beginning showed no great aptitude. But suddenly he began a string of knockout victories, leading to a title shot against William 'Gorilla' Jones in 1932, which he won. The next with a good claim was Fred Apostoli from San Francisco, who stopped Thil in the tenth round in New York in 1937. He lost to Ceferino Garcia of the Philippines in 1939, the man who resisted the challenge of Henry Armstrong. Ken Overlin and Billy Soose also held strong claims, before Tony Zale finally unified all opinion and became undisputed champion in 1941.

Anthony Florian Zaleski, of Polish ancestry, was born on 29 May 1913 in Gary, a steel city in Indiana, and worked in the mills while successfully boxing as an amateur. He turned professional in 1934, shortening his name to Tony Zale, and took no fewer than 28 fights in his first year. Not surprisingly he lost some, found it all a bit much, and went back to the steel mills. Two years later, however, he tried again and, with a more sensible program, gradually worked his way to National Boxing Association recognition as champion and then to universal recognition. He was tremendously strong, with a knockout punch in each hand, and could withstand such punishment that it seemed he himself had been forged in the mill. He was aptly called 'The Man of Steel.'

Zale's name will always be coupled in boxing history with that of Rocky Graziano, with whom he had a series of fights among the most exciting ever seen. Their rivalry began a decade of outstanding middleweight battles and champions. Graziano was born as Rocco Barbella in New York on 1 January 1922, so was nine years younger than Zale. He was a juvenile delinquent, an army deserter, an inmate of reformatories and prisons and generally a rough handful until boxing gave him a legitimate outlet for his aggression. The army having decided to do without him, Graziano turned to professional boxing in 1942.

Zale, who was his opposite in nature, upright and religious, and Graziano, had their first slugfest on 27 September 1946 at Yankee Stadium. Over 30,000 clamored to see the two punchers battle it out. The first round was an indication of how these two men who scorned defense would treat each other. In less than a minute Graziano was thudding to the floor from a left hook and he took terrific punishment till just before the end of the round when he threw a desperate right which staggered Zale. Only the bell saved the champion as Rocky piled in with more rights. The second round was as explosive, with the bell again saving Zale. For the next three rounds Zale took tremendous punishment from Rocky's blazing fists, but then in the sixth put all of his remaining strength into a right to the solar plexus. Graziano stood paralyzed and breathless and Zale finished him with a left hook.

Of course the delighted fans demanded a rematch. At the Chicago Stadium on 16 July 1947, record indoor receipts of

BELOW: *Rocky Graziano, one of the most colorful of boxing champions, both in the ring and during a career as a celebrity afterward. He was suspended after failing to report an attempted bribe to throw a fight. The fight was in fact called off. The boxing reporters and public stood by Rocky, who is pictured here (left) discussing his prospects with his manager, Irving Cohen.*

LEFT: *Tony Zale, middleweight champion, starts training at Pompton Lakes, New Jersey, for his first fight with Rocky Graziano. 'The Man of Steel' is forced to carry all his leather gear with him. He could hardly guess that his name would forever be coupled with Graziano's after some great battles.*

ABOVE: *Rocky Graziano hits the canvas in his first fight with Tony Zale at the Yankee Stadium, New York, on 27 September 1946. Zale won a tremendous contest in the sixth round.*

RIGHT: *The same fight, but the other man on the floor. Zale down in the second round in a period of the fight when Graziano was on top.*

ABOVE: *Marcel Cerdan (left), one of the greatest of all middleweights, about to suffer his first defeat after over 100 bouts. He lost his European title to Cyril Delannoit of Belgium at Brussels in 1948. Later he recovered it, and in his whole career Cerdan lost a total of only four fights.*

LEFT: *Marcel Cerdan (right) getting a good right home to Tony Zale's chin on his way to winning the world middleweight championship at Newark, New Jersey, on 21 September 1948.*

RIGHT: *Cerdan (left) facing defeat again, this time to lose his world title to Jake LaMotta at Detroit, Michigan, on 16 June 1949. Cerdan was forced to retire before the tenth round after injuring his shoulder in the first. This time he had no chance to avenge the defeat – he was killed in an air crash on his way to the return fight.*

$414,000 were paid by 18,547 spectators. They were not disappointed. It was the previous fight in reverse. After four rounds of warfare Graziano had one eye puffed and the other pouring blood. The referee gave him one more round and he fought like a madman, knocking Zale groggy. The blood was staunched and he had to be given another round. In this round, with the fans cheering themselves hoarse, the referee was forced to drag Graziano off a Zale so battered he was draped over the middle rope as Graziano piled in. There had to be a decider, and this time Zale fought his greatest fight, knocking Graziano out in the third round. After these fabulous battles Zale lost his title on 21 September 1948 to Marcel Cerdan, having reigned, off and on, for eight years.

Marcel Cerdan was born at Sidi-bel-Abbes, Algeria, where the French Foreign Legion was stationed, on 22 July 1916. He turned professional at 17 and was French and European welterweight champion at the outbreak of war, but had to wait until peace returned for a shot at a world title. Meanwhile he played soccer for Morocco. By 1948 he was 32 and a middleweight. Zale, the champion, was even older. At Jersey City Cerdan injured his right hand in the third round of their title fight and boxed virtually one-handed thereafter. However as

the bell sounded to end the eleventh Zale went down from a succession of hooks. He could not come out for the twelfth and Marcel was the new champion.

Cerdan was France's second outstanding fighter after Carpentier – the complete craftsman, an immaculate boxer with power and durability. He was an idol to all Frenchmen and women and his friendship with Edith Piaf, the legendary singer, was the talk of the papers and the cafes (one of which Marcel owned).

His first challenger was Jake LaMotta. They met at Detroit on 16 June 1949. Once again Cerdan fought under a crippling handicap after pulling a ligament in his shoulder in the first round. LaMotta proved too strong to beat with one hand. Cerdan fought on bravely but had to retire on his stool before the tenth round. He lived for the day he would get his revenge. A return fight was fixed, and Marcel and his manager were on their way to New York to reclaim the crown, when his Constellation airliner crashed into a mountain in the Azores and all 48 passengers and crew died.

Cerdan's record was outstanding: apart from two dubious disqualifications he was beaten only twice – the first defeat he avenged, the second he was not allowed to. All France

mourned his death and a favorite chair in his cafe was always left empty in his memory.

Jake (real name Giacobe) LaMotta was born in New York on 10 July 1922, the same year as Rocky Graziano. His father was Italian and his mother Jewish and he was brought up in the Bronx, where he and Graziano were schoolmates at reform school. LaMotta, too, was a delinquent but he took up boxing early, becoming an amateur champion before turning professional at 20. He was the first to beat Sugar Ray Robinson.

LaMotta, like Graziano, was a brawler – but a good one. He was called 'The Bronx Bull.' He disposed of most of the contenders in the middleweight division and was forced to take on heavier men because he could not obtain a title fight. The mob who controlled boxing froze him out because he wouldn't appoint their nominees as a manager, preferring to manage himself with his brother's help. Eventually, according to his own story, he had to throw a fight with Billy Fox, whom he should have beaten easily, and also pay $20,000 under the

counter for his title fight with Cerdan. He cashed in afterward and his defense against Laurent Dauthuille of France provided one of the great reversals in championship boxing. Completely outpointed and taking a beating in the final round, he suddenly caught his man with a tremendous punch thrown in desperation and followed up to knock him out with 13 seconds of the fight remaining.

In 1951 LaMotta was challenged by Sugar Ray Robinson, who had beaten him four times since LaMotta had inflicted that single defeat on Sugar Ray's record almost exactly eight years before. Jake fought defiantly but the referee saved him from his own bravery in the thirteenth round.

Had he lived, Cerdan would have found a niche in show business. Both Graziano and LaMotta did, in their ways. Graziano, with his forthright speech, became a TV star on the Martha Raye show and elsewhere and LaMotta appeared in films and entertained at a topless nightclub. Both wrote autobiographies from which films were made: Paul Newman was Graziano in *Somebody Up There Likes Me* and Robert de Niro was LaMotta in *Raging Bull*. A film was also made of Cerdan's life in which his son played the part of the great boxer.

It was truly a golden age of middleweights.

BELOW: *A tearful Jake LaMotta after becoming world middleweight champion at Detroit. On the right is his brother and manager Joey, his trainer Al Silvani is behind, while on the left is the recently retired unbeaten heavyweight champion Joe Louis, who was to make a comeback from his retirement.*

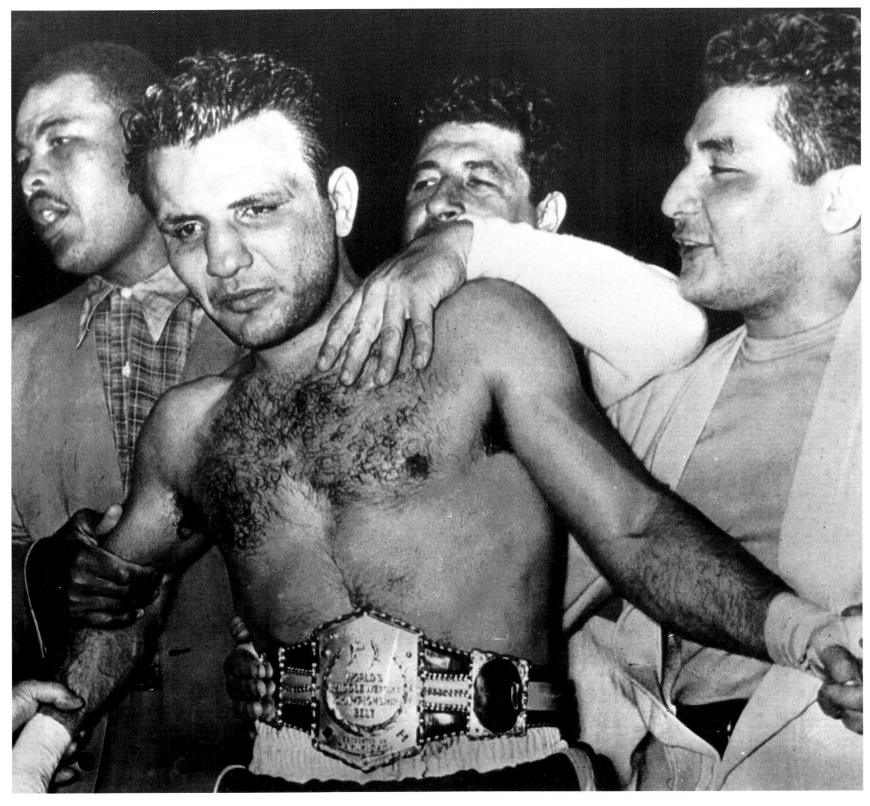

The Joe Louis Succession

When Joe Louis picked up his career as heavyweight champion of the world after the war he was rematched on 19 June 1946 with Billy Conn. The promoter and boxing public no doubt hoped to see a repeat of the scintillating match of five years and one day earlier. But neither man was what he had been, especially Conn, who was knocked out in the eighth. However, in his next fight, Louis looked more like the old Bomber when he knocked out Tami Mauriello in the first round. Louis then met Jersey Joe Walcott, a veteran of nearly 34 years old with an undistinguished career in a match originally billed as a ten-round exhibition for charity. Nobody bought tickets, so to provoke sales the match became a 15-rounder for the title.

The date was 5 December 1947 and the venue Madison Square Garden, New York. The bout was the first heavyweight title fight to be televised. Jersey Joe astonished everybody by boxing brilliantly and flooring Louis twice and most people, including Louis, who was halfway out of the ring before the verdict, thought he had won. But the champion got the split decision. Louis was embarrassed enough to apologize to Jersey Joe and to give him a return six months later, when Jersey Joe

BELOW: *Joe Louis resumed his career as champion after the Second World War and in his second defense knocked out Tami Mauriello in the first round at* *New York City on 18 September 1946. This photograph shows Mauriello being lifted clean off his feet by a powerful left from champion Louis.*

ABOVE: *Joe Louis was trying to regain the heavyweight championship of the world when he tackled Ezzard Charles, the new champion, at the Yankee Stadium on 27 September 1950. Louis was making a comeback, having retired without losing his title in the ring. Charles won on points.*

RIGHT: *A pensive Ezzard Charles being attended by his trainer, Jimmy Brown. Charles found it hard to recover from the death of Sammy Baroudi after Charles had knocked him out. He continued his career at the request of Baroudi's parents, and generously donated his next purse to them.*

LEFT ABOVE: *Jersey Joe Walcott has Joe Louis down in the third round of his title challenge at the Yankee Stadium, New York, on 25 June 1948.*

LEFT: *The eleventh round of the same fight and the roles are reversed as Walcott goes down and is counted out. After retaining his title in his twenty-fifth successful defense, Louis retired.*

103

LEFT: *Ezzard Charles in training for his world heavyweight championship fight with Jersey Joe Walcott on 22 June 1949. Charles and Walcott were to battle it out for the title vacated by Louis and for the special privilege of becoming the first new heavyweight champion for 12 years.*

RIGHT: *Charles's hair stands on end as Walcott comes swinging in, evil intent written on his face. Charles won the 1949 Chicago encounter and became the new champion.*

could not rekindle the inspiration and was knocked out by Louis in the eleventh round.

Louis now decided to retire, having made 25 defenses, a record in any division. The defeat by Schmeling, spectacularly avenged, was the only blot on his record. He negotiated a deal whereby he signed the two leading contenders for the title as a condition of retiring and then sold the rights of the fight to promoter Jim Norris, who thus was able to control the heavyweight championship for some years.

Jersey Joe fought Ezzard Charles for the vacant title on 22 June 1949 at Chicago and Charles won on points in an unimpressive contest. Jersey Joe thus had the unique unenviable record of losing three consecutive heavyweight title fights.

Ezzard Charles, born at Lawrenceville, Georgia, on 7 July 1921, was unbeaten as an amateur and became a Golden Gloves champion as a middleweight. He turned professional in 1940 and after a good career as a light-heavyweight he began to box in the heavyweight division. He boxed out of Cincinnati, and because of the deadliness and speed of his punching, became known as 'The Cincinnati Cobra.' Indeed one opponent died after a knockout, and Charles found it difficult thereafter to recapture the venom of his punches. He remained a smooth performer and was also called 'The Cincinnati Flash.'

He was a busy champion and dispatched Gus Lesnevich, the former light-heavyweight champion, and Pat Valentino within

four months of winning the title. Meanwhile Europe and Great Britain had refused to recognize the arrangement between Louis and Norris and named Lee Savold as champion after his victory over Bruce Woodcock. However Louis, in financial difficulties partly through unpaid tax, decided to make a comeback and all bodies agreed to regard the winner of a match between him and Charles as champion.

The fight was on 27 September 1950 in New York. The 36-year-old Louis was too slow and no match for Charles, who had idolized him when he began to climb the ladder years before. Indeed only Charles' respect for the old warrior saved him from a probable knockout. Nevertheless Louis' financial problems were such that he was forced to continue boxing after this defeat. Charles beat Nick Barone and Lee Oma and followed with another meeting with the 37-year-old Jersey Joe Walcott, beating him on points. He then gave a title shot to his old light-heavyweight opponent Joey Maxim, whom he had already beaten four times, but who was now the world champion. Charles got the decision over 15 rounds.

Charles was being as busy as Louis had been before the war. He undertook his seventh defense in under a year on 18 July 1951 at Pittsburgh, but it was only against the ubiquitous Jersey Joe Walcott, making his fifth attempt at the title. Walcott shocked the boxing world with a left hook in the seventh round that knocked out Charles and won him the title.

105

Jersey Joe Walcott was born in Merchantville, New Jersey, on 31 January 1914 – at least that was his official age, but he had been boxing in 1930 and some think his birthdate was earlier than he claimed. His real name was Arnold Cream, but naturally he changed that, choosing Joe Walcott, the name of the old welterweight king, to whom he bore a remarkable resemblance. To distinguish him from his hero he preceded it with his state, 'Jersey.' Through most of his career he proved to be a good defensive tactician, but that was about all, and he made so few ripples on the boxing pond that he retired in 1944 to work in a soup factoy in Camden, New Jersey, where he lived with his large family.

It was the fortuitous opening of a boxing arena in Camden that persuaded Joe to resume boxing – he agreed to help out the promoter by appearing in six fights. Strangely he kept winning, and even beat Joe Baksi, a contender. He was then offered the charity exhibition fight with Louis already mentioned, in which he beat the champion in the opinions of everyone except two of the three judges. Walcott's long career brought him a strange record. On 22 June 1936 he outpointed Phil Johnson and on 8 February 1950 he knocked out Phil's son, Harold, who was later to become world light-heavyweight champion.

Jersey Joe had obviously continued to learn and had added a punch to his repertoire. After 21 years of mostly routine performances he was now, at 37½, the oldest man to be crowned heavyweight champion of the world. Despite the advancing years he did not rush to cash in on his new status but waited nearly a year before he gave Ezzard Charles a return in Philadelphia. Surprisingly he again beat Charles, earning a decision, and the prospect of a 40-year-old champion was around the corner. But also waiting was a young blockbuster called Rocky Marciano. . . .

LEFT: *Ezzard Charles sinks to the canvas in his third title fight with Jersey Joe Walcott, on 18 July 1951.*

BELOW: *The end for Charles in the seventh round of the same fight. Walcott had triumphed at last.*

RIGHT: *Jersey Joe Walcott, the oldest man to win the world heavyweight championship. In an extraordinary career he challenged four times and was beaten four times before he took his last chance.*

Ancient Archie
Spans the War

Jersey Joe Walcott wasn't the only postwar champion of advanced years whose age was a matter of conjecture. 'Ancient' Archie Moore, the light-heavyweight champion through most of the 1950s, was 45 when he was finally relieved of his laurels – or possibly 48, according to whether you believed his version of the story or his mother's.

In the 1930s, when Moore began his professional career and was working his way up from welter through middleweight, the light-heavyweight title was held by two good men – Maxie Rosenbloom and John Henry Lewis. Rosenbloom, who was champion from 1930 to 1934, was an exceptional boxer but frequently an incorrect puncher. This led to him being given the nickname 'Slapsie Maxie.' He won over 200 fights but only 18 by the knockout route. On retirement Rosenbloom appeared in a number of films.

John Henry Lewis held the title from 1935 to 1939. During his spell as champion he beat British challengers Jock McAvoy and Len Harvey, the latter losing a close verdict while boxing with an injured hand. Lewis was a great and busy champion who developed cataracts in his eyes and was half blind when he took on his friend Joe Louis for the heavyweight title. Louis knocked him out in the first round. It was Lewis's last fight.

The title was disputed after that. Melio Bettina was recognized in New York and Len Harvey in Europe. Harvey, a Cornishman, was one of England's greatest boxers who from 1929 to 1942 was successively the British middle, light-heavy and heavyweight champion. He was due to fight Lewis in a return when the champion's eye problems became too bad.

However, Harvey's victory over McAvoy for the vacant championship in 1939 was less than two months before the Second World War broke out, and after three years inactivity in the Royal Air Force, he retired in 1942 when he lost a wartime fight to Freddie Mills.

Meanwhile Billy Conn outpointed Bettina before giving up the New York title to move up to the heavyweight class and have his epic battle with Joe Louis. Gus Lesnevich was the next to rule for more than a fight or two. He took the title from Anton Christoforidis of Greece in 1941. In 1946 he fought Harvey's conqueror Mills, in London, in one of the most exciting and savage fights ever seen. Mills was saved by the bell in the second round after being down four times, but fought back so strongly that he got on top before, in the tenth, a battered Lesnevich swung the battle again, and the referee stepped in with Mills down and four seconds to go to the end of the round. Lesnevich twice defended against Blackjack Billy Fox, the boxer to whom LaMotta had been forced to throw a fight, and then gave Mills a return. This time Mills, who had been fighting heavyweights, took the title.

After 18 months Joey Maxim knocked out Mills. Maxim lost in a heavyweight title fight with Ezzard Charles and then resisted a challenge to his own title from ex-middleweight champ Sugar Ray Robinson, before he was outpointed by Archie Moore on 17 December 1952, four days after Moore's 36th birthday.

Archie Moore was born at Benoit, Mississippi, on 13 December 1916, although his mother claimed he was born three years

RIGHT: *In one of the first outstanding fights that took place in Britain after the Second World War, Gus Lesnevich (left) arrived in Harringay, London, to defend his world light-heavyweight title against Freddie Mills (right), who had a claim to it himself.*

BELOW RIGHT: *The great Mills-Lesnevich fight. After see-sawing one way and the other the fight was won by Lesnevich (left) when the referee stepped in in the tenth. Mills won a return.*

BELOW FAR LEFT: *One of Britain's greatest boxers, Len Harvey, preparing for his British heavyweight title fight with Jack Peterson in 1933. Harvey, the light-heavyweight champion, won the fight on points.*

BELOW LEFT: *John Henry Lewis, the world light-heavyweight champion, before his fight with Len Harvey in 1936. Lewis won but was refused a license for the return with Harvey because of deteriorating eyesight. Lewis was forced to retire and eventually became blind in later life.*

earlier. His real name was Archibald Lee Wright and he followed a typical boxer's road of poor home, running wild and reform school, where he began boxing as a welterweight. He took the name Moore from his uncle Cleveland Moore, with whom he lived when his parents separated. He turned professional in 1935 and gradually built up to light-heavyweight. He was badly managed at times in his career (he had eight managers altogether), and often managed himself. It was not an easy time for a self-managed black boxer to get a title fight. From about 1943, after recovering from a serious accident and pneumonia, Archie was a logical contender for light-heavyweight honors but it was not until the end of 1952 that he had a suitable opportunity. Then he had to outpoint Joey Maxim no less than three occasions at six-monthly intervals before he could call the title his own.

Moore was the complete boxer. He was brilliant defensively, and by developing his arms and shoulders by press-ups and walking on his hands, he made himself a knockout specialist, no fewer than 145 of his victims taking the full count, which was a record at the time.

By writing letters to newspapers he pressed his claim for a fight with heavyweight champion Rocky Marciano and always felt that he should have won it. He put Marciano down in the second round and the referee mistakenly gave the champion a mandatory count of eight, which wasn't applicable, and Marciano recovered. When Marciano retired Moore was matched with Floyd Patterson for the vacant heavyweight title but he was knocked out in the fifth.

Moore's greatest victory was his defense against Yvon Durelle of Canada. The rough Durelle knocked Moore down three times in the first round and again in the fourth. An

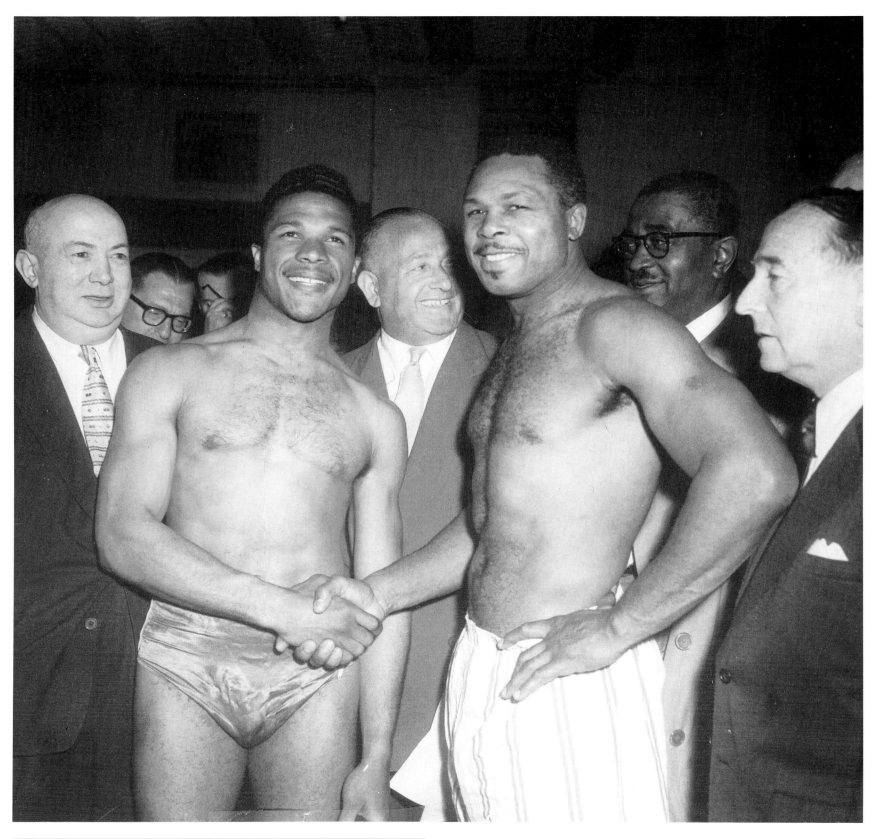

LEFT: *Joey Maxim became light-heavyweight champion when he knocked out Freddie Mills in London on 24 January 1950. Maxim was champion for nearly three years before being outpointed by Archie Moore.*

ABOVE: *Archie Moore (right), one of the world's most durable boxers, who remained a champion until his mid-40s. He is seen before a title defense against Yolande Pompey of Trinidad (left). Moore won in the tenth.*

apparently beaten Archie then got up to box brilliantly and knock out Durelle in the eleventh round.

After he had defended his title once a year from 1954 to 1959, Archie had recognition taken away by the National Boxing Association for 'inactivity,' the NBA naming Harold Johnson as champion, a man Moore had succeeded in beating four times in five contests.

Moore was recognized elsewhere, and defended in 1961, but in 1962 he again fought a heavyweight, Cassius Clay, and was stopped in the fourth. Clay was 20, Moore at least 45. Ancient Archie was then deprived of his light-heavyweight crown by the EBU for not defending against Johnson. Soon he retired, went into films (he played the role of Jim, the slave, in *Huckleberry Finn*) and he also worked for the government.

Willie Peps Up the Action

Some of the most exciting action in the weights below the middleweight level in the immediate postwar years came in the featherweight division, where there were two outstanding performers, Willie Pep and Sandy Saddler, who fought a bitter series of title bouts.

Willie Pep (real name Palaleo) was born in Middleton, Connecticut on 19 September 1922. When he was a boy his mother sent him to a gym to learn how to look after himself and he developed such a talent for boxing that he won his state flyweight title at 16 and at 18 turned professional. On 20 November 1942 he outpointed Chalky Wright in Madison Square Garden to win the New York version of the world featherweight championship, the youngest boxer for 40 years to hold a world title. He did not win many of his battles by the knockout route but by clever boxing – he was so fast and elusive that they called him Willie the Wisp. When he unified the title by knocking out Sal Bartolo in New York in 1946 he had lost only once, to tough lightweight Sammy Angott. Multiple injuries in an air crash in 1947 threatened his boxing career but within six months he was back in the ring fighting again.

Sandy Saddler, born on 23 June 1926 in Boston, Massachusetts, was nearly four years younger than Pep. His West Indian father took young Sandy to Harlem where he boxed successfully as an amateur and turned professional when 17. He was something of a freak as a featherweight because he stood 5 feet 8½ inches and had a reach of 70 inches. He was a destructive puncher, with 103 of his 144 wins coming inside the distance.

Saddler challenged Pep for the title on 29 October 1948 in New York, and won surprisingly easily by a fourth-round knockout. He had been heavily backed, leading to suspicions of a 'fix,' and when the two were rematched on 11 February 1949 they were reminded by the New York Commissioner for Boxing that the good name of the sport was in their hands.

This was a magnificent contest in which Pep gave a dazzling display of boxing craft. Although badly marked by Saddler's

BELOW: *Willie Pep goes down in the fourth round of his featherweight title defense against Sandy Saddler (right) at Madison Square Garden, New York, on 29 October 1948. Apart from a defeat by Sammy Angott, it was the first bout Pep had lost in his 136-match career. He and Saddler endured four savage battles.*

punches, he excelled in a bout in which scintillating boxing triumphed over superior power. Eighteen months later, after two successful defenses by Pep, the pair met for a third time. The Yankee Stadium was required to hold all the fans who wanted to see the decider, but they were disappointed by a rough, dirty battle, with Saddler having the edge and winning, when Pep retired with a shoulder injury before the eighth round. It was Pep's third defeat only, but his second defeat by Saddler. Their fourth fight, in 1951, was disgraceful with both men happy to trip, wrestle and use their thumbs. Pep was forced to retire after nine rounds. Both men were suspended from boxing in New York – Pep, in fact, was initially banned for good.

Saddler was drafted into the army and in his absence there was an 'interim' title but he regained the championship in 1955. Sadly, he was forced to retire in 1957 following a car accident in which his eye was badly injured.

Hogan 'Kid' Bassey of Nigeria, the first black African champion since Battling Siki, won the vacant title but was forced to retire after the thirteenth round when defending against Davey Moore in 1959. Moore, the son of a minister, was an excellent champion who defended in Tokyo and Finland during his four-year reign, ultimately losing his title to Sugar Ramos, against whom he could not come out for the eleventh round. Sadly he collapsed in the dressing room and died two days later without regaining consciousness, the second boxer to die in a title fight within the space of a year.

Sandy Saddler's last challenge for the featherweight crown was the young Flash (real name Gabriel) Elorde, from Bogo in the Philippines, who was stopped in the thirteenth round. But in 1960 Elorde won the super-featherweight (or junior light-weight) title by knocking out Harold Gomes in the seventh round in Quezon City, Philippines. He became an outstanding champion, defending 11 times in a reign lasting over seven years and making two attempts at the lightweight title, before he was finally outpointed in a split decision by Yoskiaki Numata of Japan in Tokyo in 1967. He had taken part in a title fight of one sort or another every year for 16 years.

The lightweight division for the 20 years after the war saw a succession of good champions, including Ike Williams, Jimmy Carter, Joe Brown and Carlos Ortiz.

ABOVE LEFT: *Joe 'Old Bones' Brown was world lightweight champion from 1956 to 1962, making 11 successful defenses before losing his title to Carlos Ortiz. He was 44 when he retired in 1970 after 160 fights.*

ABOVE: *Don Jordan, world welterweight champion from December 1958 to May 1960, was a complex character who claimed he was a successful assassin. He also claimed that he was disqualified in the Helsinki Olympics for holding his hands below his waist, and that he threw his title fight with Benny Paret because of Cosa Nostra threats concerning his family.*

RIGHT: *Rinty Monaghan of Ireland, the world flyweight champion, used to sing to the fans after his fights – songs like 'When Irish Eyes are Smiling.' On this occasion he had lost a non-title fight to Terry Allen at Harringay, London, on 8 February 1949. Allen was later given a title chance, and drew with Monaghan in Belfast. Allen won the vacant title.*

FAR RIGHT: *Dado Marino of Honolulu (left) was nearly 34 when he won the world flyweight title in 1950. He became the first grandfather to be a world boxing champion. In 1952 he lost to Yoshio Shirai (right), one of the first Japanese fighters to win a world crown.*

Williams, champion from 1945 to 1951, defended nine times, making an early trip to Cardiff to defeat Welshman Ronnie James. Toward the end of his reign he had difficulty in making the weight and had not defended for 17 months when finally stopped in the fourteenth round by Jimmy Carter. Carter, from Aiken, South Carolina, was a busy fighter who lost and regained the title twice in his five years at the top. Finally Wallace Bud Smith outpointed him in 1955 and Carter also lost the return, but Smith on his second defense was outpointed by Joe Brown, from New Orleans, Louisiana.

Brown defended 12 times in nearly six years, including once in London, where he had a very close contest with British champion Dave Charnley. By this time he was known as 'Old Bones' Brown because he was 35 years old. The following year, in 1962, he was finally outpointed by Carlos Ortiz from Ponce, Puerto Rico, who was his junior by over ten years. Ortiz, who had previously been light-welterweight champion, won the title in Las Vegas, and as well as in Puerto Rico, he defended in Tokyo, Manila, Panama City, Pittsburgh, Mexico City and New York City. One of Ortiz's unsuccessful challengers was Flash Elorde, who twice succumbed in the fourteenth round. Ortiz lost and regained his title to Ishmael Laguna before losing it for good to Carlos Teo Cruz of the Dominican Republic, who together with his family, sadly lost his life in an air crash less than two years later.

The first notable postwar welterweight champion was Sugar

Ray Robinson, who moved up to middleweight, and whose story follows in a separate section. Kid Gavilan from Cuba and Carmen Basilio from New York, who had two outstanding battles with Tony DeMarco, ruled for most of the 1950s. Don Jordan, at the end of the decade, was champion for a while. Jordan, who came from the Dominican Republic, claimed in an interview later in life with Pete Heller (*In This Corner,* Dell Publishing Co., New York, 1973) to have been born with webbed fingers and, as a hired assassin, to have killed 30 people in a month with poison darts in the neck.

Benny 'Kid' Paret from Cuba succeeded him and had three fights with Emile Griffith, in the third of which Paret was battered to a knockout defeat in 12 rounds and never regained consciousness. This was a year before Davey Moore died in the ring, as noted above.

In the postwar period Great Britain retained a hold on the world flyweight title when the wartime holder, Peter Kane, was knocked out in 61 seconds by Scotsman Jackie Paterson. Paterson was stripped of the title in 1947 for failing to make the weight for a defense against Dado Marino. On retiring Paterson went to settle in South Africa where he was killed in a street fight in 1966.

The vacant title was won by Rinty Monaghan of Belfast, who outpointed Marino in London and then defended against Paterson, who took so much out of himself in making the weight that he was knocked out in the seventh. Monaghan's last defense was a draw against Terry Allen of London. Monaghan retired and Allen won the vacant title by out-pointing Honoré Pratesi of Marseilles. Allen, however, lost the title to Dado Marino of Honolulu, when he was outpointed in the challenger's home city. Marino, at 33, was the oldest man to hold the flyweight crown and when he won a return 15 months later he was also the first world champion to be a grandfather. Marino ended Britain's domination of this weight, and his successor, Yoshio Shirai of Tokyo, began a period when Oriental boxers generally held the whip-hand.

The bantamweight division had one of its greatest champions in Manuel Ortiz from Corona, California, who outpointed Lou Salica in 1942 and defended his title 20 times, holding it, apart from a two-month period when he lost it to Harold Dade, for nearly eight years. Most of his defenses were in California and he lost his championship for good when he took it to Johannesburg and was outpointed by Vic Toweel, a member of a famous white South African boxing family. Toweel's successor was Jimmy Carruthers, a hard-hitting Australian who knocked out Toweel in the first round, again in Johannesburg, in 1952. Carruthers had to retire while still champion in 1954 because of eye trouble. His last defense had been an extraordinary one in Bangkok where the outdoor stadium was deluged by rain and the two boxers braved the elements and fought in bare feet.

Succeeding champions in this cosmopolitan division in the 1950s were Robert Cohen of Algeria; Raton Macias of Mexico; Mario d'Agata, a deaf-mute from Italy; Alphonse Halimi, another Algerian; and Joe Becerra, another Mexican, who relinquished the title in 1960.

The Brockton Blockbuster

Rocco Marchegiano was born on 1 September 1923 in Brockton, Massachusetts where his mother's parents had immigrated from Italy. He nearly died from pneumonia at 19 months old but made a marvelous recovery. After his schooldays he took jobs which built up his physique – loading coal, digging ditches – and in 1943 was drafted into the army. He enjoyed sports, particularly baseball, and while serving began boxing. According to legend he was dragged into a fight with an Australian in a bar in Cardiff and discovered his rough ability. In 1946 he had an amateur contest at home and was disqualified in the second round when he became so tired that he kneed his opponent in the groin.

Nevertheless he got into shape, had a second fight which he won in the first round and, as he was paid $50, he used the name Rocky Mack, hoping to protect his amateur status. However he failed in trials with top baseball clubs (he had a weak throwing arm!) so he turned to professional boxing and ran up a string of knockout victories. It wasn't until he had been boxing for two years and had his thirteenth fight that he was taken beyond three rounds. His pal Allie Colombo wrote for a trial to Al Weill, a New York manager who had already looked after world champions. Marchegiano did not impress him unduly but he was taken on. He was only 5 feet 10¼ inches and 185 pounds and, according to Charlie Goldman, the man who was to train him, he did everything wrong. On starting his new career he took the name Rocky Marciano, dropping the 'heg' from the middle of his real name.

His first big test was against Carmine Vingo, another Italian-American, on 30 December 1949 in Madison Square Garden. It was what was to become a typical Marciano bout, with both men giving everything in a torrid slugging match, first one then the other appearing about to collapse. Finally, in the sixth, Vingo was knocked out and taken unconscious to hospital where he nearly died. The incident had its effect on Marciano, who befriended his rival.

The next bout three months later for the man now being called 'The Brockton Blockbuster,' was one of his best against the also unbeaten Roland LaStarza. It drew a large crowd to Madison Square Garden and Marciano won the narrowest of decisions, each boxer having the vote of one judge by a single round and the third judge scoring it five rounds each but giving the fight to Marciano on supplementary points.

After several more excellent wins, Marciano faced Joe Louis on 26 October 1951. Louis had won eight successive comeback bouts since his defeat by Ezzard Charles, but Marciano knocked out the 37-year-old in the eighth, thus ending the ex-champion's career.

BELOW: *Rocky Marciano (right) and Joe Louis shake hands for their fight on 26 October 1951. Neither was world champion at the time. Marciano knocked out Louis in the eighth round, and Louis retired for good. James D Norris, President of IBC, is between them.*

RIGHT: *Rocky Marciano, whose rugged style of fighting lacked any resemblance to 'sweet science' or 'the noble art,' nevertheless overcame every opponent who stood before him. He is the only heavyweight champion to have retired without ever having been beaten.*

On 23 September 1952, Rocky stepped in against Jersey Joe Walcott (even older than Louis!) in Philadelphia for the world championship. Walcott had the challenger down in the first round but Rocky fought back until he began to have difficulty with a substance in his eye, probably caused by his own corner. By the thirteenth, Walcott was clearly in front, but then Marciano caught him on the ropes and a swinging right struck the champion on the chin with such force that he slid down the ropes and was counted out with his forehead on the canvas. It was an awesome punch and cemented the Marciano legend.

Walcott was knocked out in the first round of a return in Chicago in May 1953, and in September Roland LaStarza was given a much-deserved chance. He outpointed the clumsy, fouling Marciano for six rounds, but then Marciano's savagery began to tell. The challenger's arms took such a battering that bones were broken and finally, in the eleventh, LaStarza was knocked from the ring. When he climbed back the referee stopped the contest.

The 32-year-old Ezzard Charles was chosen as a 'soft option' for a June 1954 defense in the Yankee Stadium, New York, but the battle was far from soft. Nearly 50,000 saw Charles inflict a deep wound by Marciano's left eye in the fourth that could easily have ended the fight. Charles, in turn, was cut in the eighth. It was only Marciano's comparative youth and ruggedness that finally put him on top but he could not finish Charles.

A return only three months later began heavily in Marciano's favor but in the sixth his nose was split so badly that blood gushed from it. His corner pleaded with the referee to allow the fight to continue and Marciano hammered Charles in the seventh. In the eighth he received another cut in the corner of the eye and now, desperate lest the fight be stopped, he threw everything at Charles, finally flooring him with a right. A further flurry of punches and Charles was counted out.

In 1955 the British champion Don Cockell was knocked out in the ninth at San Francisco but only after a lenient referee had allowed Marciano to inflict every conceivable foul for which he could have been disqualified half-a-dozen times. It was a fight which diminished the reputation of American boxing, and Marciano, in particular, in British eyes.

Marciano's last defense was against Archie Moore, the light-heavyweight champion, on 21 September 1955. It was a battle which drew 61,574 fans to the Yankee Stadium, New York. They paid over $2 million – the second biggest gate in history at the time and beaten only by the Dempsey-Tunney fight 28 years earlier. Once again the referee did Marciano a favor, by forgetting the rules. Ancient Archie floored Marciano in the second round and Marciano, clearly not in control of his senses, rose at 'two.' Moore should have been allowed to attack but the referee continued to count as if the mandatory 'eight-count' rule applied – a rule used for the protection of boxers, allowing them at least an eight-second rest after a knockdown. Marciano recovered and Moore was subsequently knocked out in the ninth but Moore always asserted, perhaps with a little self-delusion, that the error saved Marciano from a knockout.

Marciano retired and resisted attempts to persuade him to make a comeback. He won all 49 of his professional contests, the only heavyweight champion with a perfect record. In private life he was shy and gentle, in direct contrast to his ring persona. His finances were found on his death to be in a mess, perhaps because gangsters were lurking behind his management. He was killed in 1969 when the plane carrying him to a meeting crashed, the day before his 46th birthday.

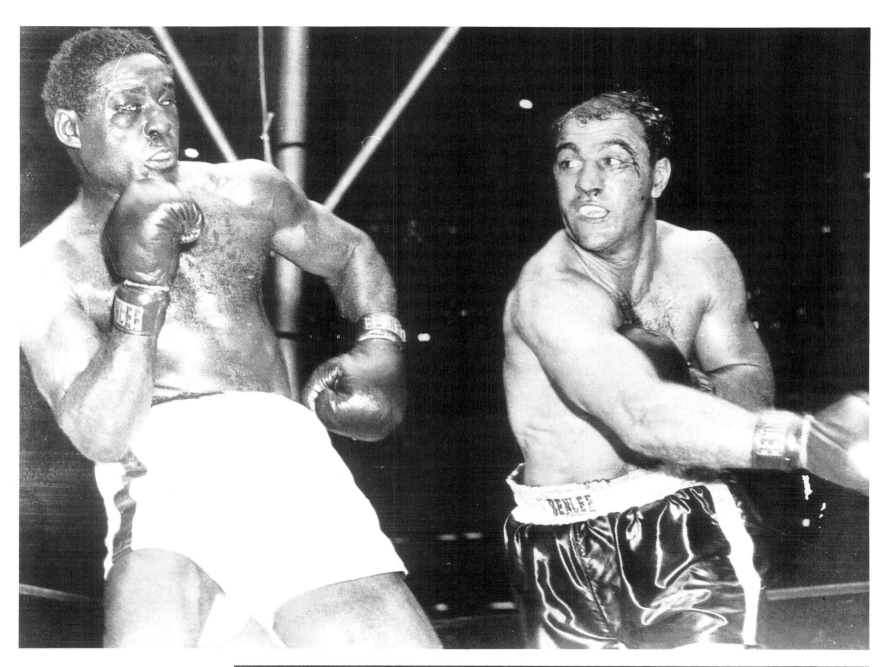

ABOVE LEFT: *Marciano about to become world heavyweight champion. It is the thirteenth round at Philadelphia in September 1952, and Walcott, poleaxed by a right, is seen here sliding down the ropes to the canvas.*

ABOVE: *The second of two tremendous battles between Marciano (right) and Ezzard Charles. This is 17 September 1954. Marciano's nose has been split and his eye cut, but Charles's eye and nose appear to be in a worse state. Marciano won with a knockout in the eighth round.*

RIGHT: *The penultimate round of the penultimate fight of Marciano's career. The challenger is British champion Don Cockell, under attack in a corner. Cockell put up a game show against some rough Marciano tactics, but was stopped in the ninth at San Francisco on 16 May 1955.*

The Great
Sugar Ray Robinson

The man who was frequently described in his prime as the greatest pound-for-pound boxer in the world was born on 3 May 1921 in Detroit, Michigan, and was named Walker Smith. His parents separated when he was 12 and he went with his mother to New York. He was an undisciplined boy and engaged in street fighting, at which he acquired some skill. Then he was introduced to George Gainsford who ran a gym where local amateur boxers trained.

Young Smith used to watch the boxing but his mother was not keen on him taking part. One day, however, a boxer failed the medical and Gainsford offered him the chance to take the fight as a substitute. As Walker Smith did not possess a license, he had to use somebody else's – a boxer called Ray Robinson. He won and kept the name, going on to win two Golden Gloves championships. He was unbeaten in 85 amateur fights. After one performance somebody said that he was 'a sweet fighter' and the reply, either from Gainsford or from a lady spectator (according to whose faulty memory you trust), was 'Yes, as sweet as sugar.' Thus the great Sugar Ray Robinson was born, piece by piece.

He turned professional in October 1940 and rapidly won his first 40 bouts. He was then outpointed by Jake LaMotta. Robinson then had another 91 fights before his second defeat, avenging the LaMotta blot on his record with five subsequent victories over him. Robinson had to wait till 20 December 1946 before getting a world title chance, however. He was at the time a welterweight and was matched with Tommy Bell for the vacant title, winning comfortably on points. He made five successful defenses of this crown in four years before deciding to challenge the middleweights, where the purses were a good deal more lucrative.

The champion was Robinson's old adversary Jake LaMotta who had taken the title from Marcel Cerdan, as previously described. On 14 February 1951 Sugar Ray took on LaMotta in Chicago and outclassed him in what was called another 'St Valentine's Day Massacre.' Robinson was in his prime and he outboxed the Bronx Bull for the first ten rounds or so, then went on the offensive to batter his opponent into submission in the thirteenth round. LaMotta was helpless but won his small victory by refusing to go down. Mercifully the referee stepped in and stopped the fight.

Robinson then treated himself to a European holiday in

which he intended to dispose of any possible European boxers with an eye on his crown. His progress was like that of royalty, or perhaps like that of a modern pop idol. His entourage included sisters, manager and wife, trainers, secretary, mascot (a dwarf) and hairdresser. The larger towns of France, Germany, Italy, Switzerland and Belgium received the king and his court, which traveled in convoy, led by the fighter's huge pink Cadillac, with the top folded back whenever the weather permitted. The local middleweight idol would be soundly beaten by the visiting royalty who would bank his check, acknowledge the respects of the populace and move on.

Unfortunately for Robinson the British and European middleweight champion was far too good to be dealt with in this imperious manner. Randolph Turpin, seven years younger than Robinson, was an ex-naval cook who, when not troubled by mental anguish caused by his relations with women and money, or usually both in combination, was as good a middleweight as any there has been.

On 10 July 1951 at the Exhibition Hall, Earls Court, Turpin was brilliant and completely outfought Robinson, to win on points. Such was Robinson's reputation that it was one of the greatest nights in the lives of the 18,000 spectators and the millions of British fight fans who listened to the radio commentary (so notoriously misguided that Henry Cooper, an ambitious 17-year-old amateur at the time, could recall it with pride and amusement in a television interview 36 years later). Sugar Ray, after all, was unbeaten for 91 fights over eight years, and in fact had lost only one of 217 amateur and professional contests in his life.

Robinson won the title back at the Polo Grounds in New York 64 days later, the referee stepping in in the tenth when,

ABOVE RIGHT: *Sugar Ray Robinson arrives with his wife in London for his fight with Randolph Turpin in 1951. The handsome Robinson looks well-groomed and utterly confident, as befits a great world champion who had lost only one fight in 217 as amateur and professional, and that one defeat had occurred eight years earlier.*

RIGHT: *On what many believe to be the greatest night in British boxing, Turpin (right) outfought Robinson in a brilliant display to take the title.*

LEFT: *Robinson fought Jake LaMotta six times and won five times; although LaMotta was always brave Robinson was the better technician. Robinson took the title in 1951. In this photograph Sugar Ray is sinking a hard left to LaMotta's midriff.*

behind on points, Sugar Ray was attacking desperately with an eye so badly cut that it threatened to lose him his third fight. A smashing right caught Turpin on the chin, and while the Englishman was taking punishment on the ropes, the referee stopped the fight in Robinson's favor. A record crowd of 60,347 saw the battle and paid $727,627.

Sugar Ray disposed of Carl 'Bobo' Olsen and Rocky Graziano and then challenged Joey Maxim for the light-heavyweight title. The fight, on 25 June 1952 at the Yankee Stadium, was extraordinary. At 104 degrees it was the hottest day of the year. Thirteen rounds of boxing affected Robinson more than Maxim. After being well ahead on points, Robinson was dropped in the thirteenth more from heat exhaustion than from anything else, and, in a state of distress, could not come out for the fourteenth. He lasted longer than the referee, who was forced to give up for the same reason three rounds earlier.

In December Robinson announced his retirement and switched to cabaret and dancing, but two years later, because of tax demands and because he was a better boxer than dancer, he began a comeback which took him to a title shot with the new champion, Carl 'Bobo' Olsen. Robinson, now approaching 35, won by a knockout in the second round to regain the championship. He won a return in the same way but in 1957

lost the title on points to Gene Fullmer. However, he again won it back with a fifth-round knockout and then faced Carmen Basilio who, like Robinson, had been welterweight champion.

Basilio, from New York, was a short man but extremely durable. He and Robinson did not like each other much and their fight was a savage encounter. Basilio, six years the younger, beat Robinson on points to become the new champion. It seemed the end at last for the old warrior but, astonishingly, in an equally savage return battle which went the whole 15 rounds, the near 37-year-old won the decision. He had won the middleweight title for the fifth time, a record for any division.

A year later the NBA relieved him of the title for inactivity and in January 1960 he also lost the New York and European recognition when beaten on points by Paul Pender in Boston. He tried to regain it six months later but again lost the decision. In December 1960 he attempted to win the other half of the title, which had been assumed by Gene Fullmer, and was given a draw in a bout in Los Angeles. Three months later he was outpointed in the return. He was now practically 40 and although he had no more title fights he kept going till he was 44. By the end he had lost 19 fights in 201, but only heat exhaustion had ever prevented him going the whole distance. Sugar Ray Robinson could pride himself on his superb career.

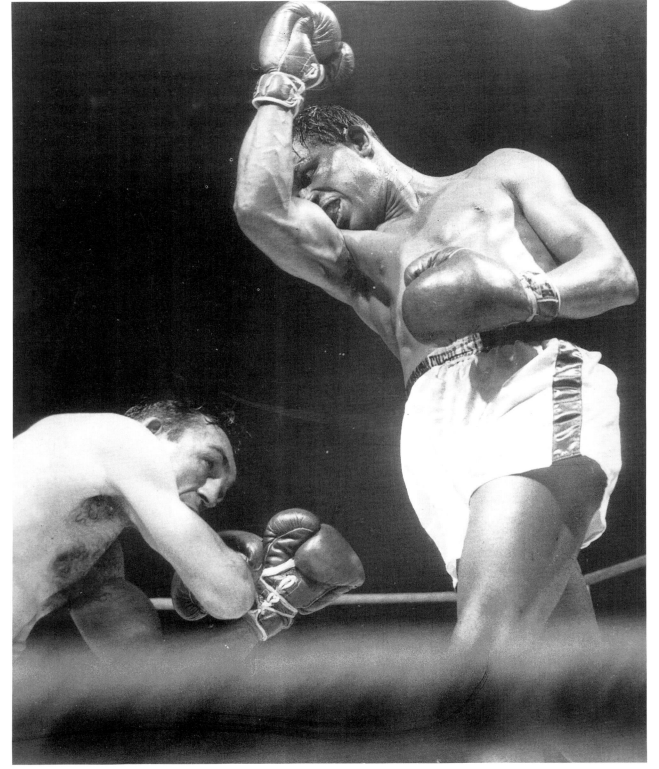

LEFT: *Robinson has missed with a right against the crouching Carmen Basilio. The two boxers had two bloody battles, Basilio winning the first and Robinson the second. Robinson's victory gave him the middleweight title for the fifth time, a record for any division.*

RIGHT: *Floyd Patterson, a very complex character who was a skillful fast-punching boxer. He was the youngest heavyweight champion and the first to regain the title after losing it.*

Patterson Breaks the Records

When Rocky Marciano retired, leaving the heavyweight championship vacant, the authorities were quick to arrange the succession. Floyd Patterson was matched with Tommy 'Hurricane' Jackson in an eliminator, won a split decision, and then fought Archie Moore for the championship. On 30 November 1956 the young Patterson was too quick for Ancient Archie, who had turned professional the year Patterson was born, and won by a knockout in the fifth round.

The new champion was born on 4 January 1935 at Waco County, North Carolina, the third son of ten children. The family soon moved to a tough neighborhood in Brooklyn where Floyd often played truant from school and was sent to a special school for retarded children. It had good sporting facilities and he learned to box there. His two older brothers boxed and were hard on the young Floyd, often making him cry with their harder blows. Eventually his brothers turned professional under Cus d'Amato, who ran a local gymnasium. Floyd tagged along, did as much training as he could, and d'Amato decided to coach him. He became an excellent amateur, won a Golden Gloves championship and took the gold medal in the middleweight class at the 1952 Helsinki Olympics.

Three months later he turned professional and d'Amato, realizing he was still growing, began grooming him for the heavyweight title. He had a unique style, stalking his man with his gloves held so high before his face that he had to peer around them – it was described as a 'peek-a-boo' style. He fought from a crouch and when he saw an opening, he would leap in with long punches. He threw punches fast and could land several in combination before his opponent could recover from the first.

When Patterson won the title he was the first Olympic gold medalist to win the heavyweight crown and, at 21 years 10 months and 26 days, he was the youngest ever holder of it. His victory brought a new perspective to the heavyweight scene. The United States government was taking action against the International Boxing Club under the antitrust laws. This was the body run by Jim Norris who had made the arrangement with Joe Louis to promote the title fight resulting from Louis' retirement. Since then this body had staged over 80 percent of all heavyweight title fights. D'Amato decided to be independent of the IBC, which meant that Patterson's defenses were against boxers who were free of options held by the IBC. This ruled out some of the leading contenders. D'Amato was accused of giving his champion soft defenses, which was the inevitable result of his policy, but it was not the prime reason for it. In fact Patterson probably suffered from this policy so far as his historical rating is concerned, for there is no reason to suspect that he could not have beaten Zora Folley, say, or Eddie Machen, both highly ranked heavyweights he never met.

Patterson gave a return to Tommy Jackson, the referee intervening in the tenth to save Jackson. That was at the Polo Grounds, New York, and D'Amato then took Patterson to Sick's Stadium, Seattle, to fight Pete Rademacher, the 1956 Olympic champion who was having his first professional contest. Rademacher put Patterson down but was knocked out in the sixth round. Then it was off to Wrigley Field, Los Angeles, to face Roy Harris, who also shocked Patterson by knocking him down before being forced to retire in the twelfth.

Brian London, an ex-British champion, then defied the British Boxing Board of Control, which did not consider him a suitable challenger, by fighting Patterson in Indianapolis. He suffered an eleventh-round knockout and a £1000 fine, but still made an excellent profit.

Another foreigner, the Swede Ingemar Johansson, was then imported. The match was at the Yankee Stadium, New York, on 26 June 1959. Johansson's arrival was something new for the New York boxing public and press to take in. He arrived with an intimate circle of family and friends, including the stunning Birgit Lundgren, his fiancée. They all stayed at training camp, where training to Ingemar was more like a package holiday than the usual grunt and sweat.

He was an interesting boxer. A bigger and heavier man than Patterson, he had reached the Olympic heavyweight final in the year that Patterson won the middleweight title, but his fate was very different. Apparently apprehensive of the punching power of his opponent, Ed Sanders, he had not made a fight of it and had to face the shame of being disqualified for not trying.

Patterson was a 4-to-1-on favorite in the betting, but the betting boys had overlooked the recent record of Johansson. He had knocked out some good men, including Eddie Machen and Henry Cooper and clearly had a very destructive right, called 'Ingo's Bingo' or 'The Hammer of Thor,' according to taste. What's more, Patterson had been put down by such men as Pete Rademacher and Roy Harris.

It should have been no surprise, therefore, that Patterson

went down when Ingemar's right caught him on the mouth in the third, or that he should rise so bemused that he didn't know where he was, and stood rubbing his nose like a little boy embarrassed at school. Six more times Johansson knocked the helpless Patterson down in that round before the referee did what he could have done three or four knockdowns earlier – stopped the fight.

Johansson, born on 16 October 1932 in Gothenburg, was Sweden's first boxer of note and he thoroughly enjoyed his triumph. Patterson, who was nothing if not dedicated, returned to his training and began to build himself up for the return. This took place at the Polo Grounds, New York, a year later, on 20 June 1960.

This time Patterson was able to work in close to Johansson's body and to avoid that thundering right hand. In the fifth, one of his leaping left hooks floored Ingo, and when the Swede climbed to his feet another put him out for the count. He took a little while to recover, to Patterson's consternation.

ABOVE: *Patterson had three title fights with Ingemar Johansson and on each occasion each man showed he had the ability to put the other on the canvas.*

Johansson won the first fight, and this photograph is from the second; Patterson's powerful left jab is helping him to regain the crown.

The rubber match, at the Convention Hall, Miami Beach, on 13 March 1961, saw both men get in their blows early. Patterson was down twice in the first round, but retaliated by flooring Johansson. Both men got in punches from then on but Patterson delivered the clean left hook which counted, knocking out the challenger in the sixth. It was the end of the road for the likeable Swede who left professional boxing to enjoy life to the full as a businessman.

Patterson had established another record by winning his title back. He was the first man to lose and regain the world heavyweight championship.

Nine months after the third Johansson fight he dispatched another opponent, Tom McNeeley, knocking him out in four rounds in Toronto. But round the corner was his nemesis.

Sonny Liston, The Ugly Bear

Patterson's nemesis was Charles 'Sonny' Liston. He was born, according to the records, on 8 May 1932 at St Francis, Arkansas, in a shanty town. Little is known of his childhood and even his date of birth is not certain – he had a daughter of an age which suggests he must have been older than the record states. His farmhand father was said to have had 24 other children. Sonny ran away from working in the fields at 13 and lived with his mother in St Louis where he was unhappy at school. His education was several years behind boys of his own age, and he ran away from school and led a life of crime on the streets. Eventually he was convicted of armed robbery and put in a penitentiary. The chaplain channeled his frustrations into boxing and he won a Golden Gloves championship in 1953.

Liston turned professional and compiled an impressive record. By the time Patterson was heavyweight champion Liston had lost only one fight in 34, his seventh, when Marty Marshall broke his jaw. Even so, Liston had fought on for six rounds to lose only on points. This defeat he had avenged twice. The 34 fights had occupied nine years, nine months of which had been spent in prison for assaulting a policeman. Underworld figures were never far from Liston during his boxing career.

Liston stood 6 feet 1 inch and weighed around 216 pounds. He possessed a big chest and shoulders, a long reach and enormous fists. But perhaps his biggest physical asset was his face and eyes. A taciturn unsmiling character, he had a look of menace, and his cold baleful eyes would be directed at his opponent at weigh-in and preliminaries in an unblinking stare of calculating malignity. Many of his opponents must have been unnerved in his presence and by the complex, almost furtive person that Patterson was.

D'Amato was not keen on Patterson facing Liston but Liston was so clearly the logical challenger and the newspapers were building him up as unbeatable. Patterson could have dodged him on the grounds of his criminal record – New York would not allow Liston to fight for the title there. But Patterson's pride would not allow him to run away forever and on 25 September 1962 the two met in Chicago. Nearly 19,000 fans watched the fight in Comiskey Park.

They did not get much for their money. An apprehensive Patterson found that his usually stinging blows had no effect on Liston, who came in delivering murderous blows to the body until Floyd was forced to lower his guard. Immediately a sweeping left hook landed on his chin and down went the champion. All his attempts to rise could only get him to a crouching position. The fight had lasted 126 seconds and Liston was the new champion.

Patterson, a man of great pride, was prepared for this humiliation. It was said he spent hundreds of dollars a year on theatrical disguises and on this night he needed his skill in makeup. He slunk out of the stadium in false beard and spectacles, unable to face the public after his defeat.

There was a return clause in the contract but most expected that Patterson would not exercise it, so total had been the demolition job wrought by Liston. But on 22 July 1963 at the Convention Hall, Las Vegas, he stepped through the ropes again to face this stone-faced man with the fists to match. He managed to do slightly better, in that he got up after the first knockdown and had to be floored three times. Also the fight lasted four seconds more at 130 seconds.

ABOVE: *The awesome Sonny Liston, master of the cold-blooded stare that turned opponents to jello.*

ABOVE: *Patterson's head is still shaking from a heavy blow by Liston, whose right is coming from somewhere near the floor to put the lights out for Patterson. Liston took the title at Chicago on 25 September 1962 in 126 seconds.*

LEFT: *Liston (left) does not look quite as big and menacing against Cassius Clay at Miami Beach in 1964, and he has picked up a bump under his eye. Liston suddenly folded up after the sixth round and retired with a shoulder injury.*

ABOVE RIGHT: *Clay's mental state was a matter of conjecture in his first fight with Liston. He was hyperactive at the weigh-in, hyped up during the fight and, as the picture shows, inclined to be a little overexcited when he won.*

124

It was the end of Patterson as a world champion although he twice more attempted to win back the crown.

Liston, who looked so utterly impregnable, was challenged by a loud-mouthed young braggart who both intrigued and irritated the boxing world with a series of flamboyant wins and outlandish publicity. He taunted Liston by calling him an 'Ugly Bear.' His name was Cassius Marcellus Clay and Liston took him on at the Convention Hall, Miami Beach, on 25 February 1964. Liston was the 7-to-1-on favorite. But Clay was not only a magnificent physical specimen himself, being taller and slimmer than Liston and almost as heavy, but he was at least nine years younger.

He also had a fanatical belief in himself. He was as frightened of Liston as the rest, but in him the fear translated itself into hyperactivity, not submission. For six rounds he kept the lumbering Liston at bay and in the interval before the seventh a suddenly tired and old-looking Liston retired on his stool.

Clay went berserk on winning the title. There was a return at Lewiston on 25 May 1965 and Clay, now calling himself Muhammad Ali, was supremely confident. The fight was at the unusual venue of Lewiston because several more fashionable states had refused it. It seemed that the boxing world wanted to be rid of Liston. If so, he had the last laugh. In the first round he went down from a punch that hardly anyone saw

and many doubted existed. Ali stood over him, snarling, until the referee (Jersey Joe Walcott) removed him to a neutral corner, by which time the timekeeper had counted Liston out. The ending was chaotic as Ali attacked Liston again when he rose, and the timekeeper had to insist to Walcott that the fight was over. Walcott then separated the boxers. By then 132 seconds had passed. The official time was later given as one minute but the film shows the fight lasted 112 seconds, including the count. It also shows a punch but hardly one capable of having such a devastating effect.

There are many theories about that most controversial of all heavyweight title fights. The least popular is that it was honest. Some think it was an underworld coup of some sort, others that Liston was snubbing the public one last time. He did in fact resume his career, winning 15 of 16 more contests. Only three men ever beat him.

A year after his last fight he died, taking the secret of the second Ali fight with him to the grave. His wife found him dead from a drug overdose in the kitchen of his Las Vegas house on 30 December 1970. The coroner could say only that he had been dead about six days, so both the birth and death dates of this mysterious man are uncertain. Nobody will now know the whole truth about him but looking at what is known it is likely he was as much sinned against as sinning.

ABOVE: *'The Greatest' (Ali) was the best thing to happen to boxing in the 1960s and 1970s, and his most remarkable victory was probably this one over George Foreman in Zaire in 1974.*

PART III

From
The Greatest
to
Iron Mike

Simply 'The Greatest' Champion

Boxing received its biggest boost in the 1960s with the arrival on the scene of a brash young man who was to dominate the sport for about 15 years. His name, Cassius Marcellus Clay, was a relic of slave days, coming from a Senator Clay, to whom his family had 'belonged.'

He was born on 17 January 1942, the son of a sign-painter, at Louisville, Kentucky. He led a happy childhood exemplified by the gift of a $60 bicycle for his 12th birthday. Unfortunately he left it outside a store and it was stolen. He tearfully reported the theft to a policeman, an Irishman named Joe Martin, and threatened to take revenge against the thief. Martin, who ran a local gym for boys, persuaded the young Cassius to start boxing lessons there so that he could look after himself if he ever found the culprit. He proved to be an outstanding boxer, despite a heart murmur which interrupted his progress when he was 14, and at 18 he was selected to represent the United States at the Olympic Games.

He was afraid of flying but Martin persuaded him to go to Rome and he not only won the gold medal, but proved to be one of the most gregarious and liked competitors in the village. He was so proud of his medal that he refused to take it off and the gold began to wear away. When asked at the press conference why he should be so proud of a country which barred men of his color from eating at certain restaurants and sitting in certain places on buses, he defended America stoutly.

Received as a hero at home in Louisville, he was shown off to visitors and his defense of the 'American way of life' was emphasized. All this turned sour when he and a friend, after one such public relations exercise, were refused service at a restaurant, abused by the proprietor and chased off by a white motorcycle gang with whom they had a scrap. Clay at last had to take his medal off to wash away the blood in the Ohio River. Afterward he walked to the middle of the bridge and threw the medal away. In his autobiography *The Greatest*, he wrote that from that time his holiday as a 'White Hope' was over.

A syndicate of white Louisville millionaires sponsored his professional career and engaged the accomplished trainer Angelo Dundee to look after him. On 29 October 1960 Tunney Hunsaker was his first professional opponent, losing a decision over six rounds. Soon the exuberant Clay met a wrestler, Gorgeous George, well known for his publicity gimmicks and boasting, and Clay, anxious to make himself famous and become heavyweight champion as quickly as possible, copied his antics, bragging endlessly and predicting the round in which he would beat opponents, often in verse. His catch phrase, 'I am the greatest,' which boomed in the middle of a rapid patter when nobody else was allowed to speak, became famous. Or perhaps notorious is a better word, because most fans were annoyed by his boasting and longed to see his lip buttoned. 'The Louisville Lip' became his nickname, or alternatively, on the 'Gorgeous George' theme, 'Gaseous Cassius.'

FAR RIGHT: *Clay in expansive mood, after his defeat of Henry Cooper at Wembley in 1963. His next fight was to be his world title challenge to Liston, and he is predicting, that Liston 'will fall in eight.'*

RIGHT: *Cassius Clay, who later changed his name to Muhammad Ali, is pictured here as a young boxer at the age of 12 years. He had just taken up the sport.*

BELOW: *Clay in manic mood, still shouting as he leaves the ring after taking the title from Liston in February 1964.*

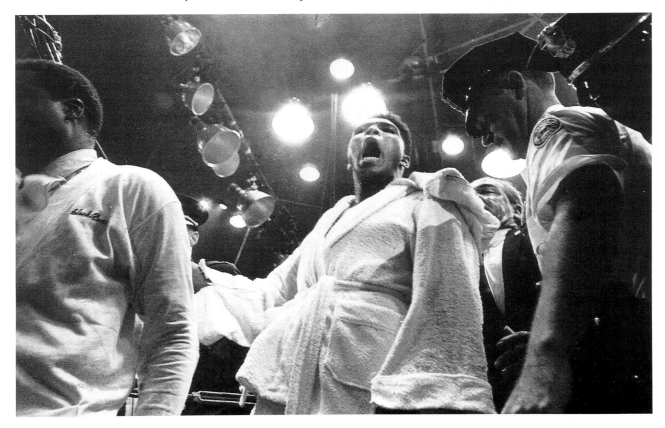

LEFT: *The punch British fans remember, as does Ali, or Clay as he then was, since this was the nearest he came to defeat in his best years. Henry Cooper's hook floors him in the fourth at Wembley in 1963, but the bell and a long interval for a split glove to be replaced saved him from the knockout.*

RIGHT: *Ali gave Floyd Patterson a merciless beating on 22 November 1965 at Las Vegas. He did not like Patterson's apparent meekness before the white race. Patterson (right), obviously on the receiving end, appears meek enough before Ali in this picture.*

BELOW: *Ali defeated George Chuvalo on points over 15 rounds at Toronto on 29 March 1966, taking all the Canadian's heavy punches to the body and outpointing his tired challenger in the later rounds.*

Clay's style in his early days was based upon his athleticism. With his hands held low he moved around quickly and punched with power, speed and precision from all angles. It was a style not unlike that used by Jimmy Wilde 50 years before but he had been a flyweight. Clay was surprisingly heavy – only Willard and Carnera among heavyweight champions before him were significantly heavier – but he moved with the bounce and athleticism of a lightweight. 'He floats like a butterfly and stings like a bee' was a famous description of his style. He stood 6 feet 3 inches and could pride himself on his perfect physical shape.

Clay built up a succession of victories without a fright until he came to London in 1963 to meet Henry Cooper, the British champion. Cooper had Clay down and groggy at the end of the fourth round and only a split glove, which prolonged the interval between rounds, and the use of illegal smelling salts saved Clay. Later he got to work on Cooper's eye, split earlier in the fight, and the referee had to step in. His best win before then was a knockout of Archie Moore who, as predicted, 'went in four.' It is astonishing to recall that Moore was not only 28 years older than Clay but six years older than Angelo Dundee!

The fight following the Cooper victory was the world championship challenge to Sonny Liston. Clay was demented at the weigh-in, dancing around and abusing Liston. His pulse rate and blood pressure soared. The commission doctor said that he was unbalanced and acting like a man scared to death. He was fined $2500 for unseemly conduct and the contest was almost stopped because of his apparent hysterical condition.

If it was a ploy it was brilliantly conceived, because Liston, completely upstaged for once, fought without conviction. He plodded while Clay danced. There was another sensation from the volatile young challenger in the interval after the fourth round. Some of Liston's medication had got into his eye, and he screamed to Dundee that he couldn't see and to cut his gloves off. Dundee, however, pushed him out for the fifth round and Clay managed to survive it by keeping his straight left permanently in Liston's face.

When Clay's eyes cleared in the sixth Liston must have known he was not to beat this extraordinary fighter who seemed to live on his nerves and who could do anything he liked. Liston looked weary. As the seventh was about to start he spat out his gumshield and retired, claiming a shoulder injury.

He was the first heavyweight champion to retire on his stool, if one excepts Willard who had the excuse of broken bones and permanent injury to his hearing. As for Clay, he went berserk, tearing round the ring, mouth agape, screaming 'What did I tell you?' and 'I'm the greatest.'

Much happened before the return. Clay's stomach suddenly swelled up like a football and he needed an emergency operation for acute hernia. He also joined the Black Muslims and announced he was renouncing his slave name of Clay and would henceforth be known as Cassius X. Later he changed this to Muhammad Ali, the name under which he fought Liston in the return at Lewiston, Maine.

That fight, already described, ended in Liston's first-round knockout by a 'phantom' punch. Ali, now utterly composed and confident, proved his claim to be at least among the greats by beating all comers and even traveling to do it. He beat Floyd Patterson in Las Vegas, George Chuvalo in Toronto, Henry Cooper in London, Doug Jones in Houston, Brian London in London, Karl Mildenburger in Frankfurt, Cleveland Williams in Houston, Ernie Terrell in Houston and Zora Folley in New York – certainly an impressive string of victories.

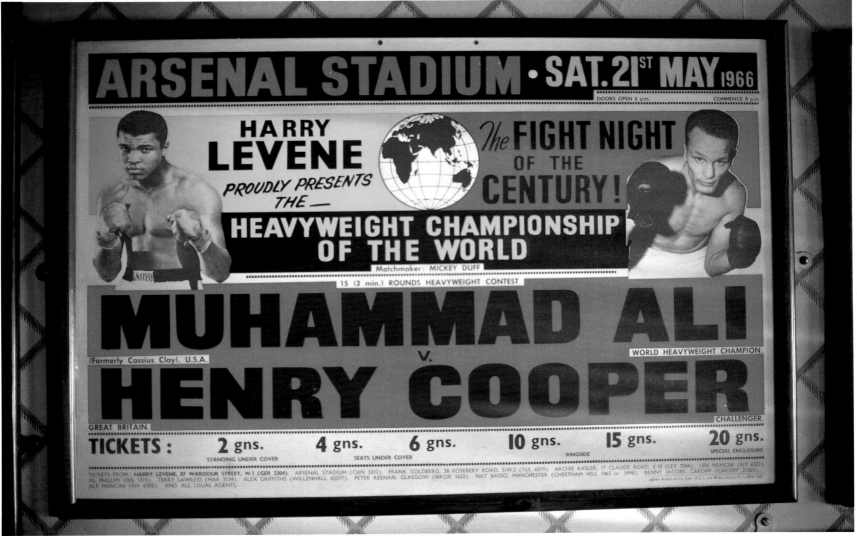

The Patterson and Terrell bouts were unpleasant and revealed a new side of Ali. Patterson would not use his new name and Ali called Patterson a 'white man's nigger,' and subjected him to 12 rounds of systematic punishment before the referee intervened. The Terrell contest was to unify the title again; before the Liston return the World Boxing Association (formerly the National Boxing Association) withdrew recognition from Ali on the grounds, so the President said, that Ali had signed for the return in the original contract, so violating a WBA by-law, and also because he was provoking worldwide criticism by his conduct. In other words the WBA did not like the Black Muslim connection. Terrell subsequently beat Eddie Machen to take the vacant WBA title. Ernie Terrell was another who refused to recognize Ali by his new name and when the two met on 6 February 1967 Ali gave Terrell a vicious lesson, punctuating his punches with the question 'What's my name?' and declining to knock out Terrell so that he could administer 15 rounds of pain.

While this activity was going on (the defenses listed above were packed into less than two years) Ali was fighting the United States Army draft board. At first classified I-Y after failing the intelligence test, he was subsequently reclassified I-A in February 1966, but claimed exemption as a minister of religion and conscientious objector. As far as he was concerned, he had no quarrel with the Vietnamese.

On 9 May 1967 Ali was convicted for failing to submit to the draft and sentenced to five years' imprisonment, against which he immediately appealed. The WBA again withdrew recognition. With Ali unable to defend his title, the WBC and the BBBC followed suit and declared the title vacant in 1969. Ali, still unbeaten and perhaps the best heavyweight of all time, was a boxing exile.

LEFT: *When he was world champion Ali came to London again to fight Henry Cooper in 1966. Cooper fought well, but again his fragile skin tissue around his eyes let him down. By the sixth round he was bleeding profusely and the referee stopped the fight.*

LEFT BELOW: *The poster for the Ali-Cooper world heavyweight title fight at Highbury Stadium, the home of Arsenal Football Club, in 1966.*

RIGHT: *Ali momentarily on the defensive during his title fight with Ernie Terrell. Ali was annoyed because Terrell would not acknowledge Ali's new name and deliberately set out to inflict as much pain on his opponent as he could.*

The Olympic Champions Take Over

After it had thankfully ditched Ali for a second time, the WBA decided on an eight-man tournament to be run on a 'knockout' basis, to find a new champion. The men they chose to fight it out were Joe Frazier, Thad Spencer, Ernie Terrell, Oscar Bonavena, Karl Mildenberger, Jimmy Ellis, Floyd Patterson and Jerry Quarry. Frazier decided to dodge these eliminators, however, with an eye to WBC recognition, and Leotis Martin took his place.

From these Jimmy Ellis and Jerry Quarry reached the 'final,' but before it took place the New York authorities and other bodies decided to recognize the winner of a bout between Joe Frazier and Buster Mathis as champion. Mathis, a giant of 243 pounds, had been the only man to defeat Frazier as an amateur, inflicting two defeats on him but breaking his thumb the second time, thus losing the chance to represent the United States in the 1964 Olympic Games in Tokyo. Frazier took his place and won the super-heavyweight gold medal, despite suffering a broken hand.

On 4 March 1968 the two men, both unbeaten as professionals, drew 18,000 fans to the fourth Madison Square Garden, built over Pennsylvania Station on New York's 7th Avenue.

The fight was on the first boxing night held there, a double world championship bill. Frazier knocked out Mathis in the eleventh round to become the New York champion. On 27 April 1968 Jimmy Ellis outpointed Jerry Quarry at Oakland to become the WBA champion. That Ellis was Ali's sparring partner indicated the stature of the man in the wilderness.

Frazier was the more active of the two champions in 1968 and 1969, beating Manuel Ramos, Oscar Bonavena (who took him the distance), Dave Zyglewicz and Jerry Quarry, while Ellis outpointed Jerry Quarry and Floyd Patterson who was making his last attempt to regain his crown, and Ellis did not defend at all in 1969.

Frazier was born in Beaufort, South Carolina, on 12 January 1944 and was one of 13 children. He worked in a slaughterhouse and took up amateur boxing, enjoying a successful career which led to the Olympic gold medal. He was not ideally built for a heavyweight boxer, being under 6 feet tall. He weighed over 200 pounds, but much of this seemed to be in his sturdy legs which made him hard to knock over. Ellis, born on 24 February 1940, at Louisville, Kentucky, was older.

The two met at Madison Square Garden on 16 February

RIGHT: *Joe Frazier (left) and Jimmy Ellis, the WBC and WBA heavyweight champions respectively, meet amicably a fortnight before their meeting in February 1970 that was to decide who was undisputed champion.*

BELOW LEFT: *Joe Frazier, the WBC champion, forces his challenger, Oscar Bonavena of Argentina, against the ropes in their Philadelphia encounter in December 1968. Frazier took the decision, so keeping his title.*

BELOW: *As Jerry Quarry turns away Jimmy Ellis is lifted by his handlers after winning the vacant WBC title at Oakland, California, in April 1968. It was a majority decision in his favor.*

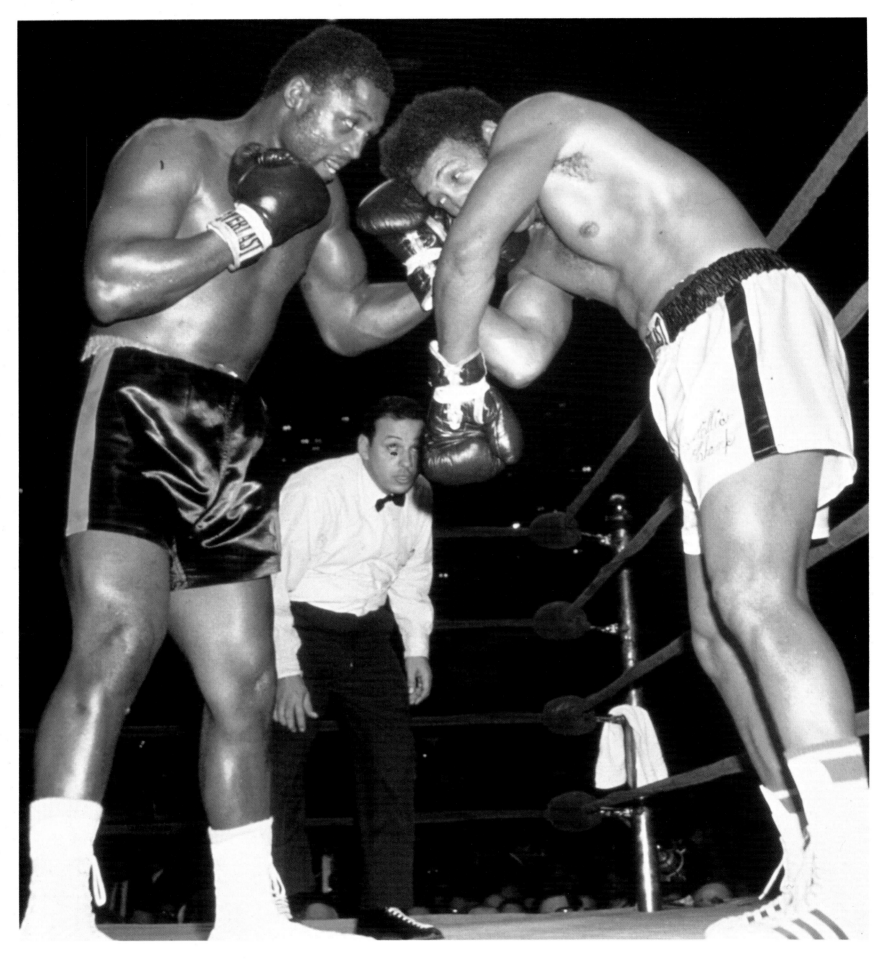

1970 and the WBC announced it would recognize the winner as world champion. Frazier won comfortably when Ellis was unable to continue after the fourth round and so became the undisputed world champion. He defended against Bob Foster, the light-heavyweight champion, in 1970 and knocked him out in the second.

Meanwhile Ali was regarded as the champion by most Americans, who were now looking on his Vietnam views with more favor, as popular sentiment turned against the war. In 1970 the State of Georgia gave him a license to box and he began a comeback with a contest against Jerry Quarry, forever the loser in championship battles, at Atlanta. Quarry did his job and was forced to retire with a cut eye. Later in the year Ali

stopped the tough Oscar Bonavena and the battle that everybody wanted, Ali versus Frazier, the match of the two unbeaten champions, was arranged for 8 March 1971.

Ali's image with most of the public had now changed from boaster to liberal hero – a man suffering from a brave stand over the war in Vietnam. Such was his aura that most expected him to beat Frazier, despite his recent long layoff from the ring. In a match watched by huge television audiences the two fought each other almost to a standstill. Frazier's better condition gave him the upper hand, and in the last round he caught Ali with a left hook which floored him and as a result made sure of the decision.

In 1972 the champion, now undisputed both in fact and

LEFT: *Frazier (left) has Ellis covering up in their unifying title fight in New York on 16 February 1970. Frazier was much too strong for Ellis, who was forced to retire after four rounds. Frazier became the first undisputed champion since Muhammad Ali had been forced into exile.*

RIGHT: *Frazier's first defense as undisputed champion was against the light-heavyweight titleholder Bob Foster. Although giving away plenty of reach, Frazier (left) was again too heavy and strong for his challenger, who was knocked out in the second round.*

BELOW: *Frazier's greatest moment. The two unbeaten 'champions,' Frazier and Ali, met on 8 March 1971 in New York, and Frazier (patterned trunks) succeeded in putting Ali down in the last round to win the verdict.*

public estimation, defeated Terry Daniels and Ron Stander. In each case the referee intervened in the fourth round. Frazier by now had emerged from the shadow of Ali. Those who had previously seen him as a champion on sufferance while Ali, like Achilles, sulked in his tent, now recognized him as legitimate and called him 'Smoking Joe.'

There was a new cloud on his horizon, however, in the big strong Olympic super-heavyweight champion of 1968, George Foreman. Foreman had boxed as an amateur only 18 times before the Olympics but won the title with no trouble. At the medal parade he had waved a tiny American flag which he clutched in his huge fist.

As a professional he had notched up 37 wins, 34 of them inside his distance. Nevertheless few gave him much chance when he challenged Frazier at the National Stadium, Kingston, Jamaica, on 22 January 1973. Frazier, who was the 3-to-1-on favorite, appeared to share this opinion and appeared in photographs with his pop group called 'The Knockouts.'

This time the millions of television viewers from all round the world saw less than two rounds. Smoking Joe came boring in but could not get near enough to Foreman to do any harm. Foreman's long reach kept him at a distance and then a long right thudded on his chin and Frazier went down. Joe leaped back onto the attack but just ran into another barrage. Finally he was standing helpless as a succession of rights put him down again. The bell saved him on the third knockdown.

In the second round Frazier continued to come forward, but, like the ebbing tide, every advance was followed by a bigger retreat. Three times he was dumped on the canvas. The last time he was lifted off his feet and landed in a crumpled heap. He struggled up again but the referee would allow no more.

George Foreman, the new champion, was born in Marshall, Texas, on 22 January 1948. He stood 6 feet 3 inches and weighed around 220 pounds. He had a tremendous right-hand punch, and at the time he became champion, he had won over 90 percent of his bouts before the end, a higher percentage of stoppages than even Marciano enjoyed. He looked unbeatable and seemed set for a long reign ahead.

ABOVE: *The photograph that deserves pride of place in Joe Frazier's album. The referee waves him away from Ali, who looks out for the count, in their first fight, in March 1971. Ali got up to last the distance.*

BELOW: *The end of his championship days for Frazier as the mighty George Foreman takes Frazier off his feet and takes his title at the National Stadium in Kingston, Jamaica, on 22 January 1973. Frazier was the 3-to-1-on favorite for this fight, but lasted less than two rounds in an exciting bout.*

RIGHT: *Ali, on the comeback trail, suffered a setback after ten straight wins, when he met Ken Norton at San Diego on 31 March 1973. Norton broke Ali's jaw early on in the fight and it swelled alarmingly, but Ali bravely fought on, although in the end he lost the decision. Six months later Ali won a return and later he was able to avenge his only other defeat by Frazier.*

The Rumble in the Jungle

While one Olympic heavyweight champion was taking the title from another, Ali, an Olympic champion at a lighter weight, had been busy since his defeat by Frazier. In 1971 he knocked out Jimmy Ellis and outpointed Buster Mathis at Houston and knocked out Jurgen Blin at Zurich. In 1972 he outpointed Mac Foster in Tokyo and George Chuvalo in Vancouver, and then knocked out Jerry Quarry, Al Lewis (in Dublin), Floyd Patterson and Bob Foster.

Soon after Foreman won the title, Ali outpointed Joe Bugner and then suffered his second defeat. Ken Norton, a superbly built 6-foot 3-inch ex-Marine from Jacksonville, Illinois, broke Ali's jaw in a contest in San Diego. Ali showed his tremendous courage in fighting on for ten rounds but lost the points verdict. Six months later he fought Norton again at Inglewood and won a split decision. It was an important revenge for Ali but clearly Norton had established himself as a title contender. Ali ended the year with a points win over Rudi Lubbers at Jakarta. Meantime Foreman's only defense in 1973 was a one-round destruction of King Roman in Tokyo.

Both Ali and Foreman had bigger tests early in 1974. Ali took on Frazier again in New York. Frazier had come back from his beating by Foreman and had outpointed Joe Bugner in London. The fight was seen as an eliminator for a challenge to Foreman. It was not quite the classic of the encounter three years earlier but it was a very hard fight, with Frazier's left hook getting home on Ali's jaw in the seventh, but Ali weathered the storm and earned a clearcut decision.

Foreman's test was against Norton, who had broken Ali's jaw and who was in Foreman's own class regarding height and weight. Norton appeared, however, to be little awed by Foreman's reputation and had little time to settle as Foreman completed an impressive defense with a second-round stoppage.

Don King, a flamboyant promoter, matched Foreman and Ali for the title in Kinshasa, Zaire, on 30 October 1974. He was helped by a huge investment in the project by the Zaire government. It was the first heavyweight title fight to be staged on the continent of Africa. Over 62,000 fans were in the May Stadium, and the overall receipts, with television fees, ran into many millions of dollars.

Few gave the 32-year-old Ali much chance in this fight billed as 'The Rumble in the Jungle.' He had performed wonders in his 'second career,' having lost 3½ years of his prime. His last

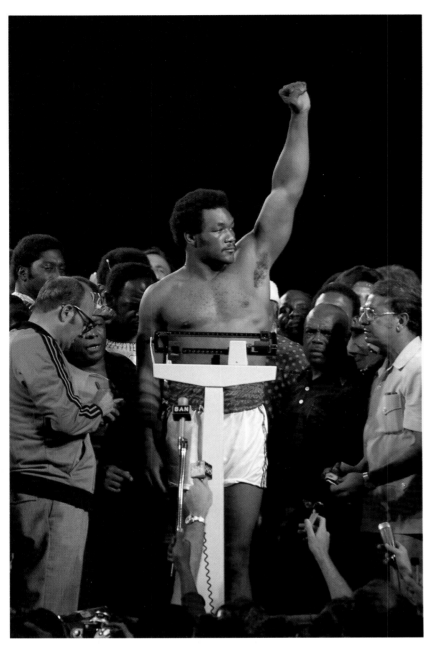

fights had all gone the full 12 rounds, however, and he appeared to have lost the sharpness and power which had destroyed so many men ten years before. Foreman, on the other hand, had boxed less than five rounds in his three crushing championship victories.

It was an exciting fight, notable for Ali's completely new tactics. Instead of dancing he fought flat footed. Foreman, boxing in the way that had served him so well so far, pressed forward with huge bludgeoning blows. Ali allowed some of those to the body to land but used his ringcraft to avoid dangerous blows to the head. Foreman landed the heavy blows with Ali spearing in occasional counters.

By the fifth round it seemed Foreman was beginning to tire. Ali now began to allow Foreman to punch him. Swaying on the ropes he took Foreman's punches, happy to encourage him to tire himself further. It was what he later defined as his 'rope-a-dope' trick. Foreman showed his lack of experience and imagination, non-plussed by Ali's tactics. He had not encountered anything like this before, and as his blows had no effect and Ali began to land some choice punches of his own, he became demoralized and even more tired. In the eighth Ali stepped forward, crossed a crisp right to the jaw and Foreman was counted out.

It was one of the most amazing performances in heavyweight boxing and it proved that a fighting brain can overcome youth and power. Foreman was never the same again. With this victory The Greatest, the second man to regain the heavyweight title, claimed that with Allah on his side he was now even more invincible than ever.

FAR LEFT: *On 30 October 1974 Ali (white trunks) put on an amazing display in Kinshasa, Zaire, to regain his title from Foreman (red trunks). Ali succeeded in confusing Foreman with his 'rope-a-dope' trick.*

LEFT: *A confident Foreman at the weigh-in in Kinshasa for his fight with the old champ, Ali.*

BELOW: *Ken Norton was given a title chance by Foreman and the two met in Caracas, Venezuela, on 26 March 1974. Norton is seen in trouble as Foreman (red trunks) moves in. He fought tentatively and was knocked out in the second round.*

The Thrilla in Manila

The new heavyweight champion was not idle. In 1975 he beat Chuck Wepner, Ron Lyle and Joe Bugner and then faced his old enemy, Joe Frazier, again. Don King promoted it at the Philippine Coliseum, Manila, on 1 October. The fight began just before 11 am in front of 28,000 fans but there were an estimated 700 million viewers hooked in by satellite television. It was a second multimillion dollar purse for Ali within a year.

The fight was billed as 'The Thrilla in Manila,' Ali pointing out that it would also be a 'chilla' and a 'killa' when he got hold of the 'gorilla.' He little knew how accurate he would be.

Ali and Frazier had great respect for each other despite all the media hype and Ali's continual taunts of Frazier, but, for this fight, Ali thought that Frazier was well past his best. He said he would not defend, but stand up to Frazier from the bell. He did, buckling his opponent in the first and in the third rounds. But he did not stop Frazier and in the fifth and sixth rounds his hooks found Ali, and Ali himself was facing defeat. He held on, fighting back in bursts, but by the tenth, although it was level on points, he looked to be drained of strength and Frazier seemed the likelier winner.

Ali, however, continued to surprise fans throughout his career. In the eleventh he found reserves and his long shots began to tell on Frazier whose great effort following the punishment he took in the opening rounds began to tire him. His eye puffed up and his mouth dripped blood. For three rounds a brave, exhausted, nearly blind Frazier could do little but stumble around, defying Ali, while an equally exhausted Ali hit him with everything he had left, which was still insufficient to put the challenger down.

At the end of the fourteenth Frazier was led back to his corner by referee Carlos Padilla and Frazier's manager Eddie Futch decided that the gallant battle would end there. Ali sank to the canvas himself at the end, admitting later that he was all in and describing his exhaustion as being next to death. He hinted at retirement. Frazier continued his boxing career for a while, retiring when he lost again to Foreman, the only other man to beat him.

Far from retiring, Ali had four fights in 1976, knocking out Jean-Pierre Coopman in San Juan, outpointing Jimmy Young in Landover, stopping Richard Dunn in Munich and outpointing Ken Norton in Munich. In 1977 he won decisions over Alfredo Evangelista, the Spanish European champion, in Landover, and the hard-hitting Earnie Shavers in New York.

On 15 February 1978 Ali took on Leon Spinks in the Hilton Pavilion, Las Vegas. Spinks was one of two brothers who had won gold medals at the 1976 Olympic Games. Leon won the light-heavyweight final immediately after his brother Michael had won the middleweight gold medal.

The contest with Spinks was a strange one. Ali, with overwhelming physical advantage, was lackadaisical, listless and lethargic. Spinks, who had had only seven professional fights, mostly against weak opposition, in which he had won six and drawn one, fought with remarkable urgency in a frenetic display of nonstop hustle and bustle. Giving 27 pounds to Ali he made the champion look slow. For most of the fight it seemed Ali was boxing to another plan, taking his time before swatting this annoying fly, but the rounds began to run out. He put on a grandstand finish in the last and the verdict was a split one – but nobody could complain at the decision for Spinks.

There was a return clause in the contract, ensuring that the

ABOVE FAR LEFT: *Joe Frazier's face after 'The Thrilla in Manila.' His manager would not let him continue after the fourteenth round.*

ABOVE: *How Frazier's face changed shape during the fight held in Manila. Ali gets in a hard straight right near the end of their fight.*

LEFT: *Ali's face shows pain of a different kind after his defeat by the raw young Leon Spinks at Las Vegas in February 1978. Ali seemed lethargic. 'You're a great fighter and a fine man,' Spinks told Ali afterward. 'Thanks,' mumbled Ali in reply to his rival, 'You ain't so bad yourself.'*

two met again seven months later. But it led to another split in the heavyweight title because the WBC stripped Spinks in the meantime for fighting Ali again instead of their approved contender, Ken Norton. So when Ali and Spinks stepped into the ring again at the Superdrome in New Orleans, it was for WBA recognition only.

The date was 15 September 1978 and Ali was by now approaching 37 years old. It was the perfect setting for him to put on a final dazzling display for his millions of fans. It was another Carnival of Boxing, with four world title fights on the bill. There were 70,000 present and 80 million television viewers. Ali did not let his admirers down. This time he moved, he danced, he stamped his authority on his opponent from the beginning. After thoroughly outboxing Spinks he tried to knock him out at the end, but the old quick reflexes were not what they had once been. He was still a very easy winner and had become the first man to win the heavyweight boxing title on three occasions.

It was the ideal time to retire, and he did. Sadly he could not resist later making a comeback to try to win a fourth time, and his career was to end with two unnecessary and fumbling defeats at the hands of Larry Holmes and Trevor Berbick. Soon afterward he began suffering severe health problems. His fans will remember him as he was in his prime. Undoubtedly, just before he lost 3½ years of his career, he was 'The Greatest.'

ABOVE: *Ali gets his arm caught in the rope when facing the hard-hitting Earnie Shavers in 1977. Ali escaped from the danger and cleverly outboxed Shavers over 15 rounds in New York.*

LEFT: *Ken Norton, Ali's old adversary, also got his title chance when Ali took him on in New York City in 1976. Although Ali was now 34, he had worn better than the 3½-years-younger Norton, and Ali (white trunks) outpointed him to keep the crown.*

RIGHT: *Ali (red trunks) and Frazier, who will be Ali's most remembered opponent. Although they had little time for each other in the pre-fight publicity, their three exhausting battles gave each boxer a healthy respect for the other, and afterward they were friends. This was the fight Frazier won, on 8 March 1971.*

The Little Men from the South

For 25 years or so from the 1950s the lighter weights in boxing were dominated by some brilliant punchers from Central and South America.

One of the smallest and one of the hardest hitters was Pascual Perez from Tupungato, Mendoza, Argentina. He was born on 4 March 1926, one of nine children from a poor family, and took up amateur boxing. He was only 4 feet 11 inches and weighed just 105 pounds, but was very strong and won the fly-weight gold medal in the 1948 Olympic Games in London. He continued boxing under an assumed name to fool his family who wanted him to progress in his job as a clerk. He was 26 when they discovered his deception and he then turned profes-sional. He lost no time after his late start, registering over 20 victories within two years. When he boxed a draw with Yoshio Shirai, the world flyweight champion, in Buenos Aires, he was given a title shot in Tokyo. On 26 November 1954 he easily won the decision and six months later he won the return.

Perez, a pocket Hercules, punched with a force which stopped 56 of the 91 opponents he faced in his career. He defended in Japan, Argentina, Venezuela and the Philippines before he dropped the title in Bangkok on his eleventh defense, when Pone Kingpetch of Thailand got a split decision on 16 April 1960. Perez lost the rematch with a stoppage in Los Angeles. The 34-year-old fought on for a few years before retir-ing. He was champion for 5½ years.

Eder Jofre, born in Sao Paulo, Brazil on 26 March 1936, was a bantamweight who turned professional on his 21st birthday.

Within three years he had won the South American title. When Jose Becerra from Guadalajara, Mexico retired from the world bantamweight championship in 1960, Jofre won the NBA ver-sion with a sixth-round knockout of Eloy Sanchez, another Mexican. Jofre, undefeated in 37 fights, was a vegetarian and another devastating puncher who won 50 of his 72 victories inside the distance.

Just over a year later Jofre unified the title with a victory in the tenth round over Johnny Caldwell, the EBU champion from Belfast, Northern Ireland. Jofre continued to rule the bantams, making eight successful defenses, until 18 May 1965 when he suffered his first defeat in 51 fights. The former fly-weight champion, Masahiko 'Fighting' Harada, outpointed him in Nagoya, Japan. Harada, from Tokyo, was an out-standing fighter, being world flyweight champion in 1962-63 and bantamweight champion 1965-68. He also lost a close challenge to Johnny Famechon for the featherweight crown.

After losing the return in Tokyo, Jofre announced his retire-ment, but after more than three years out of the ring he came back as a featherweight and in 1973 he was given a title shot against the WBC champion, Jose Legra of Cuba who was enjoying a second spell as champion. The brilliant Jofre won on points in Brasilia. Jofre was by now 37. He knocked out Vicente Saldivar in Salvador, Brazil, but was then stripped of his title for failing to defend against Alfredo Marcano. He retired soon afterward, having lost only two fights in his career – on both occasions to Fighting Harada.

ABOVE RIGHT: *Vicente Saldivar (right) of Mexico City, gets a hard left to the head of Howard Winstone of Wales at Earls Court, London, in 1965. Winstone, a future champion, was a brilliant boxer, but Saldivar was a great puncher, and won on points.*

RIGHT: *Another brilliant Welshman, Dai Dower (left), went to Buenos Aires to try to wrest the flyweight championship from Pascual Perez in 1957, but Perez caught him in the first round and the British champion was knocked out.*

LEFT: *Pascual Perez (right) of Argentina stood less than five feet tall but was one of the hardest hitters of all the flyweights. This title fight, which took place in 1960, was his last – he is about to be stopped by the champion, Pone Kingpetch of Thailand.*

Vicente Saldivar, when losing to Jofre, was himself on a comeback trail, despite being seven years younger than Jofre. He was born in Mexico City on 13 May 1943. Like Perez he too was one of a poor family of nine children. A good amateur boxer, he won a Golden Gloves title in 1959 and turned professional two years later. On 26 September 1964 he won the world featherweight title when stopping Sugar Ramos in the eleventh round in Mexico City. Ramos, from Cuba, was the boxer who had won the title in the fight in which Davey Moore lost his life.

Like the other Central and South Americans, Saldivar was a tremendous puncher who won 26 of his 37 victories inside the distance. He was champion for over three years making eight successful defenses, three of them epic battles, with a brilliant boxer, Howard Winstone of Wales. Winstone, who had lost the tops of three fingers in an accident, lacked a knockout punch at the top level. Saldivar's strength gained two narrow points victories with rallies after the skillful Winstone had built up big leads, and a third victory when Winstone retired with a cut eye in the twelfth in Mexico City. Saldivar then retired, relinquishing the title.

The championship then split. Winstone won the WBC version, but lost it to Jose Legra, who in turn dropped it to Johnny Famechon. Saldivar made a comeback and on 9 May 1970, regaining his title by outpointing Famechon in Rome. However, seven months later he was stopped in Tijuana, Mexico, by Kuniaka Shibata, from Hitachi, Japan. Saldivar retired again but after being out of the ring for 2½ years he made another comeback, leading to the losing title fight with Jofre already mentioned. Saldivar now retired for good. He lost only three times, one an early-career disqualification.

Soon after Jofre and Saldivar disappeared from the featherweight scene, Ruben Olivares took the WBA version of the title. But before this he had already distinguished himself among the bantamweights.

Olivares was born in Mexico City on 14 January 1947. He was another knockout specialist, perhaps the hardest hitter of all the bantams. He was not from a poor family, for a change.

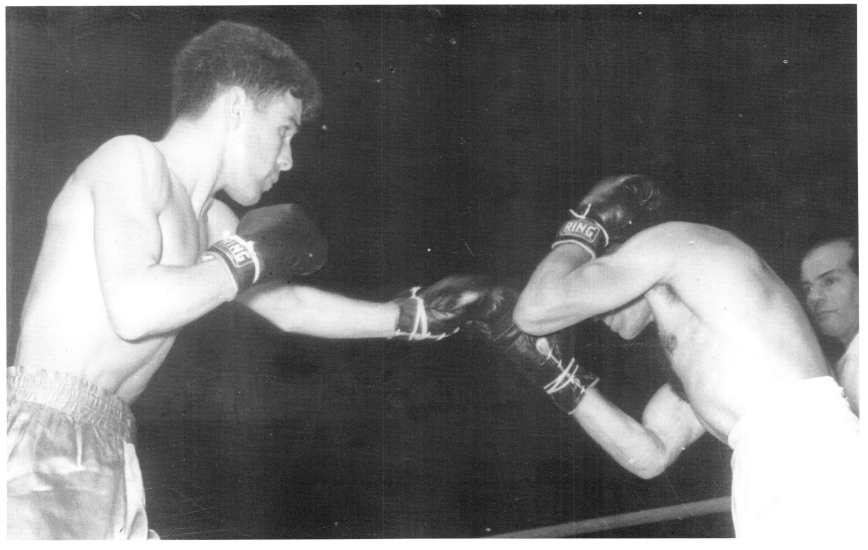

With his square shoulders and great strength he boxed merely because he enjoyed it. He married at the age of 17 and turned professional. Fifty straight wins, 49 inside the distance, earned him a crack at the championship held by Lionel Rose, a tough Australian aborigine, who had taken the title from Fighting Harada, Jofre's conqueror. Olivares won by a fifth-round knockout in Los Angeles. Olivares' first defense was against the Englishman Alan Rudkin who was stopped in two rounds in Los Angeles. Rudkin, who was a skillful boxer, had previously lost two close decisions in title fights with Harada and Rose. Olivares lost his title temporarily to Chucho Castillo, another Mexican, but ruled the division for 2½ years before losing on an eighth-round knockout to Rafael Herrera, yet another Mexican. Olivares then moved up to begin campaigning in the featherweight division.

Meanwhile the bantamweight division continued to be the property mainly of boxers from around Central America. After Herrera the title was split throughout the 1970s, champions including Enrique Pinder of Panama, Romeo Anaya of Mexico, Herrera again, Rodolfa Martinez, Alfonso Zamora and Carlos Zarate, all of Mexico, Jorge Lujan of Panama and Lupe Pintor of Mexico, who held the WBC title into the 1980s and registered the sad knockout of Wales's Johnny Owen, who died later in hospital.

Ruben Olivares, meanwhile, having moved up to the featherweights, won the WBA title in 1974 with a stoppage of Zensuke Utagawa in Los Angeles. Four months later he lost it to Alexis Arguello, being knocked out in the thirteenth in Los Angeles. Meanwhile Bobby Chacon, a colorful Californian, won the vacant WBC title, and in 1975 Olivares took this title by stopping Chacon in the second round, also in Los Angeles. However, it was to be another short reign. He held this title for only three months, losing a split decision to David Kotey of Ghana. Olivares had another shot at the title four years later but was stopped by Eusebio Pedroza, and in 1981 he retired.

Alexis Arguello, who had taken the WBA title from him, was born in Managua, Nicaragua, on 19 April 1952. He turned professional when he was only 16 and proved to be a brilliant boxer and hard puncher. He won 33 of his first 35 bouts and earned a featherweight title shot with Ernesto Marcel of Panama, on 16 February 1974, but was beaten on points. Marcel retired, however, and nine months later Arguello was champion after taking the crown from Olivares. In 19 months he made four successful defenses and then moved up a division to junior lightweight. There was an excellent WBC champion here in Alfredo Escalera of Puerto Rico who had made ten defenses, but Arguello stopped him in the thirteenth on 28 January 1978 in San Juan to become champion.

In two years Alexis defeated eight challengers, fighting away from home in New York, Los Angeles, Las Vegas, San Juan and Rimini, Italy. In 1980 he relinquished this title and moved up to lightweight. In two divisions he had given up the title having defended against six men who were to claim world titles themselves. Among the lightweights he earned a title shot against Scotland's Jim Watt, the WBC champion. In London he outpointed Watt to hold a championship in a third division.

Arguello made four successful inside-the-distance defenses of this title and then challenged Aaron Pryor, the tough WBA champion of the next weight up, the light-welterweights. After a tremendous scrap Pryor proved too strong, the referee coming to Arguello's assistance in the fourteenth round. He lost a return in 1983 with a third-round knockout. Arguello gave up his lightweight title (the third world title he relinquished unbeaten) and retired. He was a great champion, even among the outstanding men who came from South and Central America in a wonderful period of smaller men.

LEFT ABOVE: *The brilliant Alexis Arguello of Nicaragua gave up three world titles unbeaten as he moved up to new weight divisions. It was only when he moved up to the light-welterweights that he took on more than he could handle. Arguello (left) was stopped by Aaron Pryor in Miami in 1982.*

LEFT BELOW: *Hard-punching Ruben Olivares of Mexico City.*

BELOW: *Lupe Pintor (left) of Mexico just misses the head of Carlos Zarate of Mexico with a left during an exciting fight at Caesars Palace, Las Vegas, in 1979. Pintor succeeded in taking the WBC bantamweight title after ten defenses by Zarate.*

BELOW RIGHT: *Vicente Saldivar of Mexico, a great featherweight champion.*

The Milliner from the Virgin Islands

In the 1960s another boxer followed in the footsteps of Sugar Ray Robinson through the welter and middleweight divisions – Emile Griffith.

Emile Alphonse Griffith was born in St Thomas, Virgin Islands on 3 February 1938. He went to New York in 1949 and became an apprentice making ladies' hats. The owner, seeing his physique, insisted he take up amateur boxing and he was so good that in 1958 he became a Golden Gloves champion and turned professional. A defeat in his fourteenth fight in 1959 and another in 1960 were minor blots on his record, and on 1 April 1961 he had earned a welterweight title shot against Benny Kid Paret of Cuba. Griffith won by a thirteenth-round knockout at Miami Beach, catching Paret with a left hook after being behind on points. Griffith defended later in the year against Gaspar Ortega and then gave a return to Paret, who won a split decision in New York in September 1961. Six months later came the rubber match, a fatal one for Paret.

Griffith was a brilliant boxer who lacked a knockout punch. Although 23 of his 85 career victims failed to last the distance, he overwhelmed his opponents by boxing and relentless punishment rather than by single blows. There was little love lost between Griffith and Paret, who taunted the ex-milliner with homosexuality and indulged in some publicity nonsense along those lines when the boxers were stripped for the weigh-in. In his interview with Peter Heller for the book *In This Corner* (Dell Publishing Co Ltd, New York, 1973) Griffith described how in the third fight Paret knocked him down and then put his hand on his hip, laughing. His trainer told him that if he got Paret into trouble he was to keep punching until the referee intervened. This is what happened in the twelfth round with Griffith sinking blows into Paret, who was helpless on the ropes. When the referee finally stepped in and stopped it, Paret dropped to the canvas and did not regain consciousness until he died ten days later. Griffiths said he felt responsible and never really stopped a fighter after that. As this fight was shown on television it had a big effect on the public conception of boxing in the United States.

Griffith twice more defended in 1962 and then dropped a very close decision to a flashy Cuban boxer, Luis Rodriguez, in Los Angeles. Three months later there was a rematch in Madison Square Garden and Griffith took an even closer split decision. He was the first to win the welterweight title three times. A rubber match with Rodriguez in Las Vegas was another split decision which many thought the champion was lucky to get.

Griffith made three more defenses, all won by unanimous decisions, including one against the British champion Brian Curvis at Wembley, before deciding to follow the Robinson route and take on the middleweights.

Since Robinson's failure to win a middleweight title for a sixth time by being outpointed by Gene Fullmer, the title had changed hands more rapidly than usual. Fullmer defended his NBA title against Fiorentino Fernandez and the luckless Benny Kid Paret, before dropping the title to Dick Tiger.

Meanwhile Paul Pender, who had also beaten off Robinson for the New York/EBU version, had come out on top after three battles with Terry Downes, winning the first and third in his native Boston and losing the second on Downes' home territory in London. Pender forfeited this title by failing to defend within the stipulated period, and when Dick Tiger won a third title fight with Fullmer, having drawn one and won two, he was recognized as champion by all bodies. Tiger, a very popular Nigerian who boxed out of Liverpool, was a great champion who was also to be undisputed light-heavyweight champion of the world. Sadly Tiger was to die of cancer only five months after his retirement in 1971.

As middleweight champion Tiger lost and regained the title in contests with Joey Giardello, before he was challenged by Emile Griffith on 25 April 1966. In a brilliant bout Griffith put Tiger down for the first time in his career before gaining the decision and becoming champion at two weights simultaneously. This did not last long because the New York Boxing Commission insisted he should choose between his titles, and he chose the middleweight. Shortly afterward the WBA withdrew their recognition of him as welterweight champion because he did not defend his title within six months.

In the middleweights Griffith continued his luck with split

ABOVE RIGHT: *Emile Griffith, who was persuaded into boxing after getting a job in a hat-making factory, and won the world title at welter and middleweight in the 1960s.*

LEFT: *Kid Paret on his way down from a Griffith right in the thirteenth round at Miami on 1 April 1961. This fight gave Griffith the welterweight championship, but the rivalry between the boxers was to prove fatal to Paret.*

RIGHT: *Dick Tiger (right) catches Gene Fullmer with a good right to the face in the title fight at Candlestick Park, San Francisco, on 23 October 1962. Tiger took the decision and the middleweight championship.*

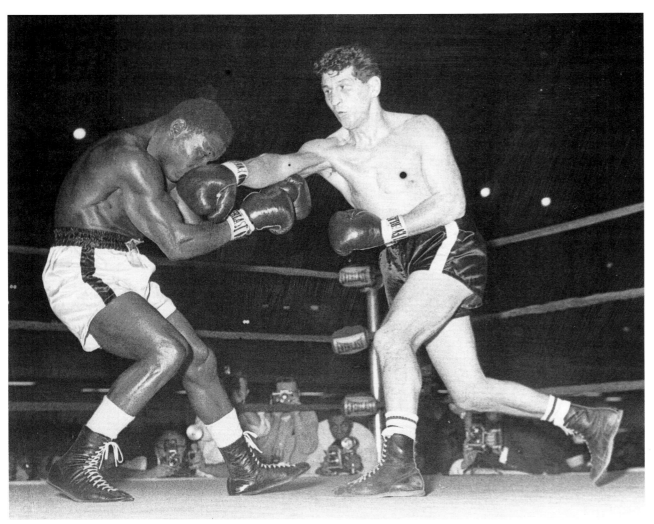

LEFT: *Joey Giardello lands a right on Dick Tiger's face at Atlantic City on 7 December 1963. Giardello took the middleweight title on points.*

BELOW RIGHT: *Nino Benvenuti (right), the stylish Italian, defending the middleweight crown against Luis Rodriguez in Rome on 22 November 1969. Rodriguez was knocked out in the first round.*

FAR RIGHT: *The popular British champion of the 1960s, Terry Downes, took the world title from Paul Pender, before losing it to Pender again.*

BELOW: *Griffith (left) and Benvenuti in their title fight on 29 September 1967 in New York. Griffith won this one to regain his crown, but Benvenuti won a rubber match three months later.*

BELOW RIGHT: *Dick Tiger (left) slams the head of Griffith at Madison Square Garden on 15 July 1970. Griffith succeeded in winning this battle of the two great ex-champs on points.*

decisions by earning two against Joey Archer, before losing the title on 17 April 1967 in Madison Square Garden to Nino Benvenuti, a classy Italian who had won the welterweight gold medal in the 1960 home Olympics. In a great display Benvenuti dropped Griffith before winning a clear decision to the delight of New York Italians. Griffith regained the title with a decision five months later but Benvenuti took the rubber match on 4 March 1968 to end Griffith's long reign as world champion. Benvenuti remained champion for nearly three more years before losing to Carlos Monzon, who also beat Griffith twice in attempted comebacks.

Tiger, Benvenuti and the milliner from the Virgin Islands were great champions in the 1960s and Monzon was to continue the middleweight tradition in the 1970s.

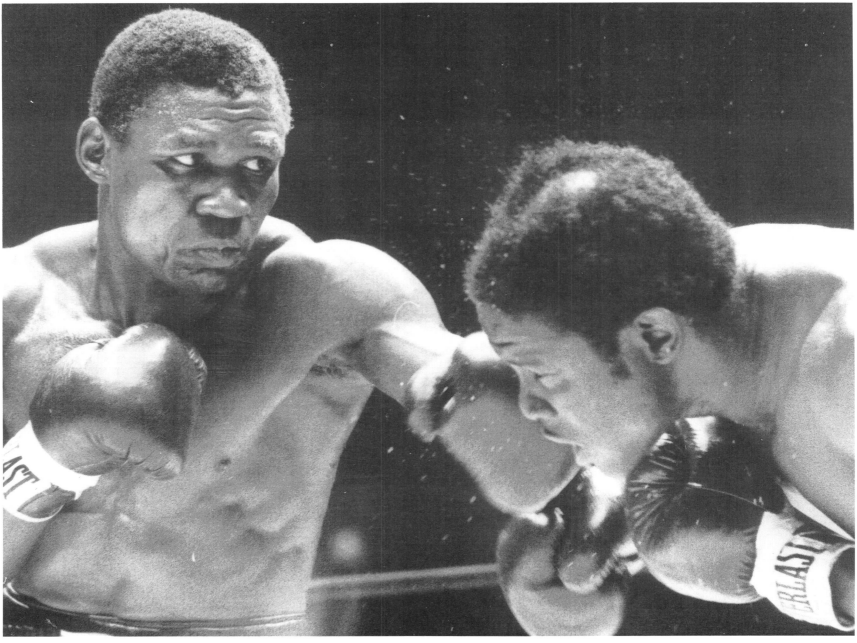

The Long Reign of King Carlos

Carlos Monzon was born at San Jairir, Santa Fe, Argentina on 7 August 1942. He was one of a family of ten children and times were hard. However, Monzon did not learn his boxing as a tearaway scrapper on the streets, as many from such backgrounds did. The young Monzon was astute enough to realize as he grew into a tall strong boy that boxing offered a way to a better life and he set out to make it a career.

When he was 21 he turned professional and got as much experience as he could, taking ten or 12 fights a year. He lost three early decisions but was mostly successful, and by the time he had built up 80 fights he had won more than half by the short route. Defeats of Jorge Fernandez won him the Argentine and South American titles, and on 7 November 1970 he was ready to travel to Rome to take on the pride of Italy, Nino Benvenuti, for the world middleweight championship. Nino was confidently expected to win but the home supporters suffered a severe shock when Monzon outboxed him and delivered a right to the chin in the twelfth which knocked out the local hero.

Monzon was tall for a middleweight and boxed well behind a long straight left. He was an excellent counter-puncher and those who tried to bustle past the left jab found a hard right cross less easy to ignore. Having beaten Benvenuti in Rome, the new champion gave him a return in Monte Carlo and this time won more quickly, flooring Benvenuti early and forcing the referee to stop the contest in the third round.

Emile Griffith, the previous champion, also needed the referee's assistance in the fourteenth in Buenos Aires and then it was the turn of the former light-middleweight champion, Denny Moyer, who also had cause to thank the referee when he intervened to save him further punishment in the fifth. This contest was held back in Rome where the Argentinian was clearly at home.

Next Monzon went to Colombes, France, where the European champion, Jean-Claude Bouttier, did not wait for the referee but retired in the twelfth. That was in June 1972 and two months later the next European champion, Tom Bogs of Denmark, was another to be stopped by the referee. He lasted five rounds in Copenhagen.

Having beaten the best Europe could offer, Monzon returned to Buenos Aires where the American champion, Benny Briscoe, had the distinction of going the distance, but he clearly lost the decision. However it was back to Monte Carlo again for Monzon's first defense of 1973. Emile Griffith was making another challenge and he too lasted the 15 rounds. Whether or not it was because Monzon was getting soft, his next challenger, Jean-Claude Bouttier again, also saw it through to the final bell. That contest was in Paris where Carlos fought again 4½ months later, taking on the brilliant welterweight champion, Jose Napoles of Cuba. Napoles might have stood a chance with a run-of-the-mill middleweight, but

LEFT: *Carlos Monzon gets in under Benvenuti's guard with a hard punch to the body in Monte Carlo on 8 May 1971. Monzon won in the third to retain the title he had taken from Benvenuti six months earlier.*

ABOVE RIGHT: *Emile Griffith was the first to challenge the new champion. Monzon makes the perspiration spray from his opponent's head with a right in the eighth round at Buenos Aires on 25 September 1971. The referee stopped the fight in Monzon's favor in the fourteenth round.*

RIGHT: *Monzon traveled in his defenses and Copenhagen had a rare chance to see a world title fight when Danish champion Tom Bogs was taken on on 19 August 1972. Bogs is seen being knocked out in the fifth round.*

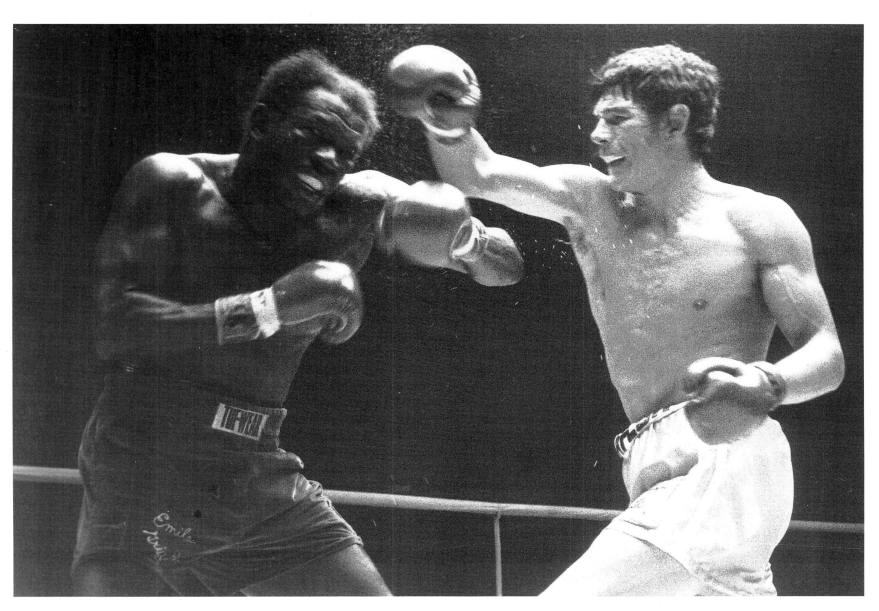

Monzon was proving himself to be one of the greatest ever and the Cuban was forced to retire in the sixth.

At this stage, having been undisputed champion for over three years, Monzon lost his recognition by the WBC for failing to defend against their nominated challenger, Rodrigo Valdes. The WBC recognized Valdes as champion after he had defeated Bennie Briscoe in Monte Carlo.

Carlos Monzon continued to beat all the challengers put before him. He retained the WBA half of the title by knocking out Tony Mundine of Australia in Buenos Aires, Tony Licata of the United States was stopped in the tenth in New York, and in 1975 the latest European champion, Gratien Tonna of France, was knocked out in the eleventh in Paris.

It was time now to meet Valdes. Valdes, born in Bolivar, Columbia on 22 December 1946, was four years younger than Monzon and during the two years he had held the WBC title he had made four successful defenses. He would have made a good middleweight champion had Monzon not been around.

The two met at Monte Carlo on 26 June 1976 and Monzon won a unanimous points decision. He had unified the middleweight championship again. Thirteen months later he won the Monte Carlo return and decided it was time to retire. He was a week away from his 35th birthday. He had beaten all the logical contenders.

King Carlos had ruled the middleweights which, over the years, has been the hardest division, for over seven years, and he relinquished the title, unbeaten, after a record 14 defenses. The only defeats in a marvelous career of over 14 years were those three early ones mentioned before.

LEFT: *Welterweight champion Jose Napoles (left) took on Monzon in Paris on 9 February 1974 but was no match for the middleweight king and was stopped in the sixth.*

BELOW LEFT: *Monzon gets a right to the head of Rodrigo Valdes at Monte Carlo on 26 June 1976. He beat the WBC champion to unify the division.*

RIGHT: *Australian champion Tony Mundine (left) was a knockout victim of Monzon in the seventh round in Buenos Aires, on 5 October 1974.*

BELOW: *Rodrigo Valdes (left) rushes in at Monte Carlo in July 1977, but Monzon counters. After Monzon's second win over Valdes he gave up the title unbeaten after nearly seven years.*

Roberto Duran, the Macho Man

Roberto Duran, like Henry Armstrong in the 1930s, fought his way up the weights in the 1970s and 1980s and although he did not win undisputed championships at three divisions, as Armstrong did, he did win partial titles at three different weights and he fought most of the best men in the world between the light and middleweight classes. He made a cult of machismo and always gave a rugged, determined performance – except on the one occasion needed to prove the rule.

Duran was born at Guarare, Panama, on 16 June 1951. He hardly had time for an amateur career, turning professional before he was 16. Not surprisingly he lost four early contests but when he developed his strength and ruggedness he began to build up a long string of unbeaten contests. These had nearly reached 30 by the time he challenged for his first world title.

Duran was a lightweight and the WBA champion Ken Buchanan of Scotland was one of the cleverest boxers ever to grace the division. Buchanan, from Edinburgh, lacked a really destructive punch. Over half of his fights went the distance but he was a brilliant tactician who won the undisputed lightweight title from Ismael Laguna in San Juan in September 1970. The following year Buchanan lost WBC recognition for not defending against their nominee, and when he met Duran on 26 June 1972 in Madison Square Garden, it was for the WBA version only.

Duran had already built up a reputation with his swaggering machismo and his disregard for the niceties of the rules. This later quality was in full evidence in the bout with Buchanan. Excellent victories in the ring had made Buchanan a favorite of

the New York fans and record indoor receipts for a lightweight battle of $223,901 were taken for the classic encounter of the superb boxer and the relentless fighter. It was the fighter who won but not without a little leniency from the referee. The decisive moment came when the bell rang to end the thirteenth. Even as the referee flung his arms around Duran to part them, so Duran sank a low blow into the champion's groin. Buchanan went down in agony and could not come out for the fourteenth, the verdict being 'referee stopped fight.'

Duran, who thought Buchanan was his toughest opponent, would not give him a return despite a Madison Square Garden contract, and the British and New York authorities withdrew recognition from him for this failure.

Whatever the manner of his assumption of the throne, Duran was a great champion and was the best of the lightweights for six years. He made 12 successful defenses of his title, beating men from the United States, Australia, Japan, Puerto Rico, Mexico, Costa Rica and the Dominican Republic in Panama City, San Jose, San Juan, Erie, Los Angeles, Miami, Philadelphia and Las Vegas. Strangely most of his opponents were stopped either very early, demonstrating his belligerence and destructibility, or very late, showing his determination and durability. His last defense, on 21 January 1978, was against Esteban de Jesus of Puerto Rico, one of the men who had beaten him and who was champion at the time. By knocking out de Jesus in the twelfth round, Duran unified the division and made himself undisputed champion.

However, he was having difficulties with the weight and

ABOVE: *Roberto Duran (facing camera) in his title challenge against tartan-trunked Ken Buchanan, the world lightweight champion, at Madison Square Garden on 26 June 1972.*

RIGHT: *Duran bending Buchanan over the ropes in the eleventh round as referee Johnny Lobianco rushes in to separate the boxers. The referee stopped the contest after the thirteenth round, when controversy surrounded a low punch thrown on or after the bell. The fight was won by Duran.*

LEFT: *Duran (right) was floored and outboxed by Esteban de Jesus in New York in a 10-round non-title bout on 17 November 1972. De Jesus won the decision, but Duran won a title fight 18 months later.*

No doubt it was frustration rather than cowardice that caused Duran's behavior but to his Panamanian fans this was a serious fall from grace. Duran had to move up another weight to try to retrieve his reputation. In January 1982 he tackled the WBC champion, Wilfred Benitez, in Las Vegas and was out-pointed. On 16 June 1983 he tried the WBA champion, Davey Moore of New York, and at Madison Square Garden Duran knocked out Moore in the eighth round to win his third world title. It was the warrior's thirty-second birthday.

However this was not enough to satisfy Duran, still smarting under the shame of his Leonard walkout, and his next step was to tackle the middleweight king himself, the awesome Marvin Hagler. Again nobody gave Duran a chance, although in fact he was only a year older than Hagler and had built his weight up to close to his opponent's. However Hagler was a natural middleweight and generally had the contest under control. But Duran, in his best arrogant manner, put up a brave belligerent scrap and took Hagler the distance, which none of Hagler's previous seven challengers had done.

Duran then returned to the light-middleweights to tackle the WBC champion, another fearsome character in Thomas Hearns. For some reason Duran relinquished his WBA title just before the fight so the contest was not held to unify the title. In any case Duran on the day before his thirty-third birthday could not cope with Hearns and was knocked out by Hearns in the second round.

There were not many places for Duran to go to now. In June 1986 he took on Robbie Sims, the half-brother of Marvin Hagler, and himself ranked fourth among the middleweights. Just turned 35, Duran put on his usual two-fisted snarling aggressive display, and lost only on a split decision, a warning for a low punch in the eighth possibly making the difference between defeat and a draw.

Duran had been boxing professionally for only a few months short of 20 years. He had faced the best and given of his best – he was almost a history of 20 years boxing in himself.

moved up to campaign amongst the welters. Four wins, including a decision over ex-champion Carlos Palomino, earned him a title chance with the outstanding WBC champion, Sugar Ray Leonard. The pair met in Montreal on 20 June 1980 and few gave much for the prospects of Duran. But not even a night of bleak rain could dampen his ardor and he put up one of his greatest performances, continually attacking, pushing the more polished Leonard around in the clinches and generally cramping Leonard's style. Although it was a very close decision it was unanimous and Duran's all-round display of machismo had won him a second world title.

It was all very different in the return match in New Orleans five months later. This time it was Leonard's dazzling boxing which came out on top. Duran, confused, unable to fight on his own terms, apparently just gave up, turning his back on Leonard and retiring to his corner in surrender. 'No mas,' he said, the Spanish for 'no more.' It was the lapse mentioned in the first paragraph – the ultimate macho man had gone home like a spoiled schoolboy.

LEFT: *Roberto Duran in action against Sugar Ray Leonard in Montreal in June 1980. Leonard was the unbeaten welterweight champion but Duran surprised him with an all-action display.*

ABOVE: *The same fight: Duran hustled Leonard and leaned on him at every opportunity, and this gave Leonard little room to box.*

ABOVE RIGHT: *Duran took the decision to become world welterweight champion eight years after he had won the lightweight title.*

FAR LEFT ABOVE: *Duran was still fighting the world's greatest in 1983. Here he is, having shaved off his beard, posing with the undisputed middleweight champion Marvin Hagler, whom he took on in 1983.*

RIGHT: *Duran acquitted himself well as a middleweight, and was the only challenger to take Hagler the distance before 1987.*

The Iron Curtain Champion

The Archie Moore succession of light-heavyweight champions began in the 1960s with Harold Johnson, the man who shared with his father the distinction of having been beaten by Jersey Joe Walcott.

Johnson, from Manayunk, Pennsylvania, won the NBA title in 1961 with a ninth-round stoppage of Jesse Bowdry after Moore had been stripped. He defended this twice and then the other authorities also stripped Moore, so when Johnson beat Doug Jones in 1962, he became recognized by all bodies. He was surprisingly beaten on 1 June 1983 by Willie Pastrano from New Orleans. Pastrano was a clever boxer who did not carry much of a punch and always looked as if he could profitably shed a pound or two. He nevertheless stopped his first two challengers, Gregorio Peralta, and the former middleweight champion Terry Downes, who was easily outpointing him when Pastrano produced a punch from nowhere in the eleventh round.

Jose Torres, an Olympic Games silver medalist in 1956, then stopped Pastrano in nine rounds in Madison Square Garden. Torres from Playa Ponce, Puerto Rico, was already 29 and was guided to the title by Cus d'Amato who had previously taken Floyd Patterson to a world title and was later to manage Mike Tyson. Torres assumed the title in March 1965 and ruled until December 1966 with three successful defenses, when he was outpointed by Dick Tiger, the former middleweight champion. Tiger, from Orlu, Nigeria, was actually nearly seven years older than Torres. Torres retired to become a sportswriter and author of a biography of Muhammad Ali, while Tiger remained champion for nearly 18 months. Tiger lost to Bob Foster in May 1968, being knocked out for the only time in his long career. As mentioned earlier, three years after this defeat he died from cancer.

Bob Foster, from Albuquerque, New Mexico, was an outstanding champion who was the best in the division for over six years. Born on 15 December 1938 he was in his thirtieth year when he became champion but he seemed to be in his prime. In 1969 and 1970 he made four defenses which lasted a total of only 18 rounds and he was stripped by the WBA for failing to defend against top-rated contenders. This might have had some validity so far as light-heavyweights went, but on 18 November 1970 Foster challenged Joe Frazier for the heavyweight crown and was knocked out in the second round. This was hardly an easy fight. Foster was a brilliant boxer with a destructive punch in his own class. He was 6 feet 3 inches tall but, although towering over the heavyweight Frazier, he did not have the power at that weight to keep his opponent away.

Foster defended the WBC title four times in 1971, while Vicente Rondon won the WBA title and also made four defenses. The two busy boxers met on 7 April 1972, when Foster made the WBA look a little sheepish by knocking out Rondon in the second round in Miami. He was again the undisputed champion.

Foster continued in 1972 by beating Mike Quarry and Chris Finnegan, the British winner of the Olympic gold medal for middleweights in 1968. In a magnificent battle at Wembley Foster knew just too much for Finnegan and produced a fourteenth-round knockout. After this he tackled Muhammad Ali, who was then on the road back to his second heavyweight title, but again Foster proved no match for the bigger man, and was knocked out by Ali in the eighth round.

Foster spent 1973 defending his title against a tough if limited South African, Pierre Fourie, getting decisions in Albuquerque and Johannesburg. In 1974 he drew with Jorge Ahumada of Argentina. By now he was 36 and when he showed no interest in facing Ahumada again or Britain's John Conteh, the WBC announced it was stripping him of the title, at which he retired and returned to being deputy-sheriff of Albuquerque.

The title now split. Conteh outpointed Ahumada at Wembley to win the WBC title, while the WBA nominated Victor Galindez of Buenos Aires as their champion after he had beaten the American Len Hutchins. Of the two, Galindez was the busier, making three defenses in 1975 against Ahumada and Fourie, previous challengers of Foster, and three in 1976. Of his first six defenses, four were in Johannesburg, one in Oslo and one in New York.

Conteh defended once in each of 1975, 1976 and 1977. He was one of the finest boxers of the day but had managerial problems and also suffered with hand injuries. In 1977 the WBC stripped him for failing to defend against Miguel Cuello. Cuello, from Santa Fe, Argentina, knocked out Jesse Burnett at Monte Carlo in 1977 to become WBC champion, but on his first defense he was stopped by Mate Parlov in Milan.

Galindez meanwhile, made three more defenses in 1977, lost and regained his title in bouts with Mike Rossman in 1978 and lost it for good to Marvin Johnson in 1979. Johnson, in turn,

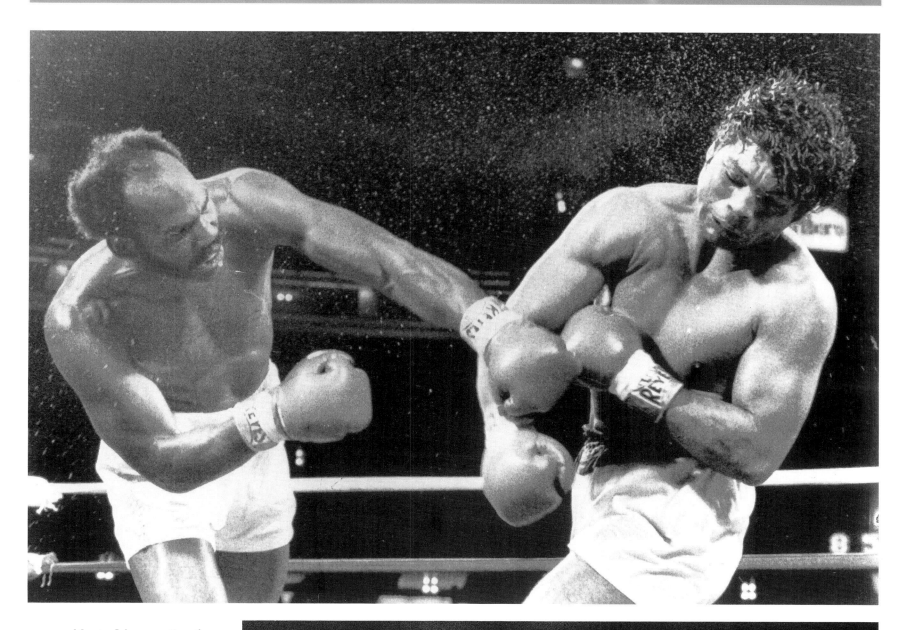

ABOVE: *Marvin Johnson scatters the perspiration of Victor Galindez in the Superdome, New Orleans, with this eleventh-round knockout punch on 30 November 1979 which won him the WBA light-heavyweight championship.*

RIGHT: *Matthew Saad Muhammad (left), who had taken the WBC title from Johnson earlier in 1979, defends against John Conteh, the champion from 1974 to 1977, and wins on points at Atlantic City on 18 August 1979.*

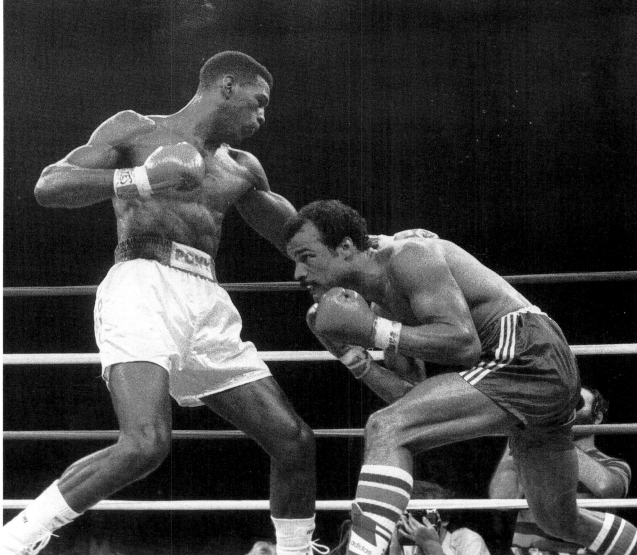

LEFT: *The undisputed light-heavyweight champion of the early 1970s, Bob Foster (right) at the weigh-in before his successful defense against the British champion, former Olympic gold medalist Chris Finnegan (left) in 1972. Foster gave up the title undefeated in 1974.*

lost his first defense to Mustapha Muhammad in March 1980. Muhammad had previously boxed under the name of Ernie Gregory, changing his name on adoption of the Muslim faith.

Mate Parlov, the new WBC champion, came from Split in Yugoslavia. He had won the gold medal at light-heavyweight at the 1972 Olympic Games and had turned professional in 1975. He was the first world champion from a communist country. He did not reign for long. In 1978 he outpointed John Conteh in Belgrade on a split decision which seemed harsh on the former champion, and was then stopped by Marvin Johnson in Marsala, Italy. On 22 April 1979 Johnson was stopped by Matthew Saad Muhammad, who successfully defended twice against John Conteh.

Matthew Saad Muhammad was from Philadelphia, Pennsylvania, and had begun his professional career as Matthew Franklin, changing his name on adopting the Muslim faith. So as the 1980s started there were two light-heavyweight champions in the world, both newly named Muhammad. With the 'alphabet boys' of the WBC and WBA and the Muslim Muhammads, boxing was becoming very complicated.

LEFT: *Matthew Saad Muhammad defeated John Conteh at Atlantic City in March 1980. Muhammad's manager, Sam Solomon, hugs the champion.*

BELOW: *Mustapha Muhammad won the WBA light-heavyweight title with an eleventh-round stoppage of Marvin Johnson on 31 March 1980 at Knoxville.*

RIGHT: *Mate Parlov (left) won a gold medal at the 1972 Olympic Games, and when he knocked out Miguel Cuello in Milan on 7 January 1978 he became the first Yugoslav world champion. In this bout his opponent is Marvin Camel, with whom he fought a draw for the new WBC cruiserweight title.*

Larry Holmes Fails to Beat Rocky

When Muhammad Ali defended his heavyweight title against Leon Spinks in 1978, the WBC would have preferred his opponent to be Ken Norton who, by gaining a decision over Jimmy Young in 1977 in a final eliminator, had established himself as their top contender. When Spinks suprisingly won the title, the WBC wanted him to defend against Norton. Therefore when it was learned that Spinks had signed a contract for a rematch with Ali, the WBC stripped him of the title. On 29 March 1978 the WBC declared Ken Norton heavyweight champion of the world. He appears as such in most reference books but others, unwilling to grant a boxer championship status without him having won a title fight, prefer to regard the Ken Norton-Larry Holmes contest on 9 June 1978 in Las Vegas as for the vacant WBC crown.

This fight was a brilliant bout and Holmes took the decision with a surprising and impressive display. While Ali won back his title (WBA version) and was rightly regarded by the public as the true champion, the WBC branch of the championship was to prove in the end, that is after Ali, to be the most plausible.

Larry Holmes was born on 3 November 1949, one of 11 children, in Cuthbert, Georgia. His amateur career was not outstanding, and he did not turn professional until he was 23. He then proceeded to notch up win after win, but for some reason was not regarded as 'box-office' and could not get a shot at the title while Ali, Frazier and Foreman ruled. Standing 6 feet 3½ inches and weighing around 210 pounds with no fat, Holmes had the physical attributes; he was a fine boxer with a cool brain and he possessed a knockout punch in each hand. He also had the technical abilities.

When Holmes finally got his chance and took the title he was in his twenty-ninth year and had been a professional for over five; he was unbeaten and had won most of his contests inside the distance.

His first defense took place at Caesars Palace, Las Vegas against Alfredo Evangelista of Spain, the European champion, who was knocked out in the seventh round. Then in 1979 Osvaldo Ocasio from Puerto Rico lasted the same distance at the Hilton Pavilion, Las Vegas, this time the referee interceding to stop the fight. Mike Weaver, a hard hitter but vulnerable himself, had lasted 12 rounds at Madison Square Garden when the referee stopped the fight, and Earnie Shavers, another hard-hitting battler who had on a previous occasion gone the distance in a challenge to Ali, was stopped in the eleventh at Caesars Palace.

Four defenses in 1980 failed to go the distance. Lorenzo Zanon of Italy was knocked out in the sixth at Caesars Palace, and at the same venue Leroy Jones was rescued by the referee in the eighth. A local heavyweight, Scott Ledoux, was stopped in the seventh at Bloomington, Minneapolis, and Holmes ended the year by taking on Muhammad Ali at Caesars Palace. Ali was trying to win a title for the fourth time, although it was not the same title he had given up, which had been the WBA

BELOW: *Larry Holmes, facing camera, defending his WBC title against Mike Weaver at Madison Square Garden, New York City on 22 June 1979, a year after he won the vacant title. Holmes won when the referee stopped the fight in the twelfth round.*

RIGHT: *Larry Holmes distorts Ken Norton's face with a right uppercut in their heavyweight title fight on 9 June 1978 at Las Vegas. Holmes put on a performance that was surprising and impressive, and he won the decision and the vacant WBC title.*

version. Ali, 38 years old and out of action for two years, was not the force of old and Holmes noticeably declined to punish the ex-champion unnecessarily, frequently looking at the referee in a plea for him to end it. Finally Ali's corner ended it, retiring their man at the end of the tenth round.

Holmes was proving himself a real champion and boxing fans began to reassess him. Like Charles, Tunney and Corbett, Holmes suffered in the public estimation by following a legend, but no champion can do more than beat convincingly the opponents put in front of him. He continued in 1981 by outpointing Trevor Berbick of Canada, who at least had the distinction of dropping him to the canvas, and destroying the former champion Leon Spinks in three rounds at the Joe Louis Arena, Detroit. He ended the year by beating Renaldo Snipes, a big unbeaten challenger with a heavy punch who was saved by the referee in the eleventh at the Civic Arena, Pittsburgh.

Another big unbeaten fighter, the 26-year-old Gerry Cooney, was built up as a threat to Holmes and endured the modern 'white hope' label. He had a tremendous punch and was extremely game, but Holmes thoroughly outclassed him at Caesars Palace, and Cooney's manager climbed into the ring in the thirteenth to force the referee to stop it. Tex Cobb caused a surprise by taking Holmes the full 15 rounds at Houston and Lucian Rodriguez of France, the European champion, stayed the scheduled 12 rounds at Scranton, Philadelphia. Fighting almost every two or three months, Holmes outpointed Tim Witherspoon at the Dunes Hotel, Las Vegas, knocked out Scott Frank at Harrah's Hotel, Atlantic City, and forced the referee to stop the fight in the first round when he took on Marvis Frazier, son of Smoking Joe, at Caesars Palace.

Holmes now announced that he would not fight under the WBC banner any more and shortly afterward he was named champion by a new body, the International Boxing Federation. The formation of this body which became known as the IBF, meant that three world heavyweight champions would soon be in existence, representing the WBA, WBC and IBF, known derisively by those who prefer the old ways as 'the alphabet boys.'

Holmes was now thought to be getting past his best and seemed to choose easier opponents. James 'Bonecrusher' Smith and David Bey were stopped and Carl Williams outpointed. This win took Holmes to 48 in an unbeaten career and he announced his intention of beating the great record of Rocky Marciano, who retired unbeaten as heavyweight champion with 49 victories in 49 fights. Still seeking the easy option, Holmes accepted a challenge from the light-heavyweight champion Michael Spinks. No light-heavyweight champion in history had added the heavyweight laurels, although many had tried, and Holmes used the opportunity to try to equal Rocky's record at the Riviera Hotel, Las Vegas. On 20 September 1985, however, he lost a close decision to the faster, fitter and younger Spinks. He announced his retirement but came back for another crack at Spinks, at the same time complaining about the verdict in the previous encounter. Alas, this time he lost a split decision which many observers thought he should have won, and he complained some more. Holmes retired, but on 23 January he made a comeback by taking on Mike Tyson at Atlantic City. By now a 38-year-old grandfather, Holmes was knocked out in the fourth round, and he retired again.

He did not equal Marciano's record nor did he equal Ali in the popular estimation. But he made over $50 million from boxing and was the best in the world for around seven years, and hardly anybody did better than that.

LEFT: *James 'Bonecrusher' Smith (right) shared the same fate as Weaver, a twelfth-round stoppage, when he challenged Holmes on 9 November 1984 for the IBF title. Both Weaver and Smith held a version of the title subsequently.*

RIGHT ABOVE: *Holmes has his opponent Ali helpless on the ropes on 2 October 1980 at Las Vegas.*

RIGHT: *Holmes (right) lost his title to the light-heavyweight champion Michael Spinks in 1985 and also lost a return in 1986, two decisions he bitterly disputed.*

Marvelous Marvin Hagler

When Carlos Monzon gave up the undisputed middleweight title in 1977 after a glorious career, his old adversary, Rodrigo Valdes of Columbia, won it with a points victory over Benny Briscoe, who sported the shaven head which was soon to become the hallmark of another great champion.

This fight was in Campione, Italy, and for his first defense in 1978, Valdes returned to Italy to San Remo. By now he had been boxing as long as Monzon and he dropped the title to Hugo Corro, an Argentinian who was a good boxer and who carried enough knockdown power to win half his fights before the final bell. Corro retained the title later in the year by out-pointing Ronnie Harris of the United States, who ten years before had won the Olympic gold medal at lightweight. He then gave a return to Valdes, outpointing him again, at which stage Valdes decided to retire. Both these defenses were in Buenos Aires where Corro was at home, but for his next defense he returned to Europe and took on Vito Antuofermo.

Antuofermo was born in Bari, Italy, but had come to America and started professional boxing in New York. He had won and lost the European light-middleweight title before returning to New York to earn a shot at Corro's middleweight crown. Antuofermo was an amazingly strong, durable, all-action battler with a short reach whose method was to bore in close and deliver more damage than he took. He lacked a knockout punch so won all his victories the hard way, taking enormous punishment. He got the decision over Corro in an exhausting and bloody fight.

The new champion then boxed a draw with a man confidently expected to beat him and in retrospect it is difficult to imagine how his opponent failed: that man was Marvin Hagler. Antuofermo should have been made for Hagler but in November 1979 he retained his title at Caesars Palace with his usual courageous display.

On 16 March 1980 however, at the same venue, his courage was not enough against Alan Minter of England, whose heavier punching gained him the clear points verdict. Minter, a southpaw, was an outstanding boxer with the unfortunate handicap of being easily cut around the eyes. This had cost him six stoppages before his world title win. Minter gave Antuofermo a return at Wembley, stopping him in the eighth, and three months later he defended against Marvin Hagler.

Hagler, born on 23 May 1952 in Newark, New Jersey, was expected, in Britain at least, to be another victim for Minter, judged on their form with Antuofermo, but his powerful punching opened bad cuts around Minter's eyes and the referee was forced to call a halt in the third. It was a bad night for British boxing because a nasty element among Minter's disappointed supporters began to throw beer cans into the ring and shout racialist abuse. Hagler was hustled back to the dressing room without being proclaimed world champion from the ring. He was to prove to be yet another outstanding one in this most exciting of all divisions.

Hagler officially changed his name to 'Marvelous Marvin Hagler,' and with his shaven skull made himself a familiar participant in some of the best fights of the next seven years. Giving all serious contenders a chance he stopped Fulgencio Obelmijias of Venezuela and Vito Antuofermo, both in Boston, and Mustafa Hamsho of Syria, in Rosemont. These defenses were in 1981 and he needed less than six rounds to dispose of his two challengers in 1982. William 'Cave Man' Lee

failed to last one round at Atlantic City and Obelmijias lasted only five at San Remo, Italy, both needing the referee's intervention to help them.

In 1983 Marvelous Marvin accepted a challenge from Minter's successor as British champion, the strong Tony Sibson, and dealt out stern punishment at Worcester, Massachusetts. Poor Sibson was stopped in the sixth and needed 17 stitches around the eyes, for which he was carted off to hospital in a blizzard. This was regarded as one of Hagler's best displays and he now had a reputation as an awesome cold-blooded destroyer of the world's best talent. Wilford Scypion was the next opponent to be dismissed, the referee saving him in the fourth round at Providence, Rhode Island.

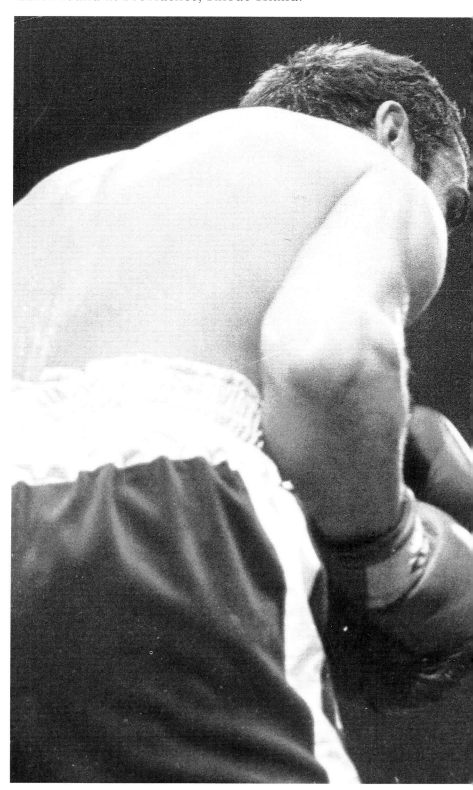

ABOVE LEFT: *Marvin Hagler's first attempt to win the world middleweight championship failed. On 30 November 1979 Hagler (right) challenged Vito Antuofermo at Las Vegas and was held to a draw after 15 rounds.*

ABOVE: *Champion Hagler took on Mustafa Hamsho (right) at Rosemont on 3 October 1981. Hamsho was a brawler and he took Hagler to the seventh round before the referee stopped the contest.*

LEFT: *Hagler in his title-winning fight with Alan Minter (left) at Wembley on 27 September 1980. Minter's problem was that he cut easily around the eyes, and the referee had to come to his assistance in the third round when Minter suffered a particularly bad cut.*

171

LEFT: *Hagler celebrates with his belts after his win over John 'The Beast' Mugabi in Las Vegas on 10 March 1986. Mugabi gave Hagler a good fight in the early rounds, but Hagler caught him in the eleventh.*

RIGHT: *Excitement in the ring after Hagler's tremendous victory over Thomas Hearns. It was a short fight but one of the most savage in history.*

BELOW LEFT: *The attentions of Hagler's gloves can clearly be seen on the face of Juan Roldan, who challenged on 30 March 1984 in Las Vegas and was stopped in the tenth round.*

BELOW: *Hagler bearing down on Hearns (right) during their epic encounter on 16 April 1985. The referee stepped in in the third round – but not a second of the action had been wasted as both men went all out for victory.*

172

Hagler ended 1983 with a defense against Roberto Duran, the veteran warrior from Panama. Most expected Hagler would be much too strong for Duran who had campaigned among the lighter weights and was not considered powerful enough as a middleweight. However, although Hagler took the decision clearly, he could not stop him. Duran fought with great bravery, carrying the fight to his opponent with his usual belligerence. It was a reminder of the performance Antuofermo had put up against Hagler four years earlier with his crowding tactics. This was Hagler's first defense to go the distance.

Hagler, with his well-muscled physique, usually attacked his opponents with such weight and variety of punch that sooner or later they were overwhelmed by his strength, and it was back to the usual style with a tenth-round stoppage of Juan Domingo Roldan of Argentina in Las Vegas and a third-round stoppage of Mustafa Hamsho in New York.

On 16 April 1985 Hagler fought Thomas Hearns at Caesars Palace, Las Vegas, in a classic fight. Hearns had been WBA welterweight champion and was currently WBC light-middleweight champion. He was a devastating hitter, called 'The Hit Man,' and was tall with a long reach. He had been beaten only once, by Sugar Ray Leonard, and many thought he would be good enough to beat Hagler, who was by now nearly 33.

Hagler had obviously decided that as a natural middleweight he was stronger than Hearns and that he would attack all out from the bell. Hearns, who was a fast starter, clearly also decided that his best chance was to attack from the bell because

Hagler was normally a sluggish starter. The result was eight minutes of the most savage boxing seen since Zale and Graziano had met in the ring.

Both men were rocked by tremendous punches in the first round. Hagler was cut but could take a big punch better than Hearns who looked the more shaken after the first three minutes of calculated mayhem. Hagler appeared the stronger in the second round but Hearns still caught him with terrific blows. It was clear the fight could not go more than a few rounds, especially when the referee twice inspected the cuts around the champion's eyes in the third. Hagler then fought with what might be described as controlled desperation, charging across the ring and delivering a left and right that spun Hearns round and had him staggering about as if drunk. Hagler chased him, two hard rights put Hearns on the canvas and the referee stopped it when Hearns was clearly still wobbly on getting to his feet.

Hagler made his twelfth defense in 1986 before another big crowd at Caesars Palace, against John 'The Beast' Mugabi from Uganda, who had won all his 26 fights without being taken the distance. It was thought he might be Marvelous Marvin's conqueror but after fighting well he began to tire and in the eleventh round Hagler knocked him out.

It was his only defense in 1986. The WBA and IBF then stripped him of the title because he declined to meet their contender, England's Herol Graham, and signed instead for Hagler to fight Sugar Ray Leonard.

173

Sugar Ray Leonard Rules

From the time Emile Griffith relinquished the welterweight title in 1965, many of the line of succeeding champions were outstanding and there emerged finally one of the greatest boxers of recent times, Sugar Ray Leonard.

To fill the vacant spot left by Griffith, the WBA organized a tournament which was won by Curtis Cokes from Dallas who on the way defeated Luis Rodriguez, a former champion and conqueror of Griffith. Cokes then won EBU and New York recognition with a decision in his home town over Jean Josselin, the European champion. Late in 1967 Cokes stopped Charlie Snipes, who was regarded as world champion by the Californian authorities, and with this win earned universal recognition.

After five defenses Cokes dropped the title to an excellent champion, Jose Napoles, who was born in Oriente, Cuba, but boxed in Mexico. The referee stopped their fight in the thirteenth round in Los Angeles. Napoles took over the title on 18 April 1969 and before the end of the year had forced Cokes to retire in a return at Mexico City and outpointed Emile Griffith, who had by now won and lost the middleweight crown. In 1970 Napoles stopped Ernie Lopez in the last round and then dropped his title to Billy Backus, a southpaw nephew of Carmen Basilio. Backus was a 9-to-1 outsider and stopped Napoles in the fourth, but it was a temporary setback as Napoles won the title back six months later.

Napoles made nine further defenses and an unsuccessful attempt on Carlos Monzon's middleweight crown, before he was stopped in 1975 in Mexico City by John H Stracey, the British champion, who recovered from a first-round knockdown to batter the champion to a sixth-round defeat. Napoles retired, having been champion for 6½ years.

Toward the end of Napoles' reign the championship had split when the WBA and WBC had disagreed over contenders. Stracey was the WBC champion but lost his title to Carlos Palomino, a Mexican boxing mostly out of Los Angeles, who destroyed Stracey with body punches. Palomino made seven successful defenses and was champion for 2½ years before he was beaten by another outstanding boxer, Wilfred Benitez.

Benitez, a Puerto Rican from the Bronx, New York, was born on 12 September 1958. He won the WBA light-welterweight title on 6 March 1976 and at 17½ was the youngest-ever world champion. He was three months past 20 when outpointing Carlos Palomino at San Juan on 14 January 1979.

Benitez was such a brilliant boxer that he should have enjoyed a long career as champion, but after one successful defense he was challenged by the great Sugar Ray Leonard.

Leonard was born at Wilmington, South Carolina, on 17 May 1956 and became an excellent amateur, winning Golden Gloves, lightweight and light-welterweight titles and the Olympic light-welterweight gold medal in 1976. He soon made his professional debut and in 2½ unbeaten years had earned his title shot. Leonard and Benitez put on an outstanding show at Caesars Palace. Both men were paid at least a million dollars. Benitez recovered well from a third-round knockdown and a cut on his forehead in the sixth caused by a clash of heads, but finally ran out of steam in the fifteenth and last round. He rose exhausted from a count and the referee stepped in with six seconds left.

Leonard was being built up as the charismatic figure to take the place as boxing's figurehead which Ali had held for so long. A presentable figure with a Cheshire cat smile, he was a boxing genius and possessed a devastating punch, as he proved in his first defense, when England's Dave 'Boy' Green was knocked out with a single punch in the fourth.

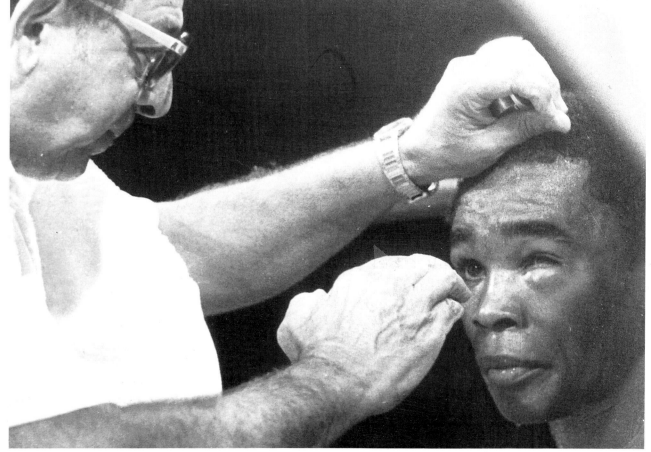

LEFT: *Manager Angelo Dundee works on Sugar Ray Leonard's eye during his welterweight title fight with Thomas Hearns on 16 September 1981. After one further defense of this title Leonard underwent surgery to re-attach the retina of his left eye, and gave up boxing. However, he was to make two brief comebacks.*

RIGHT: *The first of many outstanding title fights that Leonard enjoyed. He stands over the welterweight champion, Wilfred Benitez, at Las Vegas on 30 November 1979. Benitez was stopped with six seconds of a terrific contest remaining.*

ABOVE: *Leonard's only defeat was by Roberto Duran (left), but it was a defeat that he avenged in spectacular fashion in a return on 25 November 1980 in New Orleans. The macho Duran gave in in the face of Leonard's brilliance.*

ABOVE RIGHT: *Leonard turns in triumph at the end of a round in the 1981 contest with Thomas Hearns that unified the world welterweight title. After soaking up punishment, Leonard found reserves to floor Hearns in the thirteenth.*

LEFT: *Leonard in his corner during the Hearns bout in 1981. The left eye looks badly damaged. This may have been the start of his retina trouble.*

RIGHT: *Hearns (left) and Leonard during the same fight. Leonard won in the fourteenth round.*

Sugar Ray now suffered a reverse. Roberto Duran put up one of his greatest performances to rough-house Leonard out of his title with a narrow points win. Leonard was paid $8½ million for this fight in Montreal and re-established his earning power and regained his title five months later with an inspired performance at New Orleans. Duran was so bedazzled by Leonard's boxing and Leonard's antics in inviting Duran to try to hit him, that he gave up in the eighth round. It was a sensational and complete revenge.

Meanwhile the WBA half of the title had been held for nearly four years by Pipino Cuevas, an extremely hard-hitting Mexican knockout king. He won the title from Angel Espada of Puerto Rico in 1975 and made 11 successful defenses. Half of his 12 winning title fights did not get beyond the second round and only once went the distance. However he himself was stopped in the second round when he was tackled by another tremendous puncher, 'The Hit Man' himself, Thomas Hearns. Hearns made four successful defenses, and then the prospect arose of a unification bout between him and Leonard, the two outstanding champions.

In 1981 Leonard had moved up to the light-middleweight division and had become WBA champion by stopping Ayub Kalule of Uganda. However the Hearns fight was such a

money-spinner that he immediately relinquished his new title to accept $11 million, then the biggest purse in history, to decide who was the better welterweight of Hearns and himself.

On 16 September 1981 at Caesars Palace, yet another 'fight of the century' took place and it was one which did not disappoint the customers. Hearns started the stronger and his bombs several times shook Sugar Ray. The fight was going Hearns's way, especially when Leonard's left eye was almost closed, until Sugar Ray launched a tremendous sustained fightback in the thirteenth. Hearns went down from a slip but then was put down properly by a brilliant succession of punches. In minutes Leonard had turned the fight around. He continued his assault in the fourteenth and after one minute 45 seconds the referee stopped a marvelous fight in his favor.

Sugar Ray made one defense in 1982 before he had to undergo an eye operation for a detached retina. It was successful, but on 9 November 1982 he decided not to risk his eyesight in the ring and retired with his fortune. Yet the lure of boxing was to prove too strong and in May 1984 he returned to stop Kevin Howard in the ninth at Worcester. But Howard put him down for the first time in his career and he retired again, admitting that the old snap was missing. However three years later he was to be tempted again in memorable circumstances.

Modern Light-Heavies and Cruisers

The light-heavyweight division of the Muhammads and the name changes continued its tradition in the 1980s.

Matthew Saad Muhammad, the WBC champion, was the busier of the two champions although none of his opponents was able to take him the distance. Louis Pergaud lasted five rounds in Halifax, Canada, Yaqui Lopez fourteen in McAfee, New Jersey, Lotte Mwale four in San Diego, Vonzell Johnson eleven in Atlantic City, Murray Sutherland nine in Atlantic City and Jerry Martin eleven, also in Atlantic City.

Matthew Saad Muhammad had made 11 successful defenses in 28 months when he finally dropped his title, fighting again in Atlantic City. Dwight Braxton stopped him in the tenth round on 19 December 1981. Braxton, believe it or not, was yet another boxer in this division to change his name: the following year he fought as Dwight Muhammad Qawi. A name change seemed almost obligatory among the light-heavies. Qawi defended against Jerry Martin, Matthew Saad Muhammad and Eddie Davis, before losing to Michael Spinks and having a shot at the new cruiserweight class.

Meanwhile in the WBA branch Mustapha Muhammad lost his title on his third defense, also to Michael Spinks, one of the greatest champions in this division. Spinks was the younger of the two brothers to win Olympic gold medals in 1976 and had turned professional in 1977. He had left 16 defeated opponents behind him and was unbeaten when he outpointed Muhammad to take the WBA title on 18 July 1981. Fourteen months later Vonzell Johnson, Mustapha Wasajji, Murray Sutherland, Jerry Celestine and Johnny Davis had all been stopped

ABOVE: *Michael Spinks dominated the light-heavyweight scene in the first half of the 1980s. Spinks eventually beat Larry Holmes to take the IBF heavyweight title and he relinquished the light-heavyweight championship. He is photographed wearing his new heavyweight belt, with the IBF, WBA and WBC light-heavyweight belts in his hands and on his shoulders.*

LEFT: *Dwight Braxton (right) appears to be enjoying his upset victory over Matthew Saad Muhammad who appears to be taking a nap in their title fight in 1981. Braxton changed his name to Dwight Muhammad Qawi.*

RIGHT: *Marvin Johnson won a light-heavyweight title for the third time in stopping Leslie Stewart of Trinidad on 9 February 1986 at Indianapolis for the vacant WBA version.*

ABOVE: *Michael Spinks, the WBC champion, outpointed Dwight Muhammad Qawi, the WBC champion, at Atlantic City on 18 March 1983 and became undisputed champion.*

LEFT: *Dennis Andries (left) took the WBC light-heavyweight title with a victory over J B Williamson in 1986 and five months later defended it against Tony Sibson (right) in London. Sibson, a middleweight, could not cope with Andries and was stopped in the ninth.*

ABOVE RIGHT: *Dwight Muhammad Qawi (left), still fighting under his original name of Braxton, gave a return to Matthew Saad Muhammad on 7 August 1982 at Philadelphia. Qawi took the title in the sixth round.*

RIGHT: *Hearns (left) takes on Andries for the WBC light-heavyweight championship in Detroit on 7 March 1987. Hearns stopped Andries in the tenth round and was three-quarters of the way to his record four titles at different weights.*

between the sixth and ninth rounds. On 18 March 1983 he and the WBC champion, Qawi, fought for the undisputed title and Spinks won the decision. He then defeated Oscar Rivadeneyra, Eddie Davis, David Sears and Jim MacDonald before relinquishing the title in 1985 to move up to the heavyweights to challenge Larry Holmes.

As is customary these days, the title now split again into three. Marvin Johnson, Leslie Stewart of Trinidad and Virgil Hill took the WBA championship through 1987, while the IBF progression went to Slobodan Kacar, a second Yugoslavian to hold a light-heavyweight title, and then to Bobby Czyz. Czyz, a very exciting boxer from Wanaque in the United States, was thought to have a long reign ahead of him but as a 9-to-2-on favorite he was stopped by 'Prince' Charles Williams of Ohio on 29 October 1987.

The most interesting of the three branches of the light-heavyweight championship was the WBC line, however. It was won by J B Williamson of Indianapolis but he lost it on his first defense to Dennis Andries of London. On his second defense, on 7 March 1987, Andries came to Detroit to defend against Thomas Hearns. In a heavy punching contest the smooth Hearns eventually got the better of the lumbering and brave Andries, the referee stopping the fight in the tenth round. Hearns thus won his third world title.

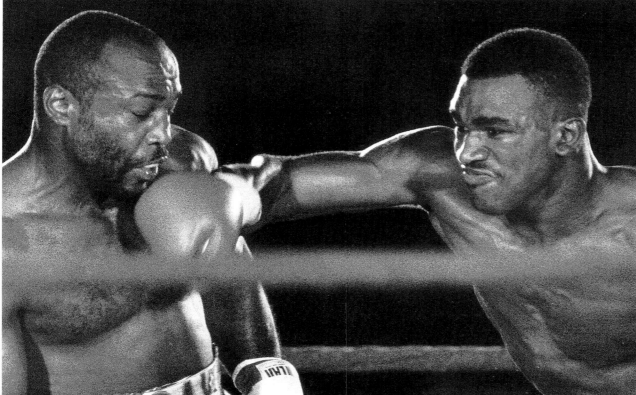

ABOVE: *Evander Holyfield (right), one of the few American boxers at the 1984 Olympics not to reach a final, became one of the best professionals afterward, winning the WBA cruiserweight title. The recipient of the right is Ossie Ocasio who challenged on 16 August 1987 at Saint Tropez.*

LEFT: *This right by Holyfield helped him win the title on points on 12 July 1986 at Atlanta. It is Dwight Muhammad Qawi who is the deposed champion, fighting now under his new name.*

RIGHT: *Pipino Cuevas of Mexico City was the WBA welterweight champion as the 1980s started. On 6 April 1980 Cuevas (left) knocked out Harold Volbrecht in the fifth round at the Astroarena, Houston.*

In 1979 a new cruiserweight division was instigated by the WBC and naturally the WBA and IBF alphabet boys followed soon after with their versions of this new championship. The actual weight limit differs between the bodies. The WBC began with a 190-pound limit but raised this to 195 pounds in 1981, while the WBA and IBF championships, started in 1982 and 1983 respectively, required the boxers to weigh in at under 190 pounds. Marvin Camel, Carlos de Leon and Ossie Ocasio were prominent in this division, until an outstanding boxer emerged in the 1980s to take over both the WBA and IBF crowns. He was Evander Holyfield, the US light-heavyweight disqualified in the semifinal of the 1984 Olympic Games. Holyfield won the WBA cruiserweight title by outpointing Dwight Muhammad Qawi at Atlanta on 12 July 1986 and the IBF title by stopping Rickey Parkey in the third at Las Vegas. When he stopped Ossie Ocasio in August 1987 it was his sixteenth straight win since turning professional and he was being discussed as a possible future heavyweight king.

Light to Light-Middle in the 1980s

When Alexis Arguello relinquished his third world title, the WBC lightweight crown, Edwin Rosario of Puerto Rico took it up by outpointing Jose-Luis Ramirez of Mexico. It was only the fourth defeat for Ramirez in over 80 contests, while Rosario was unbeaten in 22. They were two excellent battlers and met again after Rosario had twice defended successfully. This time Ramirez inflicted on Rosario his first defeat by stopping him in San Juan to become the new champion. Ramirez however, on his first defense, lost to a really outstanding fighter, one of the best of the 1980s, Hector 'Macho' Camacho who was born in Puerto Rico but was based in New York. He too was unbeaten on taking the title and defended twice against Edwin Rosario and Cornelius Bosa-Edwards, the former junior lightweight champion, before he relinquished the title in 1986 to take his unbeaten record up to campaign among the light-welter-weights. Jose-Luis Ramirez won back the vacant crown with a terrific points win over Terence Alli and held it by knocking out Bosa-Edwards in Paris in October 1987.

Ray 'Boom Boom' Mancini from Ohio, a destructive hitter who was sometimes knocked out himself, was meanwhile a popular holder of the WBA title. He was eventually outpointed by Livingstone Bramble in 1985 but in 1986 Edwin Rosario came back to win this version of the title by knocking out Bramble in the second round. In November 1987 Rosario lost the title to Julio Cesar Chavez of Mexico, who stopped him in Las

Vegas. Chavez was a previous junior middleweight champion and was building up an unbeaten run which took him past 50 professional victories.

Greg Haugen of Auburn, Washington, carried the less interesting IBF lightweight title into 1987 with a points victory over Jimmy Paul at Las Vegas.

Two excellent light-welterweight champions lost their titles in different circumstances in 1987. Patrizio Oliva of Naples, Italy, was a very classy Olympic gold medalist in Moscow in 1980 and, turning professional, won his first 43 fights which took him to a WBA world title match with Ubaldo Sacco in March 1986. Oliva won the decision and continued defending successfully until July 1987 when he was at last stopped by Juan Coggi of Argentina, at Ribera, Sicily. It was Oliva's forty-ninth fight, and having lost his unbeaten record he decided it was time to retire.

Terry Marsh, a fireman from Basildon, England, won the IBF title by stopping Joe Manley in his home town on 4 March 1987. He defended successfully in July at the Albert Hall, London, against Akio Kameda of Japan but was forced, in September, to admit that he suffered from epilepsy. He retired unbeaten, an early draw being the only slight blot on his otherwise impeccable record.

Two excellent welterweight boxers succeeded Sugar Ray Leonard in the 1980s. In February 1983 Don Curry, from Fort

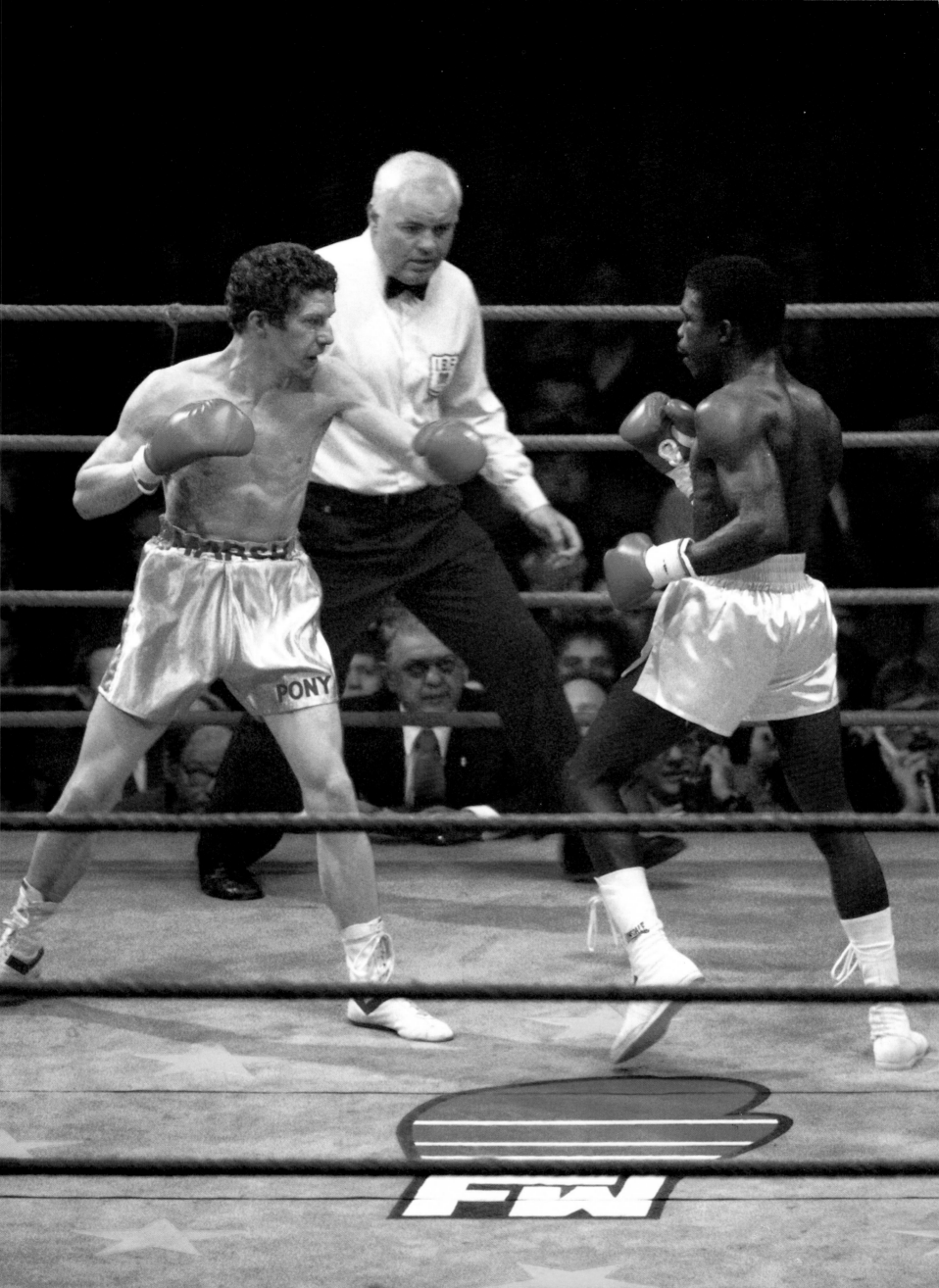

ABOVE: *One of the best British victories of the 1980s was that of unbeaten Lloyd Honeyghan (right), who went to Atlantic City on 27 September 1986 and outmaneuvered and outpunched the undisputed world welterweight champion, Don Curry (left) who was also unbeaten and previously considered unbeatable.*

LEFT: *Terry Marsh (left) met Joe Manley (right) in his successful challenge for the IBF light-welterweight title on 4 March 1987 at Basildon, Essex. After one successful defense Marsh admitted he was an epileptic, and retired undefeated.*

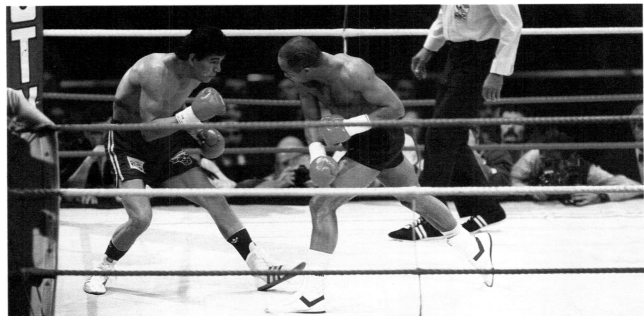

RIGHT CENTER: *Lloyd Honeyghan (right) lost his title and suffered his first defeat in peculiar circumstances at Wembley on 29 October 1987. He was not himself and tamely surrendered to Jorge Vaca of Mexico.*

RIGHT: *Two of the most active lightweight champions of the 1980s, Edwin Rosario, facing camera, and Hector 'Macho' Camacho, met on 13 June 1986 for Camacho's title. Camacho won on points.*

Worth, Texas won the WBA title in his home town, and six months later Milton McCrory from Detroit won the WBC title on a split decision over Colin Jones of Wales at Las Vegas, the two boxers having fought a draw five months earlier. Eventually Curry and McCrory met to unify the title, Curry's five defenses in the meantime including a four-round stoppage of Colin Jones in Birmingham, when Jones's nose was split, and McCrory's four defenses including trips to the European cities of Paris and Monte Carlo.

When the two champions met, Curry, 'The Cobra,' proved too strong for the cool boxing of McCrory, 'The Ice Man,' and he knocked him out in the second round. At the time Curry was being talked of as the best pound-for-pound boxer of his era, but after one defense of the unified title he faced Lloyd 'Honey' Honeyghan, the British champion, in Atlantic City. Curry was unbeaten in 25 contests, Honeyghan in 27. Curry was a hot favorite but Honeyghan outboxed and outpunched him, forcing Curry to retire at the end of the sixth round. Honeyghan was one of only two champions (Hagler was the other) to hold an undisputed world title but he relinquished the WBA title rather than face their contender, Harold Volbrecht, a South African. It was his protest against *apartheid*. Honeyghan proved a very destructive champion for three defenses but surrendered the title tamely when facing a substitute, Jorge Vaca of Guadalajara, Mexico, on 29 October 1987 at Wembley.

Honeyghan had got into a poor emotional state. Hand injuries, publicity over his four children with three mothers and disaffection with his manager caused him to fight as if he did not want to win. The ending was extraordinary with a delay of nine minutes before a verdict. In the eighth, an accidental clash of heads opened a nasty gash over Vaca's eye,

ABOVE: *Mike McCallum (right) of Jamaica built up a long unbeaten run and took the vacant WBA light-middleweight championship in 1984. Some thought his reign would come to an end against Don Curry on 20 July 1987 at Las Vegas, but McCallum, seen here getting in a right to Curry's face, won by a fifth-round knockout after a brilliant left hook.*

causing a stoppage. The referee ordered the judges to score to the end of the previous round and to deduct a mark from Honeyghan as he was held responsible for the clash of heads. Vaca won a split decision, the deducted point losing Honeyghan his crown. Despite such a strange outcome, Honeyghan's state was such that he appeared relieved rather than aggrieved to lose his title and unbeaten record.

Curry, Honeyghan's victim, had moved up to the light-middleweights, where several great boxers had fought in the 1980s. Wilfred Benitez, Davey Moore, Roberto Duran and Thomas Hearns all held versions of the title, the last two relinquishing their titles unbeaten. When Duran gave up his in 1983, the vacant WBA crown was taken by Mike McCallum, a brilliant Jamaican boxer who could punch with devastating power with either hand. McCallum's fifth defense, in April 1987, was against Milton McCrory, the old welterweight, and the sixth was against Curry. Curry had established himself in the new division in an odd manner – with two victories from fifth-round disqualifications. He took on McCallum on 20 July 1987 at Las Vegas and again the fifth round was the vital one. Curry was the favorite, despite McCallum's unbeaten record and long reign, and was leading on all scorecards during the fifth round when a brilliant left hook from McCallum knocked him flat on his back, arms spread. There was no way he could rise and McCallum 'The Body Snatcher,' was proving himself one of the best of the 1980s' champions.

The Mighty Atoms of the 1980s

In 1975 a light-flyweight class for boxers up to 108 pounds had been introduced by the WBC and by the mid-1980s there were three champions at the weight. Luis Estaba from Venezuela was an early and busy champion, and as the division established itself it was taken over largely by boxers from Central America or the East. In the late 1970s, Yoko Gushiken of Japan made 13 successful defenses of the WBA title and in the early 1980s Hilario Zapata of Panama made 11 successful defenses of the WBC version, but by 1987 the three champions were all South Korean: Jung-Koo Chang, Zapata's conqueror, a brilliant boxer who took the WBC title in 1983 and through 1987 equaled the record for the division of 13 successful defenses and was still unfinished; Myung-Woo Yuh, who took the WBA title from an American, Joey Olivo, in 1985; and Jum-Hwan Choi who took the IBF crown in 1987.

The traditional flyweight division also came to be dominated by Eastern and Central American boxers. Hilario Zapata also had a run in this class, being WBA champion for 16 months, but the longest-reigning champion in the 1980s was Sot Chitalada of Thailand, who won the WBC title by beating Gabriel Bernal of Mexico in 1984. He held the title into 1987 when Fidel Bassa of Colombia and Dodie Panalosa of the Philippines held the other versions.

In 1980 another new division, the light-bantamweights (or junior bantams according to the WBA and IBF, and super-flyweights according to the WBC) was instituted at 115 pounds, only three pounds above the flyweight limit and seven pounds above the light-flyweights. Jiro Watanabe of Japan held both WBA and WBC titles for a couple of years each. Kaosai Galaxy from Thailand was another long-running champion, taking the WBA title in 1984 and holding it through 1987.

The best of the 1980s' bantams were Jeff Fenech of Australia, who held the IBF title till 1986 when he moved up a division, and Miguel Lora of Colombia who took the WBC title in 1985 and made his fourth successful defense in July 1987.

In 1976 a light-featherweight class was revived, there having been one title fight in 1922 after which the division fell into disuse. There was a remarkable scandal in a defense in Pusan, South Korea by the first of the modern champions, Rigoberto Riasco of Panama, in 1976. His opponent was Dong-Kyun Yum of Korea and the contest was in pouring rain. The Panamanian judge awarded it to Riasco by a comfortable 147 to 143, the Korean judge to Yum by an overwhelming 150 to 143. The American referee at first awarded it to Riasco 145 to 143 but returned to the ring later to correct himself: Yum, he announced, was the winner. However back in the United States he revealed that his correction had been made under threats and, as a result, Riasco was reinstated.

The longest reigning champion in this division has been Wilfredo Gomez, who took the title from Yum, who himself had succeeded on a second attempt. Gomez, from Puerto Rico, won the title in May 1977 and successfully defended it 17 times.

BELOW: *Wilfredo Gomez (left) was one of the busiest world champions after winning the WBC light-featherweight crown in 1977. This defeat of Derrick Holmes (right), whom Gomez managed to floor no less than eight times before the referee stepped in in the fifth round, was his twelfth defense.*

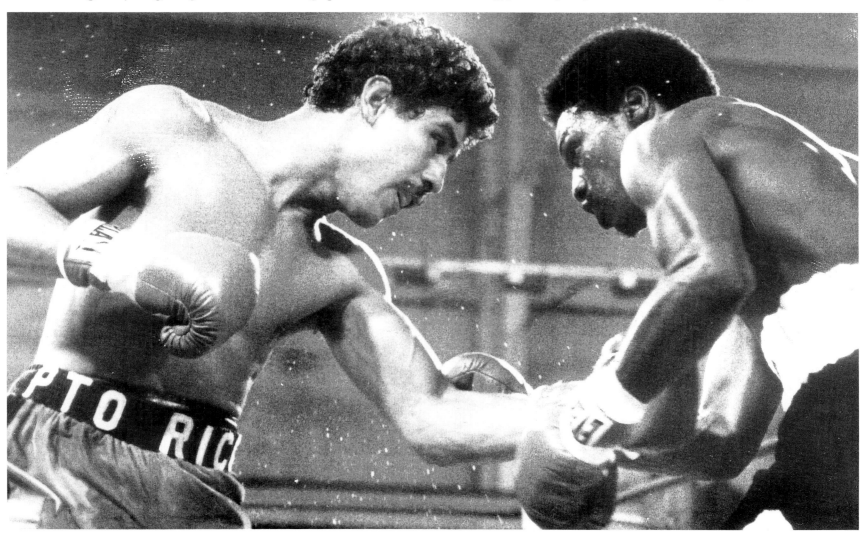

During this spell he unsuccessfully challenged Salvador Sanchez for the featherweight crown, but after relinquishing the light-featherweight title in 1983 he did win the featherweight and junior lightweight titles.

The featherweight division had some great champions in the late 1970s, after Alexis Arguello moved up a division. Danny 'Little Red' Lopez took the WBA title on a unanimous points decision from David Kotey of Accra, Ghana, in November 1976. A record crowd for featherweights in Kotey's home town saw Kotey, who won the title from Ruben Olivares, surrender it on this third defense. Lopez, a part-Indian boxer based in California, fought in an exciting hard-hitting style which destroyed many opponents but left him vulnerable himself. None of his eight successful defenses went the distance, nor did the fight in which he lost the title in February 1980. He was stopped in the thirteenth round by Salvador Sanchez, an outstanding fighter from Santiago, Mexico.

Sanchez was a two-fisted boxer with a good punch and he ruled in an era when the featherweight division was very strong. As well as Lopez, whom he also stopped in a return, he beat Ruben Castillo, Pat Ford, Juan Laporte (twice), Roberto Castanon, Wilfredo Gomez, Pat Cowdell and Azumah Nelson in a 2½-year reign. Laporte, Gomez and Nelson went on to become champions at the weight. Sanchez was killed in a road accident in 1982. An early defeat as a bantamweight was the only blot on his professional record.

Laporte took over the WBC title until in 1984 he was outpointed by Wilfredo Gomez, who had enjoyed such a long run as light-featherweight champion. Gomez dropped this title on his first defense, however, to Azumah Nelson of Accra who defended five times into 1987.

Meanwhile the WBA title had been won in 1978 by another superb champion, Eusebio Pedroza of Panama City. Born on 2 March 1953, Pedroza turned professional in 1973 and in his sixteenth fight, in 1976, was beaten by Alfonso Zamora in a bantamweight title challenge. He was a superb hard-punching boxer who, from the time he won the title in April 1978 until he lost it in June 1985, made no fewer than 19 successful defenses. He defended in Panama City, San Juan, Tokyo, Houston, Port

ABOVE: *Salvador Sanchez, a brilliant featherweight champion, after stopping Azumah Nelson in the last round of a defense at New York City on 21 July 1982. Tragically it was his last defense, as shortly afterward he was killed in a road accident.*

RIGHT: *Eusebio Pedroza (right) was another outstanding featherweight who held the WBA title for over seven years. Barry McGuigan (left) took the crown with a points win in a fight held in London on 8 June 1985.*

LEFT: *Jeff Fenech of Australia (dark trunks) won the WBC light-featherweight title when he challenged Samart Payakarum of Thailand in Sydney on 8 May 1987. The referee stopped the fight in the fourth round.*

Moresby (Papua, New Guinea), Seoul, McAfee (USA), Caracas, Atantic City, Charlotte (USA), Liguma (Italy), San Remo, Maracaibo (Venezuela) and London. It is a great pity that he never met Sanchez. The two of them were outstanding fighters who, because of the two 'ruling bodies,' could be only half a champion each.

Pedroza lost his title to Ireland's Barry McGuigan who brought some temporary unity to strife-torn Ireland with some stirring displays in the King's Hall, Belfast. One of the most popular of sportsmen, McGuigan, who as an amateur represented Northern Ireland in the Commonwealth Games and the Republic of Ireland in the Olympics, was a relentless two-fisted body-puncher. He proved too strong for Pedroza in a thrilling battle on the Loftus Road football ground in London.

McGuigan's third defense was in June 1986 against Steve Cruz, a fairly low-ranked substitute, at Caesars Palace, Las Vegas. Cruz, of San Antonio, handled the 110-degree heat much better than the paler McGuigan, who was knocked down twice in the last round and lost a narrow decision. Cruz, in his first defense, was stopped by Antonio Esparragoza of Venezuela, who, in turn, defended successfully in July 1987 against Pascual Aranda.

The junior lightweight division in the 1980s never had fewer than two champions, and from 1984, three. Among the best were Sam Serrano of Toa Alta, Puerto Rico, who from 1976 to 1983 won 15 world title bouts; Bobby Chacon and Roger Mayweather of the United States; Hector Camacho who relinquished his WBC title to move up to lightweights; Rocky Lockridge of the United States who held the WBA title in 1984 and 1985 and won the IBF version in 1987 from Barry Michael of Australia; Wilfredo Gomez of Puerto Rico, winning a world title at a third weight; and Julio Cesar Chavez of Mexico, who won the WBC title in 1984 and defended it successfully eight times to April 1987, when he took a 55-fight unbeaten record up to the lightweight division and went on to win the WBA title.

The WBA Heavyweight Line

In September 1979, about a year after Muhammad Ali had regained his heavyweight championship by beating Leon Spinks, he announced his retirement. The part of the championship he held was the WBA version, the WBC having withdrawn recognition from Spinks because he had signed for the Ali return.

The WBA thus found itself without a heavyweight champion and decided that a contest between John Tate from Marion City, Arkansas, and Gerrie Coetzee from Boksburg, Transvaal, would be for the vacant crown. Tate, standing 6 feet 4 inches and weighing around 240 pounds, was unbeaten, having stopped 15 of his 19 opponents. Coetzee, the South African champion, stood 6 feet 3 inches and weighed 227 pounds. Tate won on points over 15 rounds in a fight held in Pretoria, South Africa.

He did not hold the title long for five months later he defended it against Mike Weaver of Gatesville, Texas. Weaver stood a mere 6 feet 1 inch and weighed around 220 pounds. His record was variable for he had already lost nine fights, including a challenge to Larry Holmes for the WBC title, but in a battle between two punchers with weak chins he came out on top, although it wasn't until the very last of the 15 rounds that he knocked out Tate at Knoxville. Seven months later he went to Sun City, Bophuthatswana, to give Gerrie Coetzee another crack at the title, and knocked him out in the thirteenth.

Weaver then sat on his third of the championship for nearly a year before at Rosemont, on 3 October 1981, he outpointed James 'Quick' Tillis, a boxer from Tulsa who had won all his 20 bouts till then. Still spacing out his defenses, Weaver took on another unbeaten challenger, Michael Dokes, at Caesars Palace, Las Vegas on 10 December 1982. Michael 'Dynamite' Dokes smashed the champion down in the first round and the referee declared it all over at 63 seconds. Dokes, from Akron, Ohio, stood 6 feet 3 inches and weighed 223 pounds.

On 20 May 1983 Dokes gave Weaver a return at the Dunes Hotel, Las Vegas. This time neither fighter's punches could dispatch the other. At the end of a hard struggle two judges marked a draw, the third gave it to Dokes. A draw was the official verdict with Dokes still champion.

Gerrie Coetzee was the next challenger, traveling to Richfield, Ohio and facing Dokes in the Coliseum Arena on 23 September 1983. It was third time lucky for Coetzee as he inflicted on Dokes his first defeat and took the title with a tenth-round knockout. Coetzee had been beaten three times in his 33 fights and had also achieved a victory over Leon Spinks, the former undisputed champion.

Coetzee kept the title to himself for over a year and then took on Greg Page at Sun City. It was a strange fight. Page, from Louisville, had lost his two previous bouts, to Tim Witherspoon in a challenge for the WBC title and to David Bey who

RIGHT: *Gerrie Coetzee has a bad cut in the sixth round of his challenge for Michael Dokes's WBA heavyweight championship on 23 September 1983 at Richfield, Ohio, but Coetzee took the title with a tenth-round knockout.*

LEFT ABOVE: *Wilfredo Gomez looks surprised to be on the canvas in the first round of his featherweight title challenge in 1981. Salvador Sanchez shows him his profile. Gomez recovered, but Sanchez retained his title by stopping his opponent in the eighth round.*

LEFT: *Barry McGuigan on the canvas in the last round of his featherweight defense at Caesars Palace, Las Vegas, on 23 June 1986. Steve Cruz took the points decision and the title.*

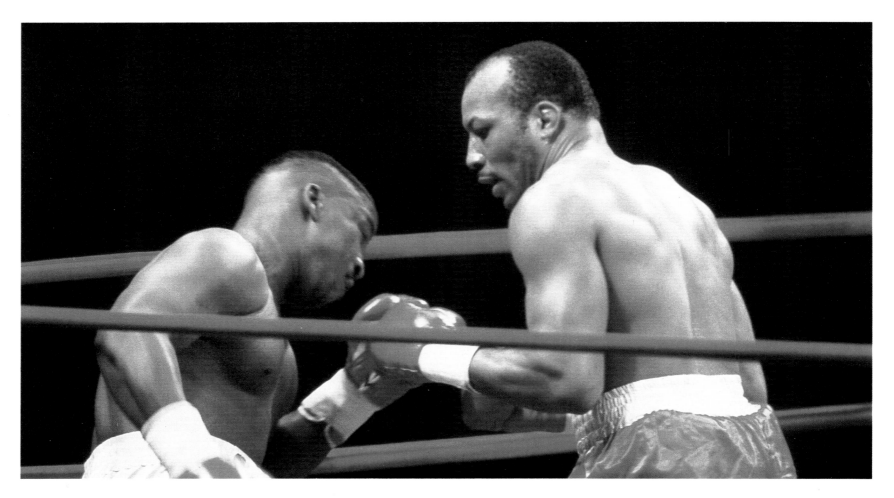

ABOVE: *James 'Bonecrusher' Smith (right) came in as a substitute for the WBA title fight with Tim Witherspoon and created a surprise by winning in the first at New York in December 1986.*

BELOW: *A poster for the double-header at the Dunes, Las Vegas, on 20 May 1983. Holmes beat Witherspoon to keep the WBC title, and WBA champion Dokes drew with Weaver.*

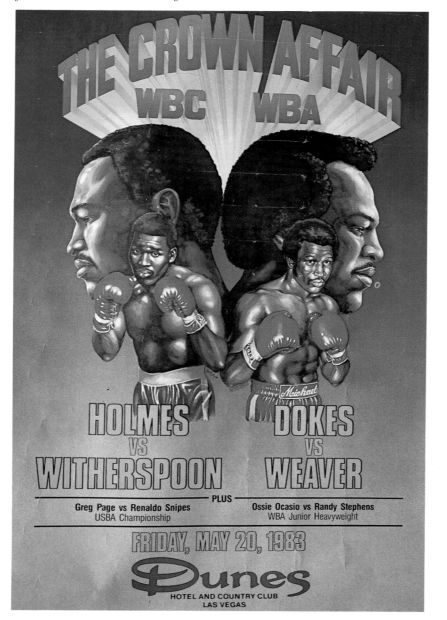

deprived him of his American heavyweight crown. Nevertheless Page stood up to Coetzee's blows and floored the champion in the sixth (after the bell) and seventh. In the eighth he knocked out Coetzee with a left hook, but the round had overrun by 50 seconds. The result stood, of course, and Page was the new champion. At 6 feet 3 inches and 240 pounds he was even bigger than his predecessors.

Page defended five months later, on 29 April 1985, and was outpointed at Buffalo by Tony Tubbs. Tubbs, from Cincinnati, was unbeaten in a five-year career and Page was his twenty-second victim. At 6 feet 3 inches and 229 pounds, Tubbs was another big man and was destined to be another loser on his first defense. On 17 January 1986 at Atlanta he was outpointed by 'Terrible' Tim Witherspoon from Philadelphia. Witherspoon was a previous WBC champion and had two blots on his record, defeats by Larry Holmes and Pinklon Thomas, both in WBC title fights. Tubbs and Witherspoon put on a dour exhibition with neither man looking to have the strength to floor the other and both looking overweight, particularly and ironically Tubbs. At the end two judges gave it narrowly to Witherspoon, the other marking it a draw, so Witherspoon became the fifth WBA champion in five title fights, an indication perhaps of the mediocrity of the line.

Witherspoon did manage a successful defense by traveling to London and stopping England's Frank Bruno in the eleventh round, but back in New York on 12 December 1986 he surprisingly lost to James 'Bonecrusher' Smith of Magnolia, who was standing in as a substitute for Tubbs. Smith had already been beaten by Witherspoon, Tubbs, Holmes and Marvis Frazier, but his plan of rushing from his corner at the bell to catch Witherspoon cold, worked. A terrific right to the head so shook the champion he never recovered and, though he tried to fight back, he was forced to take three counts in the first round, at which the referee ended the fight.

The original Witherspoon versus Tubbs contest had been one in a series arranged by promoter Don King and the Home Box Office television company to rationalize the whole heavyweight scene. Its ultimate objective was to proclaim one undisputed heavyweight champion again. For stepping in as a substitute and winning, 'Bonecrusher' Smith's prize would be a fight with Mike Tyson.

The WBC and IBF Heavyweight Kings

Larry Holmes assumed the WBC heavyweight title when Leon Spinks was dethroned and after an excellent career as WBC champion made the IBF respectable by becoming their champion. Holmes relinquished the WBC title after defending it against Marvis Frazier at the end of 1983. The WBC had ordered Holmes to defend against Greg Page, the United States champion, whose only defeat till then had been inflicted by Trevor Berbick. Holmes appeared unwilling to do so and the WBC matched Page with Tim Witherspoon on 9 March 1984 at the Convention Center, Las Vegas.

Witherspoon's only defeat had been by Holmes and in fact he gave Holmes one of his toughest defenses, one judge actually giving him the verdict by a point. The fight with Tate was a tough grueling struggle not unlike his battle with Holmes, but this time Witherspoon just took the verdict and was the new WBC champion. Witherspoon, born on 27 December 1957, had built up a reputation as a hard, bruising fighter and was known as 'Terrible Tim.'

It seemed that the WBC line was no more consistent than the WBA line when Witherspoon lost his first defense. His challenger was Pinklon Thomas from Pontiac, whose unbeaten 25-fight career had a minor blot in a draw with Gerrie Coetzee, who was the reigning WBC champion.

Thomas and Witherspoon met on 31 August 1985 at the Riviera Casino, Las Vegas and Thomas scored heavily with a solid left jab to such effect that at the end of the twelfth round he had inflicted enough damage to his opponent to take the decision. Thomas was born on 10 February 1958 and was of the usual stamp of recent heavyweights, standing 6 feet 3 inches tall and weighing 216 pounds.

Thomas made a successful defense against Mike Weaver on 15 June 1985, Weaver emphasizing the interchange of titles and challenges between the three branches of the heavyweight title.

BELOW: *Trevor Berbick (left) gets a jab to the head of Pinklon Thomas in his challenge for the WBC heavyweight championship at Las Vegas on 22 March 1986. Berbick won to get a date with Mike Tyson.*

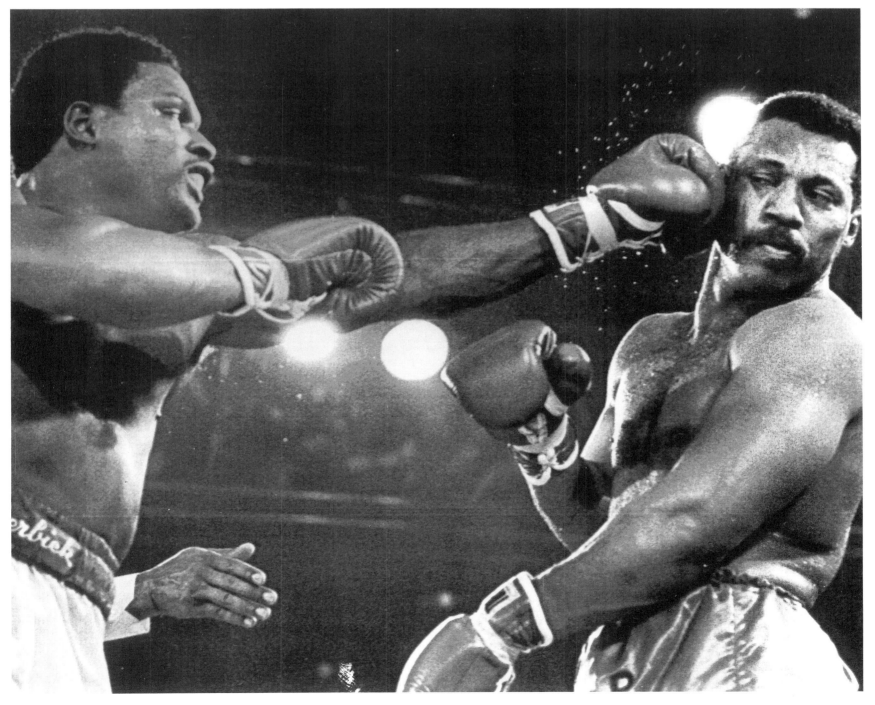

He had won and lost the WBA title and been beaten by Holmes, now the IBF champion, when he was WBC champion. The 'alphabet boys' had certainly reduced the heavyweight championship to a confusion of initials. Thomas beat Weaver at Las Vegas with an eighth-round knockout.

Pinklon Thomas's next defense was against Trevor Berbick at Las Vegas on 22 November 1986. Berbick, known as 'The Preacher,' was born in Jamaica on 1 August 1953. He had spent much of his boxing career in Canada and had won the Canadian heavyweight title in 1979, less than three years after turning professional. He had been outpointed by Larry Holmes in a WBC title challenge in 1981 and had later outpointed a sad Ali in his last fight. However he had suffered four defeats and was a 7-to-1 underdog against Thomas. Thomas, however, was listless and Berbick took the initiative and scored throughout the fight with good punches. Although all three judges scored the contest as a close one, the decision for Berbick was unanimous. His next bout was to be against the formidable Mike Tyson.

Meanwhile Larry Holmes, as previously described, continued with his impressive defenses of the third prong of the championship, the IBF title, until he was challenged by the former undisputed light-heavyweight champion, Michael Spinks. On 21 September 1985 Spinks took the title with a decision that was not to Holmes's liking. The return on 19 April 1986 was even more controversial. As before Holmes did the forcing, with Spinks being content to box at long range. As the older man began to get tired so Spinks, near the end, began to carry the attack to Holmes and it was a very difficult fight to score, with both men exhausted at the bell. Spinks took the split decision and general opinion seemed divided on the merits of it.

Spinks was born at St Louis on 13 July 1956 and began professional boxing after winning a gold medal at the 1976 Olympics. A fast and skillful boxer with a good punch he was outstanding as a light-heavyweight and defended his undis-

puted world championship ten times, beating all the logical contenders before moving up a weight and beating Holmes.

On 9 September 1986 Spinks defended his IBF championship at Las Vegas with a fourth-round stoppage of Steffen Tangstad of Norway, the European champion, although not a man in world class nor even the best in Europe.

The Don King/HBO rationalization program meant that the IBF champion was the last in the line to put his claims to the test – he was scheduled to meet the man who emerged from the WBA and WBC showdown. In effect Spinks was on line to meet Mike Tyson to decide the best in the world. But Spinks decided instead to opt out of this arrangement and earn a big pay day by taking on the revived 'white hope' Gerry Cooney, the former challenger of Holmes, his only conqueror in 29 contests. The two met on 15 June 1987 at Atlantic City.

Cooney was brave but no match for Spinks, although the fight remained a contest until the fifth round. Then Spinks stunned Cooney with two punches and followed up and floored him. When Cooney arose after a second knockdown, he was helpless and the referee stopped it. Spinks, at 208 pounds, was 30 pounds lighter than Cooney. This fight was not recognized by any of the alphabet associations as being for a world title, the IBF having stripped Spinks for his failure to meet Tyson. His manager proclaimed him the 'people's champion' and presented him with a championship belt adorned with diamonds and rubies and said to be valued at $10,000, a reminder of the John L Sullivan/Paddy Ryan/Richard K Fox argument of a century before. The authenticity of Spinks's claim to be champion was the subject of much speculation. He was small by current standards and had not beaten a top-class heavyweight in his prime, assuming Holmes at 35 to be past his peak. On the other hand *Ring* magazine, an unbiased authority, regarded Spinks as champion because his lineage could be traced back to John L Sullivan.

On the defection of Spinks the IBF decided that their new champion would be the winner of the contest at the Hilton Hotel, Las Vegas on 30 May 1987, between Tony Tucker and James 'Buster' Douglas. Both men were good boxers with dangerous punches, but on the day the taller and faster Tucker gradually got on top. Suddenly in the tenth Douglas was seen to be hurt and as Tucker piled into the attack the referee was forced to stop the fight. Tucker, from Grand Rapids, was born on 27 December 1958 and so shared a birthday with Tim Witherspoon. He remained unbeaten after 35 contests, one of which had been declared 'no contest.'

So Tony Tucker was the new IBF champion and had earned himself a spot in the HBO 'final' against Mike Tyson.

FAR LEFT: *Michael Spinks (left) and Larry Holmes tangle in the first round of their Las Vegas fight on 19 April 1986. Spinks had taken Holmes's IBF title seven months earlier in a close decision and he kept it in an even closer one.*

RIGHT: *Michael Spinks with his IBF belt which he retained after beating Steffen Tangstad in 1986. However, he forfeited the title when he refused to meet Tony Tucker.*

BELOW LEFT: *Tony Tucker won the vacant IBF championship with a tenth-round stoppage of James 'Buster' Douglas at Las Vegas on 30 May 1987 and found himself the last opponent of Mike Tyson in his clean-up of the heavyweight division.*

BELOW: *Michael Spinks (left), after beating Steffen Tangstad, opted out of the Don King/HBO heavyweight program and took on Gerry Cooney (right), who had been outboxed by Holmes. Cooney was no match for Spinks either, and Spinks got himself ready for a possible lucrative encounter with Mike Tyson.*

The $100,000,000 Fight

The WBC world middleweight title fight at Caesars Palace on 6 April 1987 was the biggest boxing bonanza of all time. On the one hand was the shaven-headed Marvelous Marvin Hagler, the man who for almost seven years had been the undisputed champion, one of the best fighters even the middleweight division had seen. On the other hand was Sugar Ray Leonard, perhaps the greatest boxing artist of the 1980s, a man whose career had been cut short over five years earlier by a detached retina in his left eye, and whose attempt at a comeback two years later had lasted for one fight: 'It just wasn't there any more,' he kept saying about his dismal performance.

The fight was controversial from its inception. Leonard had been a welterweight and there were those that thought that even at his peak he would not beat a superbly fit natural middleweight like Hagler. But Leonard was more than a boxer, he was a celebrity and when he decided he wished to challenge Hagler the box-office predictions were of huge numbers of dollars. The two men were, after all, the outstanding boxers of the 1980s.

Of course a man who in five years had had one fight and who had retired twice with eye problems had no right to be fighting for the world middleweight championship, and the WBA and IBF, who wanted Hagler to meet England's Herol Graham, agreed. They stripped him of the title. So the fight was for the WBC version which remained.

This did not affect the ballyhoo. The 15,336 seats raised $7.9 million, an average price per seat of over $500, and they were sold immediately, months before the event. About 30,000 television viewers watched the bout live on closed circuit. Over 300 million viewers in 50 countries saw it later. When all the receipts were in it was estimated that Hagler would earn between $18 and $20 million for his efforts; Leonard, as challenger, a mere $12.5 million. The revenue generated by the fight exceeded $100 million and the tourist turnover in Las Vegas was thought to be $350 million.

The fight lived up to all expectations. Leonard, the 3-to-1 underdog in the betting, put up an unbelievable show. He had built up his body to 158 pounds, only a half pound below Hagler, and retained his speed. The pattern of the fight was quickly established. Hagler advanced and Leonard ran, but every now and then Leonard would stop and put together rapid clusters of punches, bewildering in their hand speed. For four rounds Leonard dazzled while Hagler lumbered but in the fifth Hagler got an uppercut and some hooks home and from then on the fight was joined in earnest. In the ninth Leonard looked in trouble but drew on reserves and still made an impressive flurry. In the last two rounds it looked as if Leonard was almost exhausted but still he avoided Hagler's more murderous blows and retaliated with his own bursts.

At the end of an exciting bout a split decision was announced. One judge gave it to Hagler by two points, another to Leonard by two points. The third judge made Leonard an easy eight-points winner.

Never has a verdict caused so much after-fight discussion. Some critics regarded Leonard's attacks as little more than decoration and claimed that the whole performance was a confidence trick. Others were equally certain that Leonard had completely outboxed Hagler. Whichever view is taken, Leonard's had been one of the most remarkable and astonishing performances in the history of boxing.

ABOVE LEFT: *Hagler connects to the head and challenger Leonard to the body in the most awaited middleweight title fight of all, held at Las Vegas on 6 April 1987.*

ABOVE: *Leonard appears to gain a psychological ascendancy at the weigh-in, raising his arms high while champion Hagler looks upstaged.*

LEFT: *Leonard (right) taunts Hagler with his 'come and hit me' tactics that had proved so successful against another hard man, Duran.*

BELOW: *The battle is joined in earnest as Hagler backs his opponent Leonard against the ropes.*

ABOVE: *Post-fight jubilation from Leonard as he is declared the winner. He immediately retired for a second time.*

LEFT: *Hagler (left) coming forward and Leonard covering up. It was not an easy fight to score. Judge Jalo Guerre of Monterey, Mexico, became the center of a postfight storm by giving Hagler only two rounds. The other judges canceled each other out with close verdicts.*

RIGHT: *Thomas Hearns, one of the exciting performers of the 1980s, took the vacant WBC middleweight title and became the first boxer to win world titles at four weights. He met President Reagan and said that all he wanted now was to get revenge against both Hagler and Leonard.*

Of course the middleweight championship was immediately in disarray. Having achieved his ambition Leonard retired again. So neither of the two great pugilists was now a world champion. The 'alphabet boys' soon saw to it that others were installed. In October 1987 all three boxing associations recognized new champions.

First 23-year-old unbeaten Frank Tate of Houston, Texas, comfortably outpointed Michael Olijade, born in Liverpool but fighting out of Vancouver and Canadian champion, to become the IBF champion. Tate was the light-middleweight gold-medalist at the Los Angeles Olympic Games in 1984, but was not expected to beat Olijade.

A fortnight later, Sambu Kalambay, the European champion, who was born in Zaire but was based in Italy, outpointed Iran 'The Blade' Barkley of New York, in Livorno, Italy, to become the WBA champion. The 31-year-old Kalambay's best victory before then was over the previously unbeaten Herol Graham to take the European crown.

Finally at the end of October, Thomas Hearns knocked out Juan Roldan of Argentina in the fourth round in Las Vegas to win the WBC version of the title.

Thomas Hearns, born in Memphis, Tennessee on 18 October 1958, thus completed his forty-fifth win in 47 contests, 38 of them inside the distance, in a ten-year career. On the way he had won the WBA welterweight title, the WBC light-

middleweight title, the WBC light-heavyweight title, and now the WBC middleweight title. He had thus won world titles at four weights, a new record. He was duly acclaimed but his record cannot truly compare with those of triple world champions, Bob Fitzsimmons and Henry Armstrong. To begin with, the light-middleweight title is only half a title, being at a 'junior' weight inserted between welter and middle. Secondly, with three champions at this weight – IBF, WBC and WBA – he held only a third of that half-title, that is one sixth of a title. His welterweight title might be regarded as half a title, as the IBF did not have a champion at the time. If his other titles are regarded as a third of a title each, Hearns's 'score' is only one and a third world titles. Ironically his only two defeats were against Leonard and Hagler.

This observation is not to decry Hearns who, with Tyson, Leonard and Hagler, was one of the great attractions of his era, but to highlight how difficult it is for a true multichampion to establish his supremacy in the days of the 'alphabet boys.' At present Armstrong's achievement of holding world titles at three weights simultaneously could not be repeated because the three associations insist that a world champion can practice at only one weight at a time. Boxing would be more interesting if, as in the old days, there was one champion at each weight, and if any boxer could be champion at any weight or weights for which he could weigh in.

The Iron Man Cometh

Mike Tyson was born in Brooklyn on 30 June 1966 and was brought up in the hard neighborhood of Brownsville. He claims to have been retiring as a boy, discovering his aggressive instincts when an older boy killed one of the pigeons which he used to keep. The ten-year-old Tyson, his passion roused, lost his inhibitions and beat up the surprised bully. Tyson at once realized and enjoyed his feelings of strength and power. Not unnaturally, given the area in which he was living, he practiced this power in the usual way, on the streets. He became a mugger and a petty thief. At 13 he was in a detention center. It was a life which could have led to serious crime.

As with a number of others, boxing offered another way. He found Cus d'Amato's gym at Catskill in New York State. Cus d'Amato was a famous name in boxing. He had managed Floyd Patterson and Jose Torres, former world champions, and his managership of the complex Patterson, in particular, had been sensitive. He had made a stand against the part-monopoly that controlled the heavyweight championship at the time and shepherded Patterson through a long and distinguished career. D'Amato took a liking to Tyson, saw his potential, coached him and set him on the ladder to the world title.

Tyson turned professional on 6 March 1985 and his first opponent, Hector Mercedes, was knocked out in the first round. First-round victories became a habit of the hard-punching Tyson, no fewer than 12 of his first 16 bouts ending this way, only one of the others reaching the fourth. James Tillis gave him his first big test, taking him the whole ten rounds in May 1986 and Mitch Green repeated the experience only 17 days later, but it was then back to the quick destructions.

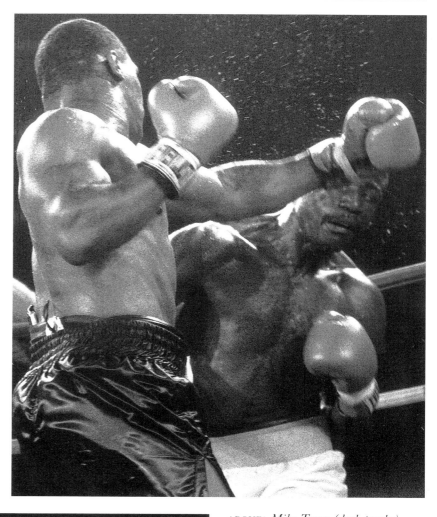

ABOVE: *Mike Tyson (dark trunks) connects to the head of Jose Luis Ribalta in the tenth round at Atlantic City on 17 August 1986. The referee stepped in to save Ribalta from further harm.*

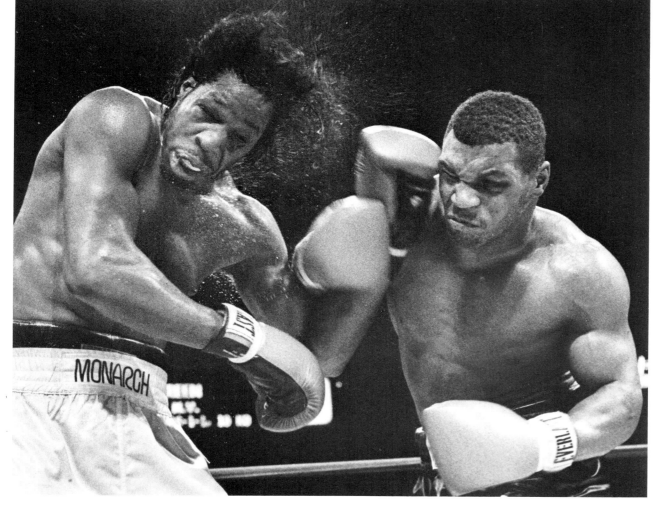

LEFT: *Mitch Green's hair goes flying as Tyson rocks him with a right in New York on 20 May 1986. Green was the first of Tyson's opponents to be on his feet at the end of the fight.*

RIGHT: *Alfonso Ratliff hits the deck in the second round of his contest with Tyson on 6 September 1986 at Las Vegas. This was Tyson's last fight before becoming WBC champion.*

BELOW: *On 16 February 1986 Jesse Ferguson (left) fought Tyson, who is here getting in a left to the side of the neck. Ferguson lasted until the sixth round, the farthest anyone had gone in the 19-year-old Tyson's first 18 fights.*

201

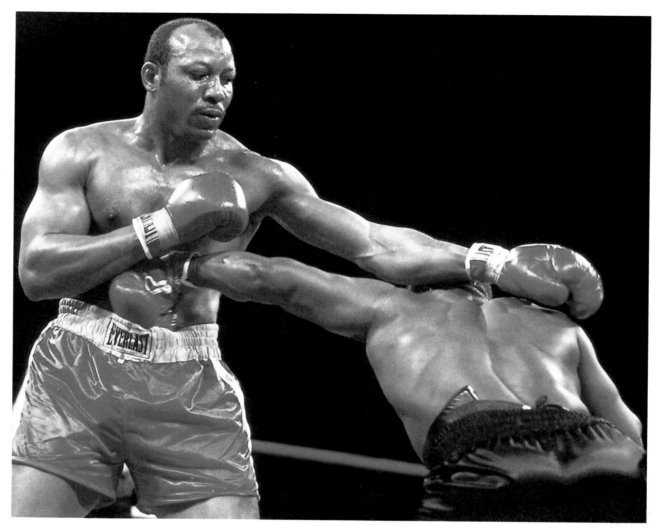

LEFT: *James 'Bonecrusher' Smith (left) spent the 12 rounds of his challenge to Tyson back-pedaling and grabbing. Here Tyson tries to get through with a left to the stomach. Tyson won the contest easily on points.*

RIGHT: *Tyson wearing the WBC championship belt after his two-round annihilation of Trevor Berbick on 22 November 1986. At 20 years and 5 months old, Mike Tyson was the youngest boxer ever to claim a world heavyweight title.*

BELOW: *Tyson throws a long left at Tony Tucker on 1 August 1987 at Las Vegas. Tucker put up the best show of the three champions whose titles Tyson annexed, but lost the decision, and this meant Tyson became the first undisputed champion since Ali.*

Cus d'Amato, who developed a very strong relationship with his boxer, had become his legal guardian and Tyson, who idolized the older man, absorbed his teaching. He assumed the dedication, put in the hard slog and developed the technique which d'Amato worked out for him. At 5 feet 11 inches Tyson is very short for a modern heavyweight, and d'Amato taught him a crouching style with which he advances with his gloves held high as he stalks his opponent. Tyson's most striking physical attribute is his massive neck which measures 19¾ inches. Opponents facing Tyson as he advances with only a hard head above a rock-like neck to hit, find him awkward, especially when he himself is delivering powerful upward blows. Tyson exercises his neck muscles by rolling around on the floor with his weight on the top of his head, and he has the nervous habit of flexing his neck muscles during a fight. Cus d'Amato also gave Mike Tyson a historical awareness of his place in the history of the heavyweight succession.

Sadly Cus d'Amato died in 1985 after Tyson's eighth fight. However Tyson was lucky to find two other knowledgeable and dedicated managers in Jim Jacobs and Bill Cayton. He likes to watch the films of old fights, of which his managers own the best collection in the world, and is an expert on the styles and records of old heavyweight boxing heroes.

Tyson's rapid demolition of heavyweights naturally caused excitement in the boxing world. Don King and HBO television had already started the $21 million promotion to find a single heavyweight king and Tyson, called 'The Iron Man,' had to be brought into the picture. His first title fight was on 22 November 1986 when he challenged the WBC champion, Trevor Berbick, at the Hilton Hotel, Las Vegas. Berbick was easily Tyson's strongest opponent to date and was expected to be a stern test for the young fighter.

Surprisingly, in view of the fact that he had the experienced Angelo Dundee, Ali's trainer, in his corner, Berbick tried to

RIGHT: *Larry Holmes (right) came back to challenge Tyson in 1988, but the old champion could show no more than that he had been a good mover in his day. In the fourth round the new champion caught the 38-year-old grandfather with one of his best punches, and Holmes did not last much longer.*

LEFT: *Tyson looks tired but happy after chasing 'Bonecrusher' Smith for 12 rounds for the WBA title. With the two-belted champion is the promoter with the startling and startled hairstyle, Don King. With Home Box Office television King had staged the fights that gave boxing back a true heavyweight champion. All that is required now is for the other divisions to be similarly rationalized.*

slug it out with the powerful challenger straight from the bell. Both boxers landed heavy blows in the first round but Berbick looked much the more hurt. In the second round Berbick continued his tactics but was caught with a right which dumped him on the canvas. Berbick was determined not to go on the defensive and moved in close for a toe-to-toe punching session. But suddenly a left high on the head had a delayed action effect. Berbick's legs went. He reeled across the ring, crashed to the canvas, rose, reeled back, fell again, rose and still continued to stagger about the ring like a drunkard. The referee stopped it. Tyson was WBC titleholder, at 20 years and 5 months the youngest to hold a version of a heavyweight title. The previous youngest was Floyd Patterson, d'Amato's old charge.

Tyson's next step on his way to the unified crown was to take on James 'Bonecrusher' Smith, the WBA champion, for both titles. The fight was at Las Vegas on 7 March 1987. The Bonecrusher was determined not to make the same mistake as Berbick and boxed exclusively on the defense, either retreating or spoiling. He showed up Tyson's inexperience as the younger boxer could not get to grips with his opponent and showed his irritation at it. In the final minute of the 12-rounder Smith put on an aggressive flurry but this was not enough and the decision was overwhelmingly Tyson's.

The dual champion, while waiting for the IBF to sort itself out, defended his titles against Pinklon Thomas, generally considered the best of the many ex-champions still trading punches. Still, with only one defeat on his record, Thomas faced Tyson at the Las Vegas Hilton on 30 May 1987. The Tucker-Douglas IBF decider was on the same bill. Thomas's left jab was frequently finding Tyson but Tyson's early punches were hard and, like others before him, Thomas switched to survival tactics. Tyson's inexperience was again shown as Thomas smothered his efforts but a left hook to the jaw in the sixth got home and as the challenger wobbled, Tyson piled in blow after blow until Thomas fell. Thomas bravely got up but the referee had no choice but to end it.

On 1 August 1987 Tyson and the new IBF champion, Tony Tucker, had the chance to unify the championship when they met at the Las Vegas, Hilton. At 6 feet 5 inches Tucker was much the taller but he started a 12-to-1 underdog in the betting. He was not in awe of Tyson and in the first minute got in a powerful uppercut which shook his opponent. But Tyson took it and Tucker reverted to the tactics of his previous opponents with plenty of grabbing. He had some success with his own blows and boxed Tyson with more flair and confidence than many before him. However at the end the decision was in no doubt and Tyson was the new undisputed heavyweight champion of the world – undisputed, that is, by the 'ruling' bodies if not by Michael Spinks's supporters. There was an amazing coronation ceremony with Muhammad Ali placing a ruby-encrusted crown on Tyson's head.

On 16 October 1987 at Atlantic City's Convention Hall, Tyson made his first defense against Tyrell Biggs of Philadelphia who had built up an impressive record. It was a bloody battle, most of the blood that of Biggs who was cut above one eye, below the other and on his lip. Just before the end of the seventh, after Biggs had been down twice and was clearly incapable of continuing, the referee stepped in and saved him. Then on 15 January 1988 the ex-WBC and IBF champion, Larry Holmes, challenged Tyson at Atlantic City. The 38-year-old, now a grandfather, moved well for three-and-a-half rounds, but then was caught with an explosive short right by the 21-year-old champion. The writing was on the wall. Five seconds from the end of the fourth round Holmes was down for a third time, ominously spreadeagled on his back, when the referee stopped the fight. It was the end of Holmes's aspirations, but the firmly established Tyson had a year mapped out for him which was expected to earn him $50 million.

Tyson was proving himself the best heavyweight since the prime of Ali, and if, as is said, boxing is as good as the heavyweight champion, then, with Tyson as king, the sport could be in for a golden period.

INDEX

Page numbers in *italics* refer to illustrations.

Acknowledgments

The publisher would like to thank Design 23, who designed this book; Mandy Little and Moira Dykes, the picture researchers; and Diana LeCore, the indexer. We would also like to thank the individuals and picture agencies for supplying illustrations, and especially the Bettmann Archive, New York, who supplied all the illustrations, except for the following:
All-Sport: pages 2(top), 4, 6(below), 149(below), 165, 169(top), 176(right),

180(below), 184, 185(top), 188(below), 189, 192(top), 194(below), 202(both), 203, 205
The Associated Press: pages 94(top), 98(top), 99, 100, 111, 117(below), 138(below), 146, 148(below), 156(below), 157(below), 159(below), 160(top), 178(top).
BBC Hulton Picture Library: pages 3, 10(top and below), 11(top), 12(top), 13(right), 14(top), 24(top), 26(main picture), 27, 28, 40(both), 44(top), 45(top), 52, 53, 56, 58, 64, 65(below), 71(top)

73(left), 74, 75, 90(below), 91, 94(below), 108(both), 109(both), 110(both), 113(top), 119(top), 124(below), 128(left), 132(top), 162
Jonathan Buckley/Joe Coughlan: page 132(below).
Joe DiMaggio: pages 148(top), 161(below), 173, 181(top), 185(below), 195(both), 198-199(all 3).
Focus On Sports: pages 2(below), 140(top), 141(top), 144(below), 145, 160(below), 161(top left), 164(below), 168, 169(below), 171(top left), 172(top and below left),

176(left), 177(both), 180(top), 188(top).
Jim Guvie/photo Joe Coughlan: pages 6(top), 7(top), 60, 192(below).
The Keystone Collection: pages 62, 85, 95, 96, 97(both), 112(both), 113(below), 119(below), 124(top), 125, 129, 130(top), 133, 147(both), 151(top), 157(top), 170-171.
The Mansell Collection: page 22(below).
Don Morley: page 153(right).
Peter Newark's Historical Pictures: pages 10(inset), 11(below), 13(left), 14(centre

and below), 25, 26(inset) 31, 32, 35(below), 36, 37, 38, 39, 42(top), 43, 44(below), 45(below), 46, 47(below), 48, 49, 50, 51, 55(both), 57(both), 59, 65(top), 69, 71(below), 76(below), 79(both), 82(top), 88(top), 89(both), 90(top), 92, 93(both), 98(below), 101, 106(top), 107, 116, 117(top), 118, 120, 128(right), 130,(below), 131, 138(top), 167.